A Synoptic Review of U.S. Rangelands

A Technical Document Supporting
the Forest Service 2010 RPA Assessment

Matthew Clark Reeves and John E. Mitchell

Abstract: The Renewable Resources Planning Act of 1974 requires the USDA Forest Service to conduct assessments of resource conditions. This report fulfills that need and focuses on quantifying extent, productivity, and health of U.S. rangelands. Since 1982, the area of U.S. rangelands has decreased at an average rate of 350,000 acres per year owed mostly to conversion to agricultural and residential land uses. Nationally, rangeland productivity has been steady over the last decade, but the Rocky Mountain Assessment Region appears to have moderately increased productivity since 2000. The forage situation is positive and, from a national perspective, U.S. rangelands can probably support a good deal more animal production than current levels. Sheep numbers continue to decline, horses and goats have increased numbers, and cattle have slightly increased, averaging 97 million animals per year since 2002. Data from numerous sources indicate rangelands are relatively healthy but also highlight the need for consolidation of efforts among land management agencies to improve characterization of rangeland health. The biggest contributors to decreased rangeland health, chiefly invasive species, are factors associated with biotic integrity. Non-native species are present on 50 percent of non-Federal rangelands, often offsetting gains in rangeland health from improved management practices.

Keywords: rangeland health, livestock, remote sensing, rangeland extent, grazing, coterminous United States, Renewable Resources Planning Act

Authors

Matthew Clark Reeves is a Post Doctoral Research Ecologist in the Human Dimensions program of the USDA Forest Service, Rocky Mountain Research Station in Missoula, Montana. He earned his B.S. degree in Range Management from Washington State University, his M.S. degree in Environmental Resources from Arizona State University, and a Ph.D. in Ecosystem and Conservation Sciences from the University of Montana. He specializes in using remote sensing and spatial analysis to understand the status and trends of natural resources and biospheric processes and is an active participant in the Sustainable Rangelands Roundtable and Society for Range Management.

John E. Mitchell is an Emeritus Rangeland Scientist with the Rocky Mountain Research Station in Fort Collins, Colorado. Prior to retiring in 2009, his research supported the rangeland component of the Renewable Resources Planning Act Assessment. Since that time, he has continued to assist with rangeland work for the Assessment and has been an active participant in the Sustainable Rangelands Roundtable and Society for Range Management. Mitchell is a Certified Professional in Rangeland Management.

Acknowledgments

This work was initiated by John Mitchell, the author of the previous rangeland portion of the RPA Assessment. After the initial planning phase, the assignment was given to Matt Reeves in 2009. Dr. Mitchell provided the impetus to design the program to evaluate the U.S. rangeland base, excellent perspective, and mentoring throughout the development of the document and contributed significantly to Chapter 3: Ecosystem Goods and Services.

Staff from a wide range of organizations contributed guidance, review, and data to populate the report. Specifically, we thank John Reitsma, Phil Cooley, and Sherm Karl from the Bureau of Land Management (BLM) National Operations Center for providing interpretation and data describing BLM land dispositions, grazing allotments, rangeland health, and grazing statistics. In a similar manner, USDA Forest Service range management staff provided data describing gross receipts from grazing Forest Service (USFS) lands, grazing statistics, allotment boundaries, and juxtaposition of USFS lands. Shelley Douthett, Kaylene Monson, and Lisa McBride, were all involved in this process. Other members of USDA also contributed: Marisa Capriotti provided data regarding conservation lands and Virginia Harris was instrumental in obtaining and understanding data from the National Agricultural Statistics Survey.

In addition to agency personnel, staff from three universities contributed data and information for the report. Adam Moreno, under the direction of Dr. Steve Running, Professor of Forest Ecology, University of Montana developed the forecasts in rangeland productivity. Wasantha Kulawardhana and Dr. Robert Washington-Allen, Assistant Professor of Ecosystem Science and Management, Texas A&M University, developed the estimated footprint of livestock herbivory. Finally, Ian Leinwand, under the direction of Dr. Dave Theobald, Research Scientist, at Colorado State University, provided the analysis of human modified rangeland and fragmentation. Acquisition of data describing oil and gas networks and invasive species was performed by Robb Lankston, whose help enabled more timely completion of the document. Impetus for the climate change effects section was provided by Dr. Jack Morgan of the Agricultural Research Service. Dr. Morgan's expertise on the subject enabled us to complete an overview of climate change effects. Kate Marcille provided editorial suggestions and was responsible for a good deal of formatting and compilation.Lane Eskew, Lindy Larson, and Nancy Chadwick patiently provided editorial assistance.

Finally, the RPA specialists and Washington Office management personnel provided continual support, answers, and guidance. Dr. Linda Langner and Margaret Connelly, both from the Washington Office, provided oversight and kept the document as up-to-date as possible. In addition, Dr. Langner provided analysis and written evaluation of the RPA scenarios. Dr. Linda Joyce provided data and support for the downscaled climate data. Dr. Kurt Riitters provided the data and analysis for the rangeland fragmentation evaluation.

Executive Summary

Chapter 1: Context, Design, and Impetus for the 2010 RPA Rangeland Assessment

The Forest and Rangeland Renewable Resources Planning Act (RPA) of 1974 requires assessments and projections of the Nation's renewable resources. Successive RPA Range Assessments have exhibited a central theme or context binding the chapters together. The 1989 Range Assessment extensively evaluated the forage supply and demand and relied on an econometric model (now retired) for forecasting purposes. It was generally concluded that the total U.S. forage supply was sufficient to meet projected demands. The 2000 Range Assessment was organized around the concept of criteria and indicators developed by the Sustainable Rangeland Roundtable and, like the 1989 Range Assessment, it concluded that forage quantity was sufficient for current and projected livestock levels. This 2010 Range Assessment addresses topics similar to its predecessors, but focuses on providing more spatially explicit data describing the status and trends of U.S. rangelands. Projections for rangeland resources are not provided here and will instead be available in forthcoming documents supporting this Assessment. As a result, this report focuses on contemporary issues, including rangeland extent and health, forage supply, and livestock numbers, while maintaining linkages with past assessments.

Chapter 2: Rangeland Extent and Global Concerns

Quantifying rangeland extent provides an area basis for estimating carbon sequestration and forage availability, serves as a baseline against which future estimates of resources can be compared, and is necessary for developing monitoring and management strategies. Extent of rangelands is also a component of at least three criteria and six indicators of rangeland sustainability. Rangeland area in the coterminous United States is between 511 and 662 million acres, depending on the definition used, and roughly one-third of these lands are protected. Since the pre-settlement era, approximately 34 percent of rangelands have been permanently modified by human activity. However, as reported in the 2000 Range Assessment, the U.S. rangeland base is relatively stable, though further fragmentation due to exurban development, oil and gas exploration, agricultural development and, to a lesser degree, residential development can be expected. Privately owned rangelands will continue a slow decline in area while publically owned rangelands will continue to be stable, and changes will usually result from land exchanges and oil and gas development. While data describing global rangelands are sparse, the worldwide situation appears less favorable than the conditions in the United States.

Globally, rangelands occupy nearly one-half of the vegetated surfaces and at least half of these lands are grazed and provide livelihood to millions of people. Since rangelands are not explicitly monitored through the United Nations, it is difficult to quantify losses of this land type. However, global pasturelands have shrunk by approximately 4.7 million acres per year since 1995, largely at the expense of expansion in agricultural land use. Changes in rangeland extent in the future are difficult to predict, but projected increases in global population will undoubtedly result in further conversion of pasture and rangelands to agricultural uses. At the same time, sharp increases in demand for red meat will require greater output of goods and services per area of land.

Chapter 3: Ecosystem Goods and Services

The concept of rangeland goods and services is a relatively new subject receiving a good deal of attention. Rangelands provide extractable goods, such as plant materials, oil and gas, and livestock feed, as well as tangible and intangible rangeland ecosystem services, such as clean water, carbon sequestration, and renewable energy. This Range Assessment focuses on a subset of ecosystem goods and services, including trends in decadal productivity and forage supply, livestock production, alternative energy, and a summary of potential climate change effects. Overall, since 2000, U.S. rangelands have maintained a relatively constant level of productivity. The Rocky Mountain region, however, experienced a significant increase in productivity, but the causes of the greening of the region are unclear.

The stable rangeland productivity has direct implications for the U.S. forage supply. The total forage supply is near 1.9 to 2.6 trillion pounds. Based on this estimate, the forage situation is positive and forage quantity is sufficient to support roughage requirements of wild and domestic herbivores now and into the foreseeable future. The degree to which climate change will affect forage supply and rangeland productivity is unclear, but research is being conducted to estimate these effects. The currently stable pattern of productivity is reflected in livestock numbers since 2000. Between 2002 and 2007, the U.S. cattle inventory remained within 1.4 percent of the estimated 10 year average of 96,563,644 animals, though the North Assessment Region lost nearly 26 percent of its cattle inventory. The situation with sheep is quite different. Since 1997, sheep numbers have declined by approximately 26 percent, reflecting the trend that has been in place since roughly the late 1930s when nearly 50 million sheep were present in the United States. Horses, bison, and, to a greater degree, goats have increased sharply owed to changing dietary preferences and ranchers seeking to diversify their operations. To increase the profitability and diversify holdings and income streams, ranchers are increasingly involved with alternative sources of revenue. One of the more notable alternative streams of revenue reflecting the concern for climate change is the ubiquitous development of energy resources that do not preclude other land uses, including wind, unconventional natural gas, and biofuel. While solar energy yields more potential than some other sources, it is generally not compatible with other land uses and is therefore not addressed in this report.

Of all the energy sources derived from rangelands, natural gas provides more output than wind and biomass combined. Though not renewable, natural gas is a cleaner alternative to both coal and oil. Many of the major gas plays in the United States occur on western rangelands. Likewise, the large, often windswept, arid landscapes make rangelands uniquely poised to provide substantial quantities of energy from solar and wind facilities. The United States is the second leading wind generating nation, but wind only accounts for 1 percent of total energy production in the United States. Energy from biomass is predominantly derived from forest or agricultural residue and therefore, very little energy is derived from biomass emanating from rangelands. There is, however, significant promise for developing biomass sources from large statured grasses such as switchgrass. The future for alternative energy development on rangelands is bright but not without further research and serious consideration. Development of these energy sources needs to be balanced with social, economic, and environmental costs.

Chapter 4: Rangeland Health

Concepts of rangeland health are still evolving. Rangeland health is characterized using a variety of qualitative and quantitative indicators, but these methods are not consistently applied across agencies. Further, the extent and remoteness of rangelands make assessing these indicators of health and vitality difficult. No national monitoring framework is in place to collect data over time and, unlike the Bureau of Land Management (BLM) and Natural Resources Conservation Service (NRCS, via the National Resources Inventory [NRI]), the USFS currently has no data collection protocol permitting evaluation of rangeland health on all NFS lands.

Data from the BLM and NRCS suggest that coterminous U.S. rangelands are in reasonably good condition as roughly 80 percent of non-Federal and 75 percent of Federal rangelands exhibit overall healthy characteristics or are moving in a positive direction. Current processes that are decreasing rangeland health include the spread of invasive species, changing fire regimes, and woody encroachment, particularly by mesquite and juniper species. These interrelated factors often induce feedbacks that perpetuate the decreased health. The expansion of invasive species could be the most critical factor influencing the future health of U.S. rangelands. Invasive plants reduce the ability of rangelands to provide goods and services required by society and can interrupt ecological processes, including nutrient cycling, pollination, and predator and prey relationships, and can reduce biodiversity, increase soil erosion, degrade wildlife habitat, and reduce the carrying capacity of livestock. There are an estimated 3310 non-native species occurring within the contiguous United States, many of which are present on roughly 50 percent of non-Federal rangelands. The 16 most pervasive species affect 126 million acres and are expanding at alarming rates of up to 4000 acres per day (approximately 1.5 million acres per year) in some regions such as the Great Basin.

Invasive plant species have continued to increase in spread and density, and estimates of expansion over time are reflected by the growth in concern over the associated problems. The size and scope of the problem, and the generally uncoordinated approach toward controlling invasive species, make determining the amount of effort committed to combating invasive species difficult. Despite this difficulty, in 2000 the total annual cost was estimated at $137 billion in losses and direct expenditures.

Despite the scope of the problem, the invasive species situation is not hopeless and substantial investments in control and mitigation efforts have been made. Programs such as the Citizen Scientist Project offer significant promise for inventorying, monitoring, and controlling the spread of invasive species. For maximum effectiveness, a national strategy for controlling invasive species should include a combination of biocontrol, herbicide application, public involvement, improved or revised management strategies and use of alternative livestock, such as goats, which readily ingest numerous invasive species.

Contents

Chapter 1: Context, Design, and Impetus for the 2010 RPA Rangeland Assessment

The Forest and Rangeland Renewable Resources Planning Act (RPA) of 1974 mandates a periodic assessment of the condition and trends of the Nation's renewable resources. The RPA Assessment provides a snapshot of current conditions and trends in outdoor recreation, water, forests, urban forests, wildlife and fish, and range resources across all ownerships in the United States. The RPA Assessment further identifies drivers of change and projects 50 years into the future, when possible. This report focuses on the status and trends of rangeland resources.

Rangelands are found in many ecoregions encompassing a diverse suite of vegetation. In general, rangelands are areas where the natural vegetation is comprised principally of grasses, forbs, grasslike plants, and shrubs that are suitable for browsing or grazing. An important distinction, however, is that the presence of current herbivory is not a prerequisite for range-land classification. Further, herbivory can be liberally applied and generally means grazing or browsing by domestic livestock or wild herbivores. Rangelands are distinguished from grazing lands, with grazing land identified as any vegetated land that is grazed or has the potential to be grazed (SRM 1998), including rangeland, pastureland, grazed forestland, native and naturalized pasture, hayland, and grazed cropland. Rangelands are therefore a subset of grazing lands and are increasingly managed for multiple goods and services, of which grazing is often a component. It follows that the term "range resources" applies to goods and services derived from rangelands that increase social, economic, and biophysical well-being (Mitchell 2000), the status and trends of which comprise the majority of this report.

The status of U.S. rangelands has arguably been of continual interest to Americans for perhaps thousands of years. Burning by Native Americans was especially useful to divert big game into smaller areas for easier hunting and to stimulate production of more nutritious fresh foliage for herbivores. Manipulating the vegetation in this manner is unquestionably a kind of "management" and had a profound impact on the function and composition of rangelands. Mitchell (2000) provided an in-depth review of the recorded history of U.S. rangelands, and therefore, we only synopsize key events here to orient the reader.

For over a half century after the Lewis and Clark expedition of 1804, the vast western ranges remained largely undeveloped. Then, in 1862, the Homestead Act was passed leading to western expansion for extracting minerals, forage, and timber, which fostered unrestricted use, leading to serious depletion of rangeland resources. Passage of the Homestead Act, fol-lowed by the Enlarged Homestead Act of 1909 and the Stock Raising Homestead Act of 1916 enabled about 285 million acres to be privately claimed, which led to settled occupation of nearly all lands containing suitable water and forage for grazing (Mitchell 2000). Collectively, these homestead acts led to a 6-fold increase in cattle production resulting in roughly 27 million head by 1890 (Poling 1991), while sheep numbers increased 20-fold peaking at 20 million head in 1890 (Stoddart and Smith 1943). The rapid westward expansion, unrestricted use of privatized rangelands, and increased livestock numbers led to a dependence on public domain lands to meet the demand for forage (Carpenter 1981), causing severe depletion of both private and public rangeland resources. This situation prompted Senate Resolution 289 in the 74th Congress requiring the Secretary of Agriculture to develop a report on the status of range resources. This report was the first in a series of unscheduled reports over the next four decades that focused primarily on forage production and consumption. Finally, in 1974, the Forest and Rangelands RPA was enacted requiring, among other things, decadal assessments of renewable resource supplies, demands, and trends. The RPA further required forecasts of expected future supply and demand of resources.

The 1980 RPA Range Assessment (USDA FS 1980) focused primarily on forage supply and demand, reflecting apprehension regarding the ability of U.S. rangelands to meet forage demand linked to increasing red meat consumption. The report caused concern by forecasting a demand for red meat that could exceed the capacity of some regions to supply suitable forage quantities. The 1989 RPA Rangeland Assessment (Joyce 1989) also predicted a sharp increase in demand for grazed forage from 431 to 665 million animal unit months (AUMs; requirement of around 780 pounds of air dry forage per month). However, the report concluded that the increased demand for red meat could be met through expansion of forage production on private lands, especially more productive pasturelands. The 2000 RPA Range Assessment (Mitchell 2000) focused less on concerns over forage production capacity and more on contemporary issues regarding indicators of rangeland sustainability.

In this report, we attempt to maintain consistency with predecessors by evaluating the forage situation and addressing critical topics that have arisen over the period since the last report. Recognizing that future renewable resource conditions are influenced by common driving forces such as population change, economic growth, and land use change, and are likely to be influenced by climate change, a suite of scenarios were developed for the 2010 RPA Assessment to assist the resource forecasting process (USDA FS 2012). The current range assessment yields little insight to the estimated effects of various scenarios on rangeland resources, but forthcoming reports likely will. This document is organized into chapters, each providing information on critical issues potentially influencing the sustainability of rangelands for future generations. Though each section can be read independently, it is important for the reader to consider the potential interactions among all the elements.

Chapter 2 evaluates the global rangeland situation and the current rangeland base of the coterminous United States while documenting the loss of rangeland systems from pre euro-American settlement and the changing nature of U.S. rangelands. We document the ownership and composition of rangelands and provide spatially explicit estimates of the current U.S. rangeland distribution. In addition, we evaluate two critical issues regarding the areal extent of rangelands: (1) the degree to which human modification has irreparably changed non-forest landscapes, and (2) the extent and magnitude of fragmentation of non-forest landscapes.

Chapter 3 is dedicated to rangeland goods and services. Though ecosystem goods and services include both tangible and intangible products, this section communicates the importance of extractable goods from rangelands and their unique contributions to the Nation's well-being. Specifically, we address key issues such as decadal rangeland productivity trends, forage supply, livestock production, renewable energy, and livestock appropriation of forage.

Chapter 4 evaluates the health of U.S. rangelands through examination of data describing various aspects of "health" on Federal and non-Federal lands. Elements of rangeland health evaluated in this chapter are: rangeland condition, invasive species, and indicators of rangeland health (Herrick and others 2010). Specifically, we rely on the newly published reports based on the NRI, standards for rangeland health from the BLM, and data describing the extent of invasive species from a variety of sources.

Chapter 2: Rangeland Extent and Global Concerns

Introduction

Over 300 definitions have been constructed to describe rangelands globally (Lund 2007). The situation is no less complicated within the United States where land management agencies do not agree on a consistent definition of rangelands. Despite the differences in philosophy and definitions, quantifying the extent of the Nation's rangelands is crucial to enable measurement of indicators of rangeland sustainability (Mitchell and others 1999). In addition, quantifying rangeland extent provides an area basis for estimating carbon sequestration and forage availability, serves as a baseline against which future estimates of resources can be compared, and is necessary for developing monitoring and management strategies (Lund 2007).

Federal agencies, policymakers, and researchers have long been interested in accounting for and monitoring natural resources at a national scale (Nusser and others 1998). A full accounting of area occupied by rangelands will prevent double counting during analyses aimed at quantifying goods, services, and biological processes such as carbon sequestration. Finally, the area of rangeland is a key indicator of sustainability at a national scale (Mitchell 2000; Mitchell and others 1999). The 2000 RPA Rangeland Assessment (Mitchell 2000) was constructed around the concept of criteria and indicators of rangeland sustainability. The concept of codified criteria and indicators to describe ecosystem sustainability was incepted for forests during the Montreal Process (Coulombe 1995). This system was later adapted to include rangelands that are summarized at http://sustainable.rangelands.org/pdf/Core_Indicators.pdf. As indicated in the previous RPA Rangeland Assessment (Mitchell 2000), the following indicators rely on rangeland area estimates:

Criterion 2: Conservation and Maintenance of Plant and Animal Resources on Rangelands

> 11. Extent of land area in rangeland.
> 12. Rangeland area by vegetation community.
> 14. Fragmentation of rangeland and rangeland plant communities.

Criterion 3: Maintenance of Productive Capacity on Rangelands

> 21. Rangeland aboveground biomass.
> 22. Rangeland annual productivity.

Criterion 4: Maintenance and Enhancement of Multiple Economic and Social Benefits to Current and Future Generations

> 33. Area of rangelands under conservation ownership or control by conservation organizations.

U.S. Rangelands

Current estimates of U.S. rangeland area vary widely from 398 million acres (Schuman and others 2002) to 770 million acres (Joyce 1989). Since the 1989 Rangeland Assessment, there has not been a comprehensive accounting of U.S. rangelands. Nor has there ever been a spatially explicit accounting of rangelands emanating from differing viewpoints at a national scale. The precise extent of rangelands is dependent on the definition used to define rangelands (Lund 2007), which necessarily causes confusion, inconsistencies, and administrative difficulties. Reeves and Mitchell (2011) sought to improve the situation by accounting for all rangelands in the coterminous United States by applying two different definitions of rangelands from land management agencies to spatially explicit data describing vegetation composition, structure, and historic makeup. Specifically, rangeland extent was characterized using rangeland definitions from both the USDA's Forest Inventory and Analysis (FIA), administered by the USFS, and NRI, administered by the NRCS (table 1). The spatially explicit vegetation data were supplied by the LANDFIRE project (http://www.landfire.gov/) and included Existing Vegetation Type, Existing Vegetation Height, Existing Vegetation Cover, and Biophysical Settings (Reeves and others 2009; Rollins 2009; Zhu and others 2006). The vegetation classification used by LANDFIRE to describe current and pre-Euro-American vegetation was Ecological Systems (Comer and others 2003; Comer and Schulz 2007) and National Vegetation Classification System (NVCS) alliances (Grossman and Others 1998). As a means of consistency with previous assessments, the areal extent of rangelands has been provided in a variety of summary units, including states, Federal lands, RPA Assessment Regions (figure 1) (Mitchell 2000), non-Federal lands, and protected areas.

The total rangeland area quantified using the NRI and FIA perspectives from Reeves and Mitchell (2011) in the coterminous United States is 662 and 511 million acres, respectively (figure 2). It should be noted that these area estimates will not be harmonized with other estimates of rangeland area from land management agencies for three reasons:

1. No other maps depicting rangeland area are available at a suitable level of detail from other agencies.

2. There is no equivalent geospatial dataset indicating where different forest types exist at 30-m resolution reflecting either the NRI or FIA perspectives.

3. The rangeland definitions were applied consistently, as objectively as possible, without regard for land use that could potentially create differences between other estimates of rangeland area.

Reeves and Mitchell (2011) outlined the caveats associated with their study, so not all are mentioned here. There are, however, several noteworthy caveats that are necessary elements of this report. First, though the LANDFIRE product suite is the most spatially comprehensive, thematically rich (398 Ecological Systems mapped) 30-m spatial resolution data produced for the United States to date, it describes the landscape circa 2001. Second, the analysis by Reeves and Mitchell (2011) assumed sufficient accuracy of the products, which at the level it was used, is quite suitable for this national assessment.

Table 1—Rangeland definitions used by the USFS FIA and NRCS NRI programs. Also included is the definition adopted by the BLM.

Agency	Definition
USDA Forest Service (through the FIA Program) [a]	**Forest land:** "Land that is at least 10 percent stocked by forest trees of any size (or 5 percent crown cover where stocking cannot be determined), or land formerly having such treecover, and is not currently developed for a non-forest use" (USDA FS 2010). The minimum area for classification as forest land is one acre. Roadside, stream-side, and shelterbelt strips of timber must be at [sic] have a crown width at least 120 feet wide to qualify as forest land. Unimproved roads and trails or natural clearings in forested areas shall be classified as forest, if less than 120 feet in width or an acre in size. Streams and other bodies of water within forest will be considered forest land if they are less than 1 acre and 30-feet wide. Grazed woodlands, reverting fields, and pastures that are not actively maintained are included if the above qualifications are satisfied (USDA FS 2010). In addition, forested strips must be "120.0 feet wide for a continuous length of at least 363.0 feet in order to meet the acre threshold" (USFS FIA 2010).
	Pasture: "Land that is currently maintained and used for grazing. Evidence of maintenance, besides the degree of grazing, includes condition of fencing, presence of stock ponds, periodic brush removal, seeding, irrigation, or mowing" (USDA FS 2010).
	Non-Forest: "This is land that (1) has never supported forests (e.g., barren, alpine tundra), or (2) was formerly tree land, but has been converted to a non-tree land status (e.g., cropland, improved pasture). Other examples of non-forest land are improved roads of any width, graded or otherwise regularly maintained for long-term continuing use, and rights-of-way of all powerlines, pipelines, other transmission lines, and operating railroads. If intermingled in forest areas, unimproved roads and non-forest strips must be at least 120-feet wide and 1 acre in size to qualify as nontree land" (USDA FS 2010).
	Rangeland: "Land primarily composed of grasses, forbs, or shrubs. This includes lands vegetated naturally or artificially to provide a plant cover managed like native vegetation and does not meet the definition of pasture. The area must be at least 1.0 acre in size and 120.0 feet wide" (USDA FS 2010).
Bureau of Land Management [b]	Land on which the indigenous vegetation (climax or natural potential) is predominantly grasses, grass-like plants, forbs, or shrubs and is managed as a natural ecosystem. If plants are introduced, they are managed similarly. Rangelands include natural grasslands, savannas, shrublands, many deserts, tundra, alpine communities, marshes, and wet meadows (SRM 1998: 23).
Natural Resources Conservation Service (through the NRI Program)	**Forest land:** "A land cover/use category that is at least 10 percent stocked by single-stemmed woody species of any size that will be at least 4 meters (13 ft) tall at maturity. Also included is land bearing evidence of natural regeneration of tree cover (cutover forest or abandoned farmland) and not currently developed for non-forest use. Ten percent stocked, when viewed from a vertical direction is a canopy cover of leaves and branches of 25 percent or greater. The minimum area for classification of forest land is 1 acre, and the area must be at least 100 feet wide " (USDA NRCS 2007).
	Pastureland: "The land cover/use category of land managed primarily for the production of introduced forage plants for livestock grazing. Pastureland cover may consist of a single species in a pure stand, a grass mixture, or a grass-legume mixture. Management usually consists of cultural treatments: fertilization, weed control, reseeding, or renovation, and control of grazing. For the NRI, pastureland includes land that has a vegetative cover of grasses, legumes, and/or forbs, regardless of whether it is being grazed by livestock" (USDA NRCS 2007).
	Rangeland: "A land cover/use category that includes land on which the climax or potential plant cover is composed principally of native grasses, grass-like plants, forbs or shrubs suitable for grazing and browsing, and introduced forage species that are managed like rangeland. This would include areas where introduced hardy and persistent grasses, such as crested wheatgrass, are planted and practices such as deferred grazing, burning, chaining, and rotational grazing, are used with little or no chemicals/fertilizer being applied. Grasslands, savannas, many wetlands, some deserts, and tundra are considered to be rangeland. Certain low forb and shrub communities, such as mesquite, chaparral, mountain shrub, and pinyon-juniper, are also included as rangeland" (USDA NRCS 2007).

[a] To be considered rangeland, a stand must first meet the non-forest criterion. In Region 5 of the USFS (California and Hawaii), chaparral is not considered rangeland (USFS 2008).

[b] Though the BLM sometimes uses this definition, area of rangeland is not estimated using this definition, nor is it applied consistently.

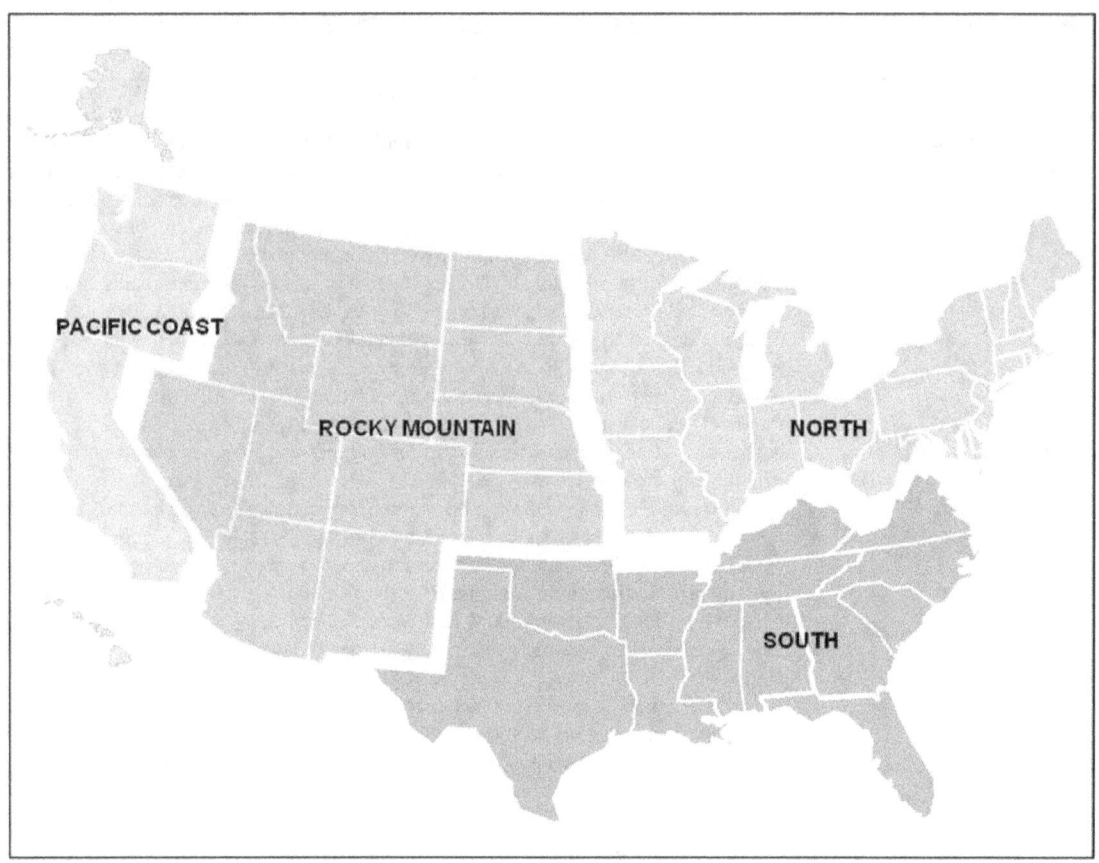

Figure 1—Spatial configuration of the RPA Assessment Regions.

Third, scientific understanding of historic disturbance regimes, principally fire, is limited but is critically important to determining the U.S. rangeland base because both the NRI and FIA definitions implicitly require knowledge of whether a site was previously occupied by tree species. To be considered rangeland using the FIA perspective, a stand must first be classified non-forest. The non-forest definition (table 1) states, "Land that does not support, or has never supported, forests…" A forest designation requires a stocking (often canopy cover is used as a surrogate) of 10 percent by trees and only 5 percent for woodlands. It follows that past stand composition had to be inferred to determine if trees were normally dominant, requiring assumptions regarding the disturbance regime characterizing the area. Determining which U.S. Ecological Systems and NVCS alliances normally exhibited less than 10 percent and less than 25 percent tree cover corresponding to the FIA and NRI perspectives, respectively, is somewhat subjective but can be informed using the extensive LANDFIRE field reference database (Caratti 2006) and our understanding of historic disturbance processes. Table 2 describes Biophysical Settings map classes that were estimated to exhibit less than 10 and 25 percent tree cover to align with the FIA and NRI perspectives, respectively. These differences in canopy cover thresholds and basic definitions are apparent in figure 3.

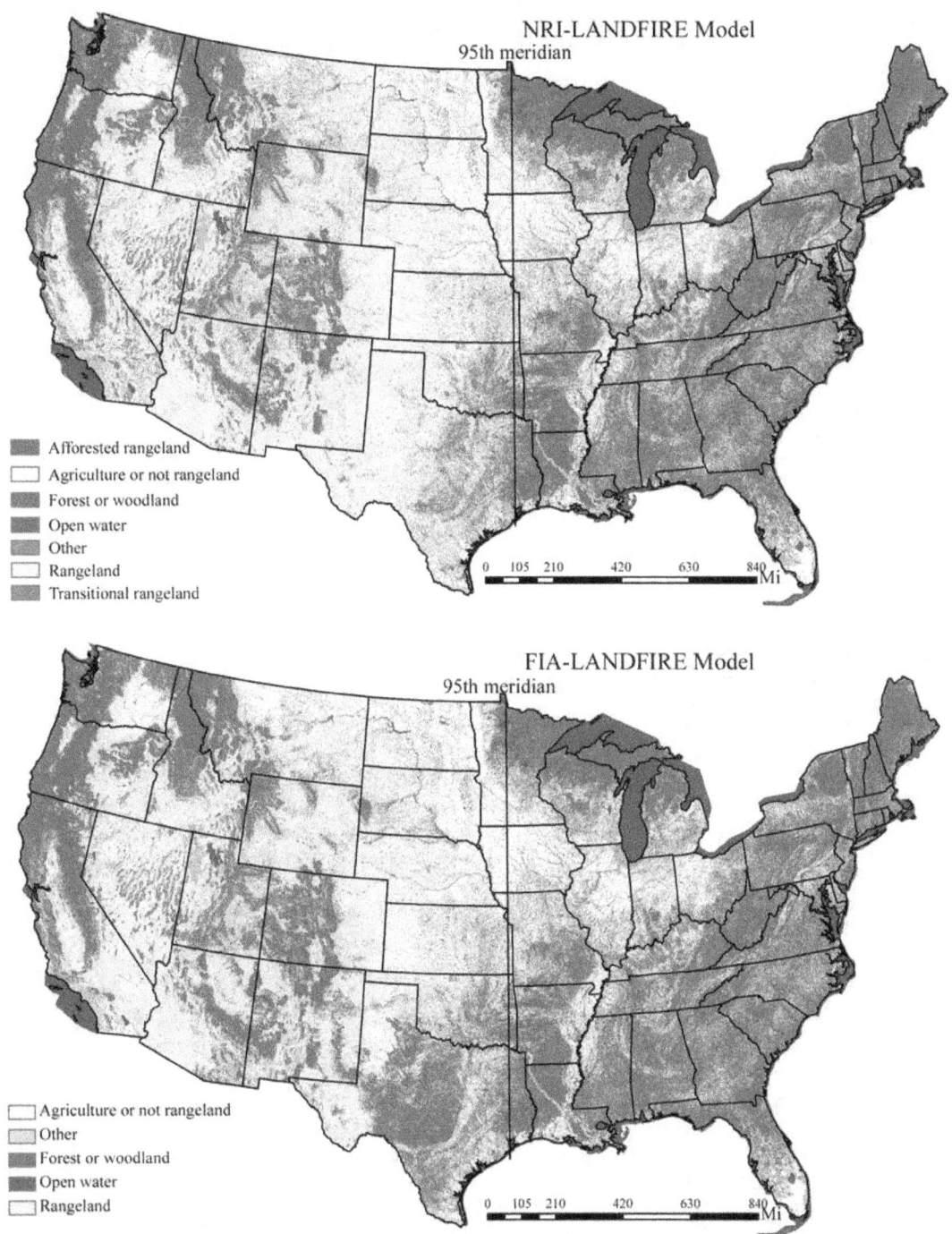

Figure 2—Rangelands of the coterminous United States, adapted from Reeves and Mitchell (2011). Panels depict the estimated rangeland extent from the NRI and FIA perspectives, respectively.

Table 2—This table describes Ecological Systems (Comer 2003) that were estimated to exhibit less than 10 and 25% tree cover to align with the FIA and NRI perspectives, respectively.

Bps name	NRI	FIA
Acadian-Appalachian Alpine Tundra	X	X
Acadian-Appalachian Subalpine Woodland and Heath-Krummholz	X	X
Alabama Ketona Glade and Woodland	X	
Apacherian-Chihuahuan Semi-Desert Grassland and Steppe	X	X
Arkansas Valley Prairie and Woodland - Prairie	X	X
Arkansas Valley Prairie and Woodland - Woodland	X	X
Atlantic Coastal Plain Peatland Pocosin and Canebrake	X	X
California Central Valley and Southern Coastal Grassland	X	X
California Maritime Chaparral	X	X
California Mesic Serpentine Grassland	X	X
California Montane Jeffrey Pine(-Ponderosa Pine) Woodland	X	
California Montane Woodland and Chaparral	X	X
California Northern Coastal Grassland	X	X
California Xeric Serpentine Chaparral	X	X
Central and South Texas Coastal Fringe Forest and Woodland	X	
Central and Upper Texas Coast Dune and Coastal Grassland	X	X
Central Atlantic Coastal Plain Nonriverine Swamp and Wet Hardwood Forest	X	X
Central Atlantic Coastal Plain Wet Longleaf Pine Savanna and Flatwoods	X	
Central Florida Pine Flatwoods	X	
Central Interior and Appalachian Shrub-Herbaceous Wetland Systems	X	X
Central Mixedgrass Prairie	X	X
Central Tallgrass Prairie	X	X
Chihuahuan Creosotebush Desert Scrub	X	X
Chihuahuan Grama Grass-Creosote Steppe	X	X
Chihuahuan Gypsophilous Grassland and Steppe	X	X
Chihuahuan Loamy Plains Desert Grassland	X	X
Chihuahuan Mixed Desert and Thorn Scrub	X	X
Chihuahuan Mixed Desert Shrubland	X	X
Chihuahuan Mixed Salt Desert Scrub	X	X
Chihuahuan Sandy Plains Semi-Desert Grassland	X	X
Chihuahuan Succulent Desert Scrub	X	X
Chihuahuan-Sonoran Desert Bottomland and Swale Grassland	X	X
Chihuahuan-Sonoran Desert Bottomland and Swale Grassland - Alkali Sacaton	X	X
Chihuahuan-Sonoran Desert Bottomland and Swale Grassland - Tobosa Grassland	X	X
Colorado Plateau Blackbrush-Mormon-tea Shrubland	X	X
Colorado Plateau Mixed Low Sagebrush Shrubland	X	X
Colorado Plateau Pinyon-Juniper Shrubland	X	X
Colorado Plateau Pinyon-Juniper Woodland	X	
Columbia Basin Foothill and Canyon Dry Grassland	X	X
Columbia Basin Palouse Prairie	X	X
Columbia Plateau Low Sagebrush Steppe	X	X
Columbia Plateau Scabland Shrubland	X	X
Columbia Plateau Steppe and Grassland	X	X
Columbia Plateau Western Juniper Woodland and Savanna	X	
East Cascades Oak-Ponderosa Pine Forest and Woodland	X	
East Gulf Coastal Plain Dune and Coastal Grassland	X	X
East Gulf Coastal Plain Interior Upland Longleaf Pine Woodland	X	
East Gulf Coastal Plain Jackson Plain Prairie and Barrens	X	X
East Gulf Coastal Plain Near-Coast Pine Flatwoods	X	
East Gulf Coastal Plain Savanna and Wet Prairie	X	X
Eastern Great Plains Tallgrass Aspen Parkland	X	
Eastern Great Plains Wet Meadow-Prairie-Marsh	X	X
Eastern Highland Rim Prairie and Barrens	X	X
Edwards Plateau Limestone Savanna and Woodland	X	
Florida Dry Prairie	X	X

(continued)

Table 2—(Continued)

Bps name	NRI	FIA
Florida Peninsula Inland Scrub	X	X
Floridian Highlands Freshwater Marsh	X	X
Great Basin Pinyon-Juniper Woodland	X	
Great Basin Semi-Desert Chaparral	X	X
Great Basin Xeric Mixed Sagebrush Shrubland	X	X
Great Lakes Coastal Marsh Systems	X	X
Great Plains Prairie Pothole	X	X
Gulf and Atlantic Coastal Plain Sparsely Vegetated Systems	X	X
Gulf and Atlantic Coastal Plain Tidal Marsh Systems	X	X
Inter-Mountain Basins Big Sagebrush Shrubland	X	X
Inter-Mountain Basins Big Sagebrush Shrubland - Basin Big Sagebrush	X	X
Inter-Mountain Basins Big Sagebrush Shrubland - Wyoming Big Sagebrush	X	X
Inter-Mountain Basins Big Sagebrush Steppe	X	X
Inter-Mountain Basins Curl-leaf Mountain Mahogany Woodland and Shrubland	X	X
Inter-Mountain Basins Greasewood Flat	X	X
Inter-Mountain Basins Mat Saltbush Shrubland	X	X
Inter-Mountain Basins Mixed Salt Desert Scrub	X	X
Inter-Mountain Basins Mixed Salt Desert Scrub - North	X	X
Inter-Mountain Basins Mixed Salt Desert Scrub - South	X	X
Inter-Mountain Basins Montane Riparian Systems	X	X
Inter-Mountain Basins Montane Sagebrush Steppe	X	X
Inter-Mountain Basins Montane Sagebrush Steppe - Low Sagebrush	X	X
Inter-Mountain Basins Montane Sagebrush Steppe - Mountain Big Sagebrush	X	X
Inter-Mountain Basins Semi-Desert Grassland	X	X
Inter-Mountain Basins Semi-Desert Shrub-Steppe	X	X
Inter-Mountain Basins Sparsely Vegetated Systems	X	X
Inter-Mountain Basins Subalpine Limber-Bristlecone Pine Woodland	X	
Klamath-Siskiyou Xeromorphic Serpentine Savanna and Chaparral	X	X
Laurentian Pine-Oak Barrens	X	
Laurentian-Acadian Shrub-Herbaceous Wetland Systems	X	X
Llano Uplift Acidic Forest-Woodland-Glade	X	
Lower Mississippi Alluvial Plain Grand Prairie	X	X
Madrean Lower Montane Pine-Oak Forest and Woodland	X	
Madrean Oriental Chaparral	X	X
Mediterranean California Alpine Dry Tundra	X	X
Mediterranean California Alpine Fell-Field	X	X
Mediterranean California Sparsely Vegetated Systems	X	X
Mediterranean California Subalpine Meadow	X	X
Middle Rocky Mountain Montane Douglas-fir Forest and Woodland - Fire-maintained Savanna	X	
Mogollon Chaparral	X	X
Mojave Mid-Elevation Mixed Desert Scrub	X	X
Nashville Basin Limestone Glade and Woodland	X	FIA
North American Warm Desert Riparian Systems	X	X
North American Warm Desert Riparian Systems - Stringers	X	X
North American Warm Desert Sparsely Vegetated Systems	X	X
North Pacific Alpine and Subalpine Dry Grassland	X	X
North Pacific Avalanche Chute Shrubland	X	X
North Pacific Broadleaf Landslide Forest and Shrubland	X	
North Pacific Dry and Mesic Alpine Dwarf-Shrubland or Fell-field or Meadow	X	X
North Pacific Maritime Mesic Subalpine Parkland	X	X
North Pacific Montane Grassland	X	X
North Pacific Montane Shrubland	X	X
North Pacific Oak Woodland	X	
North Pacific Sparsely Vegetated Systems	X	X
North-Central Interior Sand and Gravel Tallgrass Prairie	X	X
Northern and Central California Dry-Mesic Chaparral	X	X

(continued)

Table 2—(Continued)

Bps name	NRI	FIA
Northern Atlantic Coastal Plain Dune and Swale	X	X
Northern California Coastal Scrub	X	X
Northern Rocky Mountain Foothill Conifer Wooded Steppe	X	
Northern Rocky Mountain Lower Montane-Foothill-Valley Grassland	X	X
Northern Rocky Mountain Montane-Foothill Deciduous Shrubland	X	X
Northern Rocky Mountain Ponderosa Pine Woodland and Savanna	X	
Northern Rocky Mountain Ponderosa Pine Woodland and Savanna - Mesic	X	
Northern Rocky Mountain Ponderosa Pine Woodland and Savanna - Xeric	X	
Northern Rocky Mountain Subalpine-Upper Montane Grassland	X	X
Northern Tallgrass Prairie	X	X
Northwestern Great Plains Aspen Forest and Parkland	X	
Northwestern Great Plains Canyon	X	X
Northwestern Great Plains Mixedgrass Prairie	X	X
Northwestern Great Plains Shrubland	X	X
Northwestern Great Plains-Black Hills Ponderosa Pine Woodland and Savanna - Savanna	X	
Pacific Coastal Marsh Systems	X	X
Paleozoic Plateau Bluff and Talus	X	X
Pennyroyal Karst Plain Prairie and Barrens	X	X
Rocky Mountain Alpine Dwarf-Shrubland	X	X
Rocky Mountain Alpine Fell-Field	X	X
Rocky Mountain Alpine Turf	X	X
Rocky Mountain Alpine/Montane Sparsely Vegetated Systems	X	X
Rocky Mountain Foothill Limber Pine-Juniper Woodland	X	
Rocky Mountain Lower Montane-Foothill Shrubland	X	X
Rocky Mountain Lower Montane-Foothill Shrubland - No True Mountain Mahogany	X	X
Rocky Mountain Lower Montane-Foothill Shrubland - True Mountain Mahogany	X	X
Rocky Mountain Subalpine/Upper Montane Riparian Systems	X	X
Rocky Mountain Subalpine-Montane Mesic Meadow	X	X
Sierra Nevada Alpine Dwarf-Shrubland	X	X
Sonora-Mojave Creosotebush-White Bursage Desert Scrub	X	X
Sonora-Mojave Mixed Salt Desert Scrub	X	X
Sonora-Mojave Semi-Desert Chaparral	X	X
Sonoran Granite Outcrop Desert Scrub	X	X
Sonoran Mid-Elevation Desert Scrub	X	X
Sonoran Paloverde-Mixed Cacti Desert Scrub	X	X
South Florida Everglades Sawgrass Marsh	X	X
South Florida Pine Flatwoods	X	
South Texas Lomas	X	X
South Texas Sand Sheet Grassland	X	X
Southeastern Great Plains Tallgrass Prairie	X	X
Southern Appalachian Grass and Shrub Bald	X	X
Southern Atlantic Coastal Plain Dune and Maritime Grassland	X	X
Southern Atlantic Coastal Plain Wet Pine Savanna and Flatwoods	X	
Southern Blackland Tallgrass Prairie	X	X
Southern California Coastal Scrub	X	X
Southern California Dry-Mesic Chaparral	X	
Southern Colorado Plateau Sand Shrubland	X	X
Southern Rocky Mountain Montane-Subalpine Grassland	X	X
Southern Rocky Mountain Ponderosa Pine Savanna	X	X
Southern Rocky Mountain Ponderosa Pine Savanna - North	X	
Southern Rocky Mountain Ponderosa Pine Savanna - South	X	
Tamaulipan Calcareous Thornscrub	X	X
Tamaulipan Clay Grassland	X	X
Tamaulipan Mixed Deciduous Thornscrub	X	X
Tamaulipan Savanna Grassland	X	X
Texas-Louisiana Coastal Prairie	X	X

(continued)

Table 2—(Continued)

Bps name	NRI	FIA
Texas-Louisiana Saline Coastal Prairie	X	X
West Gulf Coastal Plain Northern Calcareous Prairie	X	X
West Gulf Coastal Plain Southern Calcareous Prairie	X	X
Western Great Plains Depressional Wetland Systems	X	X
Western Great Plains Depressional Wetland Systems - Playa	X	X
Western Great Plains Depressional Wetland Systems - Saline	X	X
Western Great Plains Floodplain Systems	X	
Western Great Plains Foothill and Piedmont Grassland	X	X
Western Great Plains Sand Prairie	X	X
Western Great Plains Sandhill Steppe	X	X
Western Great Plains Shortgrass Prairie	X	X
Western Great Plains Sparsely Vegetated Systems	X	X
Western Great Plains Tallgrass Prairie	X	X
Western Highland Rim Prairie and Barrens	X	X
Willamette Valley Upland Prairie and Savanna	X	X
Wyoming Basins Dwarf Sagebrush Shrubland and Steppe	X	X

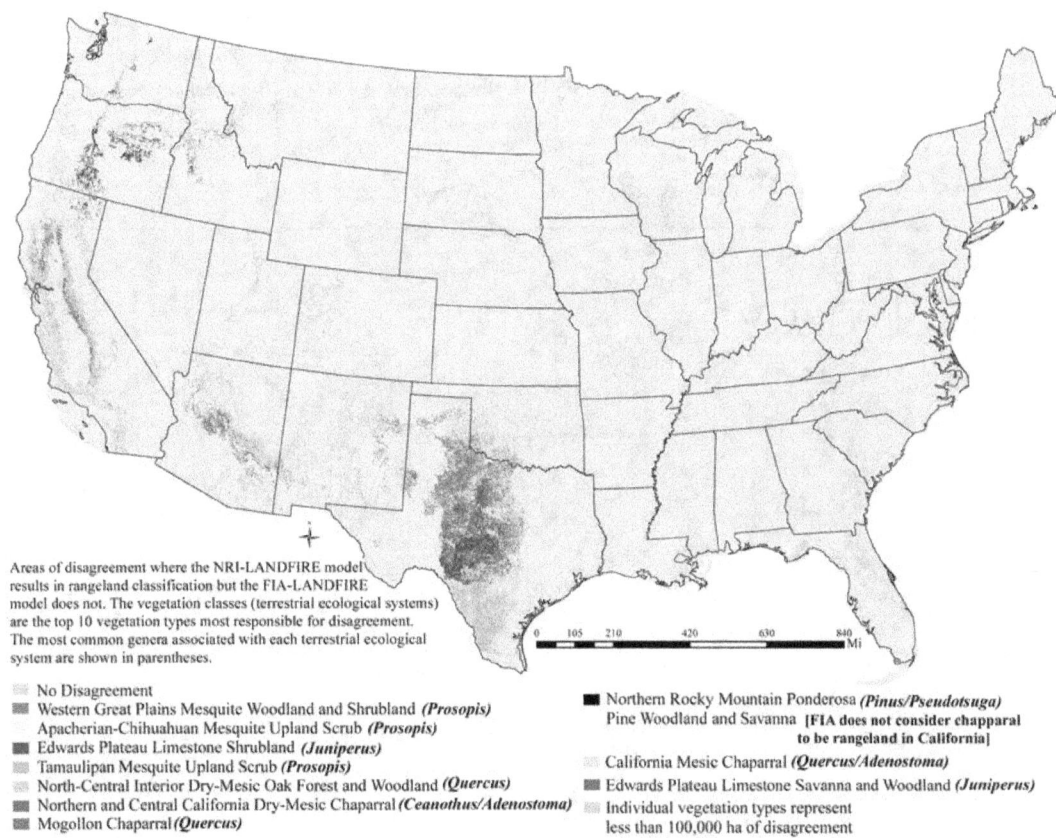

Areas of disagreement where the NRI-LANDFIRE model results in rangeland classification but the FIA-LANDFIRE model does not. The vegetation classes (terrestrial ecological systems) are the top 10 vegetation types most responsible for disagreement. The most common genera associated with each terrestrial ecological system are shown in parentheses.

- No Disagreement
- Western Great Plains Mesquite Woodland and Shrubland *(Prosopis)*
- Apacherian-Chihuahuan Mesquite Upland Scrub *(Prosopis)*
- Edwards Plateau Limestone Shrubland *(Juniperus)*
- Tamaulipan Mesquite Upland Scrub *(Prosopis)*
- North-Central Interior Dry-Mesic Oak Forest and Woodland *(Quercus)*
- Northern and Central California Dry-Mesic Chaparral *(Ceanothus/Adenostoma)*
- Mogollon Chaparral *(Quercus)*

- Northern Rocky Mountain Ponderosa *(Pinus/Pseudotsuga)* Pine Woodland and Savanna [FIA does not consider chapparal to be rangeland in California]
- California Mesic Chaparral *(Quercus/Adenostoma)*
- Edwards Plateau Limestone Savanna and Woodland *(Juniperus)*
- Individual vegetation types represent less than 100,000 ha of disagreement

Figure 3—Areas of disagreement in rangeland extent between the NRI and FIA LANDFIRE models. Areas of disagreement generally reflect different tree canopy cover thresholds and treatment of woodland species (such as *Juniperus*, *Quercus*, and *Prosopis* spp.) between the NRI and FIA rangeland definitions.

Non-Federal Rangelands

Most rangelands are privately owned and lie west of the 95° meridian (figure 4). All range-land area statistics in this section are supplied by the NRI program and not by the work of Reeves and Mitchell (2011) since the NRI is recognized as a statistical authority on the matter. According to the NRI (USDA 2009), area of non-Federal rangelands is 409,119,000 acres. The states currently exhibiting the greatest amount of non-Federal rangeland are shown in figure 5. Texas, at 98 million acres currently has the greatest non-Federal rangeland area by a wide margin, more than twice the area of the next highest state, New Mexico. There are no non-Federal rangelands (figure 5) in 27 states of the eastern United States according to USDA (2009).

Between 1982 and 2007, non-Federal rangelands throughout the United States have experienced a net loss of roughly 8.8 million acres of rangelands (table 3) (USDA 2009) representing an average annual loss of 350,000 acres. This loss constitutes roughly 2 percent of the current non-Federal rangeland base (USDA 2009). Area of non-Federal rangeland decreased sharply between 1982 and 1997, yet since the 2000 RPA Rangeland Assessment (Mitchell 2000), non-Federal rangelands have increased by approximately 200,000 acres (figure 6). It should be noted that these area estimates do not include Conservation Reserve Program (CRP) acres as those are tallied as a separate land type category (table 3). Those states that lost rangeland area between 1982 and 2007 are shown in figure 7. Florida exhibited the highest loss of non-Federal rangelands in the country at 1.75 million acres between 1982 and 2007 (USDA 2009).

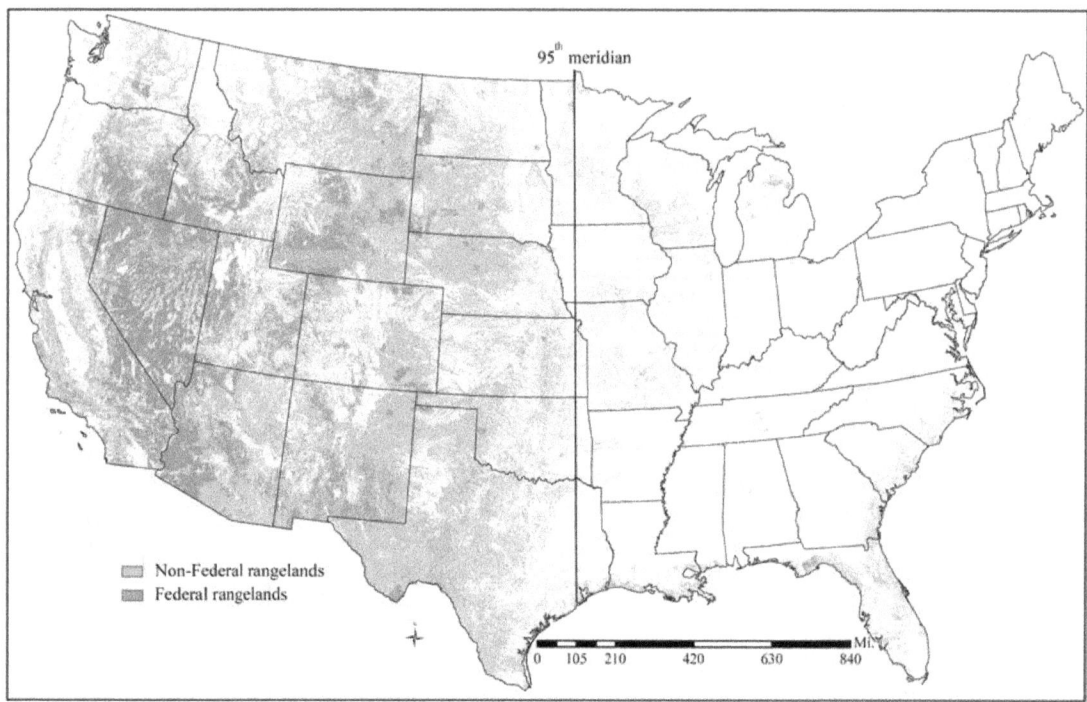

Figure 4—Distribution of non-Federal and Federally owned rangelands (adapted from Reeves and Mitchell [2011]).

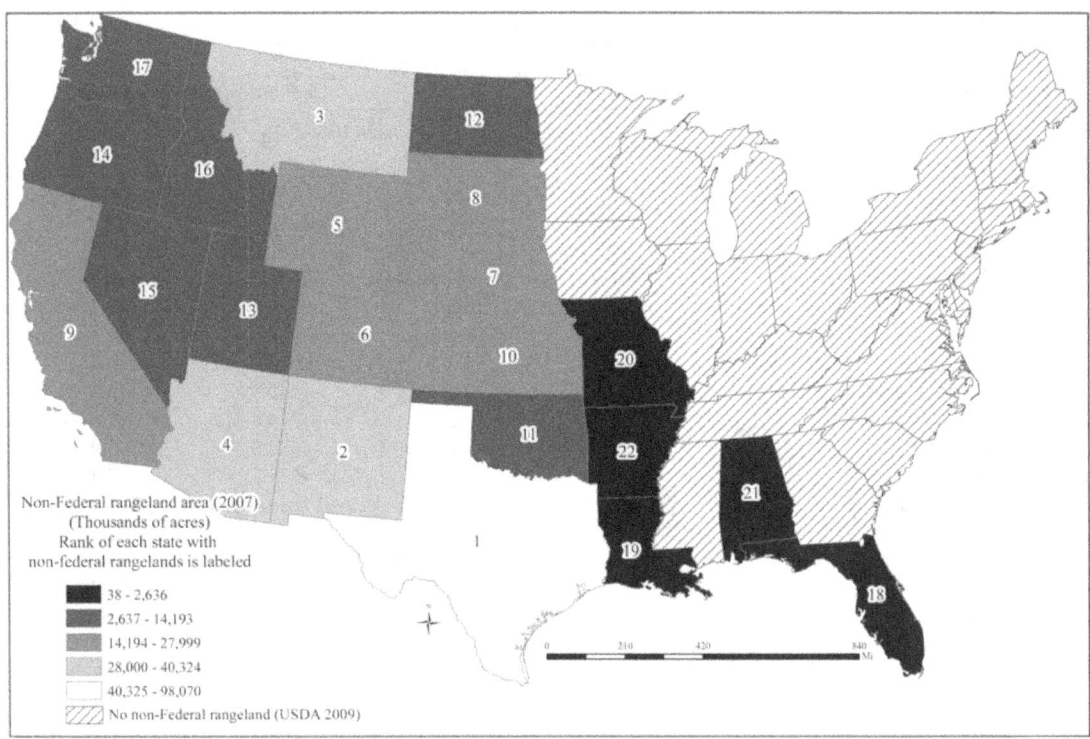

Figure 5—Ranking of non-Federal rangeland acres. Texas has the most non-Federal rangeland (NRI 2007). Hatched states indicate no non-Federal rangeland (NRI 2007). Data source: Natural Resources Inventory (2007) (USDA 2009).

Table 3—Net change in area of non-Federal rangelands from 1982 to 2007.

Assessment Region/State	Net Change in:			
	Rangeland	Pasture	CRP land	Crop land
	- Acres 10^3 - - - - - - - - - - - - - - - - - - -			
Pacific Coast				
California	-1600.2	-237.1	-941.3	327.0
Washington	-163.1	-389.4	-1294.2	71.4
Oregon	-147.5	-320.0	-746.7	110.3
Pacific Coast Total	**-1910.8**	**-946.5**	**-2982.2**	**508.7**
Rocky Mountain				
New Mexico	-1495.9	54.9	-918.7	206.3
Montana	-897.8	671.6	-3084.0	-28.8
South Dakota	-784.8	-556.2	-245.4	1.6
Kansas	-740.7	384.1	-3461.8	50.2
Nebraska	-584.1	-197.3	-705.8	54.0
North Dakota	-507.4	-5.8	-3033.6	85.1
Idaho	-177.6	103.4	-1154.1	94.6
Colorado	-92.4	-29.4	-3017.5	136.2
Nevada	39.3	-44.8	-345.9	54.0
Utah	43.6	161.3	-630.7	18.7
Arizona	75.3	4.7	-493.9	308.4
Wyoming	221.3	-178.0	-457.9	10.0
Rocky Mountain Total	**-4901.2**	**368.5**	**-17549**	**990.3**

(continued)

Table 3—Continued.

Assessment Region/State	Net Change in:			
	Rangeland	Pasture	CRP land	Crop land
	- Acres 10^3 -			
South				
Florida	-1752.3	-740	-741.7	246.8
Oklahoma	-924.7	1271.7	-2784.9	81.4
Arkansas	-3.9	-467	-683.7	66.5
Alabama	-0.3	-361.8	-2250.3	-36.5
Georgia	0	-135.8	-2585.1	-62.5
Kentucky	0	-712.3	-734.9	-122.7
Mississippi	0	-731.3	-2675.4	136.4
North Carolina	0	-66.1	-1440.5	114.3
South Carolina	0	-103	-1324.6	69.6
Tennessee	0	-312	-1382.9	145.4
Virginia	0	-289.9	-635.2	-27.4
South Total	**-2681.2**	**-2647.5**	**-17239**	**611.3**
North				
Missouri	-45.9	-1588	-1599.3	16.7
Connecticut	0	-12.2	-63.3	-3.7
Delaware	0	2.9	-105.1	11.7
Illinois	0	-953.6	-835.1	36.7
Indiana	0	-277.4	-615.0	-42.7
Iowa	0	-1245.1	-939.0	3.4
Maine	0	-141.5	-145.7	-90.6
Maryland	0	-77.3	-358.8	-1.6
Massachusetts	0	-51.6	-47.8	-56.0
Michigan	0	-724.5	-1538.0	-138.4
Minnesota	0	-62.9	-2265.3	-28.1
New Hampshire	0	-22.8	-50.4	-22.8
New Jersey	0	-84.3	-330.3	-6.6
New York	0	-1194.7	-873.5	159.6
Ohio	0	-495.6	-1330.4	-131.8
Pennsylvania	0	-602.4	-942.2	-128.8
Rhode Island	0	-12.9	-9.2	-3.4
Vermont	0	-136.8	-102.9	31.4
West Virginia	0	-459.1	-323.6	20.3
Wisconsin	0	-359.3	-1414.6	116.3
North total	**-45.9**	**6318.8**	**-8499.1**	**-13890**
U.S. total	**-8780.1**	**32850.2**	**-12280.6**	**-62523**

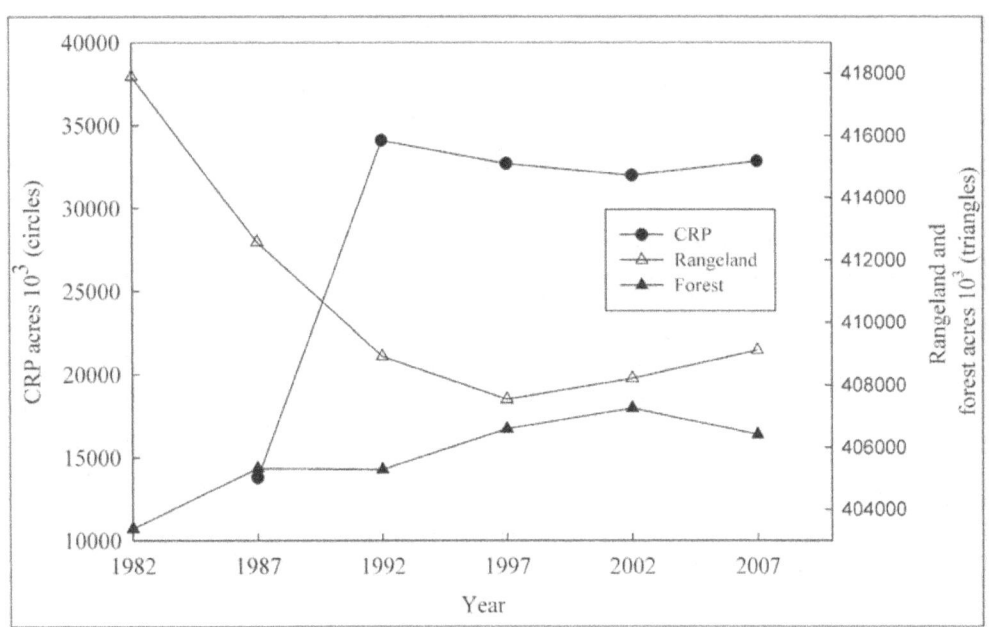

Figure 6—Trends in rangeland, forest, and Conservation Reserve Program (CRP) area in the coterminous United States from 1982 to 2007 (NRI 2007).

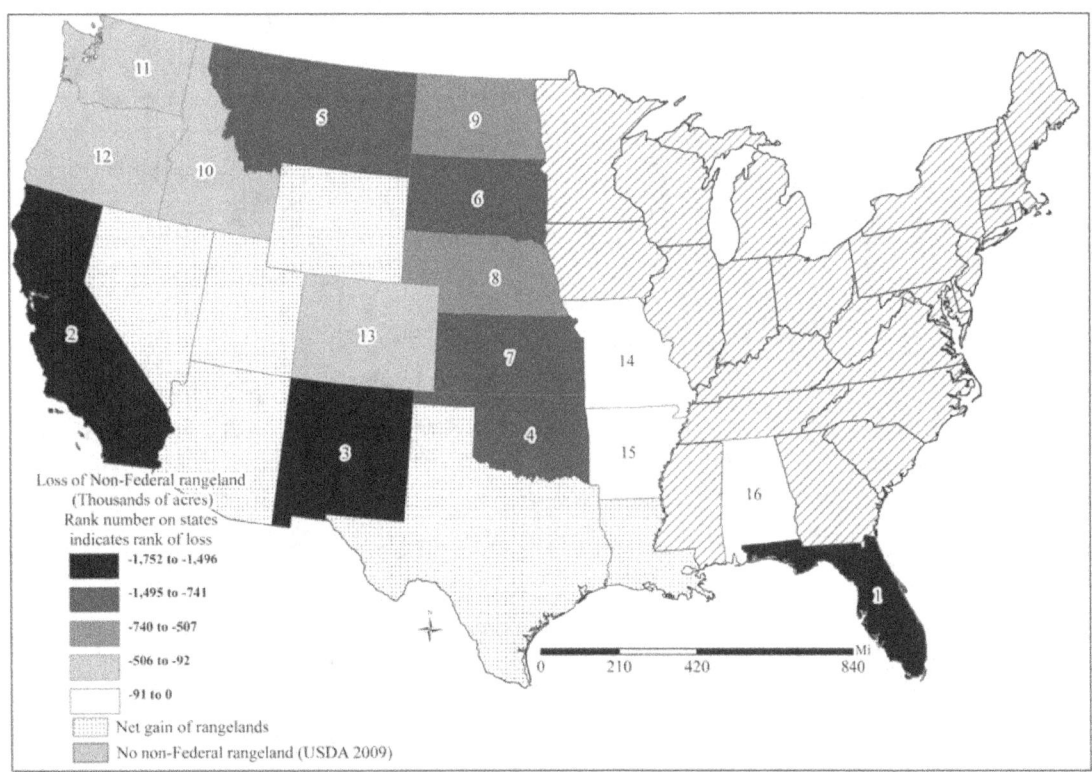

Figure 7—Net loss of non-Federal rangelands from 1982 to 2007 (NRI 2007). Gray states indicate no non-Federal rangeland (NRI 2007), while white states indicate a net gain in non-Federal rangelands from 1982 to 2007. State labels indicate the ranking of net loss of acres. Florida lost the most rangeland between 1982 and 2007 (NRI 2007). Data source: Natural Resources Inventory (2007) (USDA 2009).

The Rocky Mountain Assessment Region (table 3) exhibited the greatest loss of rangeland and the North Assessment Region exhibited the least. This is not surprising since the Rocky Mountain Assessment Region has the greatest amount of non-Federal rangeland and contains some of the fastest growing areas of the United States such as Phoenix, Arizona, Denver, Colorado, and Las Vegas, Nevada.

National Forest System Lands

Since no consistent method is used within USFS to quantify the extent of rangelands under its jurisdiction, no attempt is made to reconcile different estimates. Instead, we rely on two sources: the 1989 RPA Rangeland Assessment (Joyce 1989) and the recent work by Reeves and Mitchell (2011). The report by Joyce (1989) indicated that the USFS had 41 million acres under its jurisdiction. The analysis by Reeves and Mitchell (2011) estimated 48 million acres under USFS jurisdiction based on the NRI perspective and 28.93 million acres from the FIA perspective (table 4). Table 5 shows those 10 administrative boundaries associated with the USFS with the highest rangeland area estimates. The Tonto National Forest has the most rangeland of any single administrative unit with 1,922,861 acres according to the NRI perspective—an estimate differing by nearly one million acres from the FIA perspective. This difference reflects the disparate treatment of species common in pinyon-juniper environments and the different tree canopy cover thresholds for a forest designation between the NRI and FIA perspectives.

Table 4—Comparison of rangeland area from NRI and FIA perspectives for land management agencies with significant amounts of rangeland.

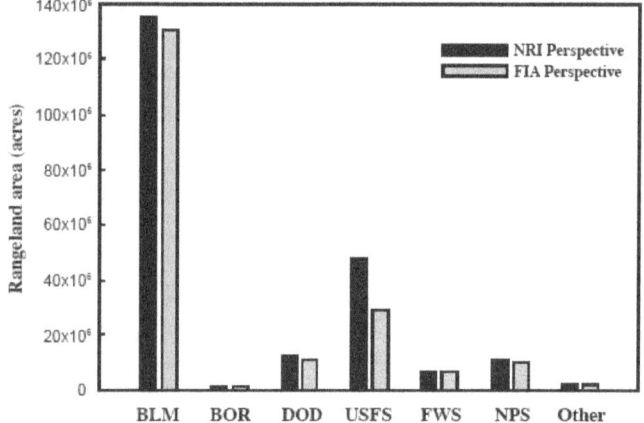

Table 5—Administrative units (top 10) of the USFS and associated rangeland area estimates from the FIA and NRI perspectives.

Administrative unit[a]	NRI perspective	FIA perspective
	---------- Acres ----------	
Tonto National Forest	1,922,861	966,450
Little Missouri National Grassland	1,626,332	1,543,288
Thunder Basin National Grassland	1,556,257	1,551,007
Modoc National Forest	1,012,663	615,693
Boise National Forest	938,687	527,350
Toiyabe National Forest	924,873	754,968
Buffalo Gap National Grassland	798,063	772,132
Gila National Forest	696,577	182,389
Apache National Forest	679,867	226,614
Fremont National Forest	672,995	196,803

[a] The administrative units used for estimating rangeland area were derived from the Federal lands database from the Protected Areas. Database Version 1.0 (USGS Version 1.0).

Bureau of Land Management Rangelands

The BLM estimates rangeland area under its jurisdiction by summing the area of grazing allotments found in each state, without regard for the vegetation type present. This means that rangelands are characterized entirely from a land use perspective. To maintain consistency with past reports, we report rangeland area on BLM lands in this manner. However, we also provide an estimate of rangeland area from a land cover perspective, as is provided for the USFS (in the prior section), using the techniques from Reeves and Mitchell (2011).

The BLM has jurisdiction over 156,661,328 acres of lands within grazing allotments. All public lands within grazing districts (figure 8) are referred to as "Section 3" and are administered under the jurisdiction of the Taylor Grazing Act (1934) and various other laws and regulations enacted after the Taylor Grazing Act. These lands are generally characterized as large tracts. BLM lands outside grazing districts are referred to as Section 15 lands (they are described in Section 15 of the Taylor Grazing Act) and are administered under the jurisdiction of the Taylor Grazing Act and various other laws and regulations enacted after the Taylor Grazing Act. The Section 15 lands typically occur in smaller, isolated patches. In addition to these lands and others in the coterminous United States, the BLM manages nearly 75 million acres in Alaska (none of which are contained in grazing districts) for a total of 249,714,362 acres under its jurisdiction. The BLM has lost roughly 12 million acres in the last decade

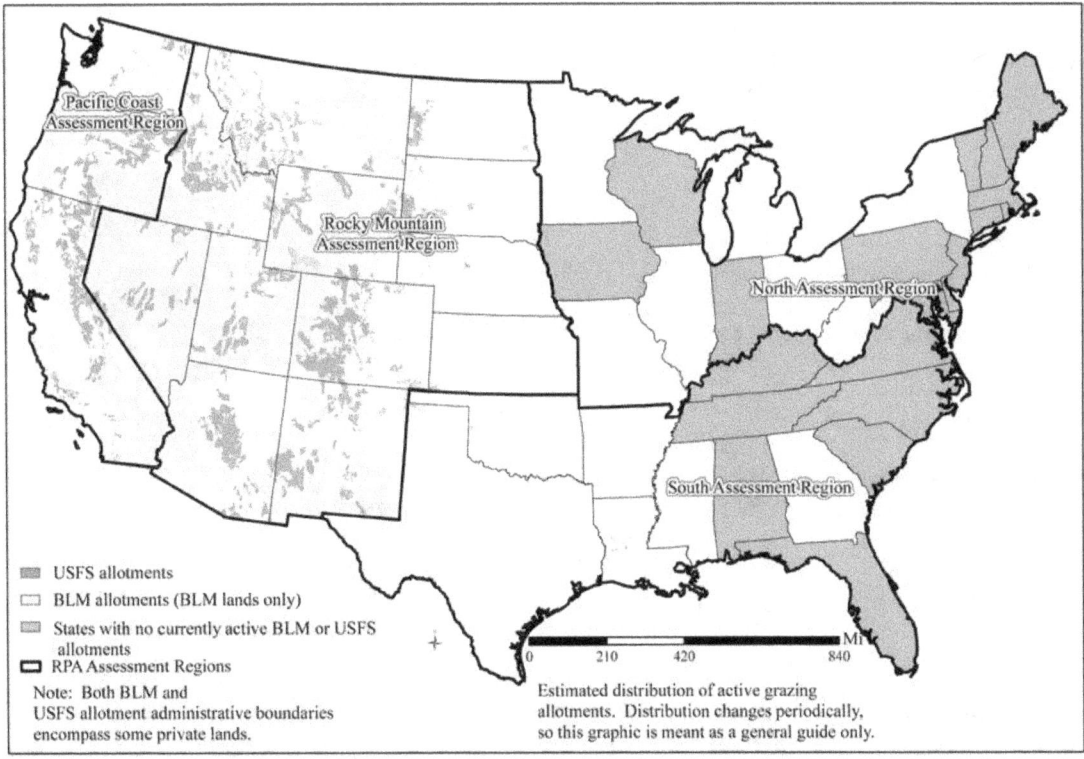

Figure 8—Grazing allotments, districts, and pastures administered by the USFS and BLM.

(BLM 2000 to 2009). Loss of lands under BLM jurisdiction is due to land exchanges or disbursements (Karl, personal communication). Area within grazing allotments has also decreased over the last 10 years, partly due to new National Monument status designations (table 6). Although quantifying the extent of lands within grazing allotments is perhaps an important metric from an administrative viewpoint, it does not address the rangeland extent on BLM lands from a land-cover perspective.

The methods of Reeves and Mitchell (2011) provide an estimate of rangelands administered by the BLM in the coterminous United States of 139 and 131 million acres from the NRI and FIA perspectives, respectively. Essentially all BLM lands are found in the western United States, with 81 percent occurring in the Rocky Mountain Assessment Region (table 7). Assuming the estimates provided by Reeves and Mitchell (2011) are reasonably accurate, roughly 70 percent of BLM lands within the coterminous United States are considered rangelands from a land cover perspective.

Table 6—Monument designations since 2000 under BLM administration.

State	Monument	BLM acres	Other Federal acres	Non-Federal acres	Total acres	Designation date
Arizona	Agua Fria	70,900	0	1,444	72,344	1/11/2000
Arizona	Grand Canyon-Parashant	808,747	208,453	31,125	1,048,325	1/11/2000
Arizona	Ironwood Forest	128,398	299	59,922	188,619	6/9/2000
Arizona	Sonoran Desert	486,600	0	9,800	496,400	1/17/2001
Arizona	Vermilion Cliffs	279,568	0	14,121	293,689	11/9/2000
	Arizona total	**1,774,213**	**208,752**	**116,412**	**2,099,377**	
California	California Coastal	607	0	0	607	1/11/2000
California	Carrizo Plain	207,237	0	39,575	246,812	1/17/2001
California	Santa Rosa-San Jacinto Mountains	94,055	83,073	102,943	280,071	10/24/2000 3/30/2009
	California total	**301,899**	**83,073**	**142,518**	**527,490**	
Colorado	Canyons of the Ancients	163,892	0	18,530	182,422	6/9/2000
Idaho	Craters of the Moon	274,693	462,832	14,799	14,810	11/9/2000
Montana	Pompeys Pillar	51	0	0	51	1/17/2001
Montana	Upper Missouri River Breaks	374,976	0	120,475	495,451	1/17/2001
	Montana total	**375,027**	**0**	**120,475**	**495,502**	
New Mexico	Kasha-Katuwe Tent Rocks	4,124	0	1,278	5,402	1/17/2001
New Mexico	Prehistoric Trackways	5,255	0	0	0	3/30/2009
	New Mexico total	**9,379**	**0**	**1,278**	**5,402**	
Oregon	Cascade-Siskiyou	53,829	52	32,117	85,998	6/9/2000
Utah	Grand Staircase-Escalante	1,866,331	13,977	153	1,880,461	9/19/1996
	U.S. total	**4,819,263**	**768,686**	**446,282**	**5,291,462**	

Table 7—Distribution of BLM lands in the coterminous United States. "AR" is Assessment Region.

State	Area (2009)	Proportion of coterminous U.S. BLM holdings (2009)
	ac x 10^3	(%)
Oregon	1,613.38	9.225
California	1,529.85	8.748
Washington	43.02	0.246
Pacific Northwest AR Total	**3,186.25**	**18.219**
Nevada	4,780.67	27.336
Utah	2,285.62	13.069
Wyoming	1,836.75	10.503
New Mexico	1,347.70	7.706
Arizona	1,220.33	6.978
Idaho	1,160.95	6.638
Colorado	834.60	4.772
Montana	796.74	4.556
South Dakota	27.44	0.157
North Dakota	5.88	0.034
Nebraska	0.64	0.004
Rocky Mountain AR total	**14,297.33**	**81.753**
Wisconsin	0.24	0.001
Minnesota	0.14	0.001
Maryland	0.05	0
North AR total	**0.44**	**0.002**
Louisiana	1.65	0.009
Texas	1.18	0.007
Arkansas	0.61	0.003
Alabama	0.35	0.002
Florida	0.31	0.002
Oklahoma	0.20	0.001
Virginia	0.08	0
Mississippi	0.02	0
South AR	**4.41**	**0.025**
Coterminous U.S.	**17,488.42**	**70**

Rangelands in Protected Status

The area of rangelands in protected area status is a key indicator of rangeland sustainability (http://sustainable.rangelands.org/pdf/Core_Indicators.pdf). Here, protected areas are identified using the Protected Areas Database of the United States (PADUS) (Version 1.0, http://www.protectedlands.net/padus/). These protected areas are broadly defined by the IUCN as: "An area of land and/or sea especially dedicated to the protection and maintenance of biological diversity, and of natural and associated cultural resources, and managed through legal or other effective means" (http://iucn.org/about/union/commissions/wcpa/). Although all protected lands can meet this definition, categories of status have also been defined to enable more succinct descriptions on the level of protection an area is subject to. Table 8 describes the different levels of protection each category receives according to the IUCN.

Table 8—Protected area categories defined by the International Union for Conservation of Nature (IUCN) (http://www.unep-wcmc.org/protected_areas/categories/index.html).

CATEGORY Ia:	Strict Nature Reserve: protected area managed mainly for science. Area of land and/or sea possessing some outstanding or representative ecosystems, geological or physiological features and/or species, available primarily for scientific research and/or environmental monitoring.
CATEGORY Ib	Wilderness Area: protected area managed mainly for wilderness protection. Large area of unmodified or slightly modified land, and/or sea, retaining its natural character and influence, without permanent or significant habitation, which is protected and managed so as to preserve its natural condition.
CATEGORY II	National Park: protected area managed mainly for ecosystem protection and recreation. Natural area of land and/or sea, designated to (a) protect the ecological integrity of one or more ecosystems for present and future generations, (b) exclude exploitation or occupation inimical to the purposes of designation of the area and (c) provide a foundation for spiritual, scientific, educational, recreational and visitor opportunities, all of which must be environmentally and culturally compatible.
CATEGORY III	Natural Monument: protected area managed mainly for conservation of specific natural features. Area containing one, or more, specific natural or natural/cultural feature which is of outstanding or unique value because of its inherent rarity, representative or aesthetic qualities or cultural significance.
CATEGORY IV	Habitat/Species Management Area: protected area managed mainly for conservation through management intervention.
CATEGORY V	Protected Landscape/Seascape: protected area managed mainly for landscape/seascape conservation and recreation. Area of land, with coast and sea as appropriate, where the interaction of people and nature over time has produced an area of distinct character with significant aesthetic, ecological and/or cultural value, and often with high biological diversity. Safeguarding the integrity of this traditional interaction is vital to the protection, maintenance and evolution of such an area.
CATEGORY VI	Managed Resource Protected Area: protected area managed mainly for the sustainable use of natural ecosystems. Area containing predominantly unmodified natural systems, managed to ensure long term protection and maintenance of biological diversity, while providing at the same time a sustainable flow of natural products and services to meet community needs.

The PADUS reveals an approximate area of 430.35 million acres of protected lands in the coterminous United States. Of these lands, rangelands occupy roughly 195.22 million acres or 45 percent of the total area or protected lands (table 9). Approximately 82 percent of the protected rangelands are found in just five states: Nevada, California, Oregon, Idaho, and Arizona. The most common Ecological Systems and NVCS alliances (Comer and others 2003) occupying the top 20 largest protected areas dominated by rangelands are listed in (table 10).

Research Natural Areas (RNAs) (http://www.fs fed.us/rmrs/research-natural-areas/) are a unique sort of protected lands administered by the USFS and found almost exclusively in the western United States (figure 9). These RNAs help protect biological diversity and represent common ecosystems in natural condition that can serve as reference areas. Based on the methods of Reeves and Mitchell (2011), RNAs are comprised of 70 and 50 percent rangeland vegetation from the NRI and FIA perspectives, respectively (table 11).

Table 9—Extent and proportion of rangelands contained within protected lands adapted from Reeves and Mitchell (2011). Only those states with greater than 1 million acres of protected rangeland area are shown (million acres).

State	Extent of protected area	Rangeland area (FIA perspective)	Rangeland area (NRI perspective)	Percent of protected area that is rangeland (NRI perspective)	Percent of protected area that is rangeland (FIA perspective)
NV	98	64	74	76	66
CA	61	26	37	60	43
OR	39	17	21	53	43
ID	34	13	15	45	37
AZ	20	8	13	66	40
UT	16	4	5	34	24
NM	12	3	5	38	22
WY	14	3	4	26	22
CO	18	3	3	19	15
MT	22	3	3	15	12
SD	3	2	2	73	61
FL	12	0.5	2	18	4
TX	6	2	2	36	29
ND	3	2	2	76	63
WA	12	1	1	12	10

Table 10—Twenty National Forest examples of protected areas and their associated rangeland area (from NRI and FIA perspectives) and vegetation composition estimates.

Area name	Rangeland area (NRI perspective)	Rangeland area (FIA perspective)	Dominant rangeland Ecological System
Tonto NF	1,854,593	840,823	Sonoran Paloverde-Mixed Cacti Desert Scrub
Toiyabe NF	1,491,460	1,155,603	Great Basin Xeric Mixed Sagebrush Shrubland
Modoc NF	986,130	550,640	Inter-Mountain Basins Big Sagebrush Shrubland
Prescott NF	742,851	175,921	Mogollon Chaparral
Sawtooth NF	689,967	540,708	*Artemisia tridentata* ssp. *vaseyana* Shrubland Alliance
Targhee NF	291,522	252,723	*Artemisia tridentata* ssp. *vaseyana* Shrubland Alliance
Uinta NF	313,912	143,255	*Artemisia tridentata* ssp. *vaseyana* Shrubland Alliance
Wild Rivers Recreation Area	238,417	180,509	Inter-Mountain Basins Big Sagebrush Shrubland
White River NF	201,090	126,341	*Quercus gambelii* Shrubland Alliance
Sevilleta NWR	190,535	166,595	Apacherian-Chihuahuan Semi-Desert Grassland and Steppe
Mendocino NF	223,390	13,949	Northern and Central California Dry-Mesic Chaparral
Rio Grande NF	162,261	137,499	Rocky Mountain Alpine Turf
Mazatzal Wilderness	205,409	83,647	Sonoran Paloverde-Mixed Cacti Desert Scrub
San Bernardino NF	246,504	46,593	Southern California Dry-Mesic Chaparral
Santa Fe NF	184,469	63,905	Western Great Plains Shortgrass Prairie
Sitgreaves NF	174,847	106,423	*Quercus gambelii* Shrubland Alliance
Superstition Wilderness	140,226	83,344	Sonoran Paloverde-Mixed Cacti Desert Scrub
Wasatch-Cache NF	167,386	95,566	*Artemisia tridentata* ssp. *vaseyana* Shrubland Alliance

Figure 9—Distribution of Research Natural Areas (RNAs) in the coterminous United States. RNAs are not shown to scale.

Table 11—Top 10 areas with most rangeland acres (from NRI and FIA perspectives) contained within Research Natural Areas (RNAs).

RNA name	State	Area of RNAs (acres)	Rangeland area NRI perspective (acres)	Rangeland area FIA perspective (acres)	Percent of RNAs as range from NRI perspective	Percent of RNAs as range from FIA perspective
Smiley Mountain	ID	3,099	2,058	2,058	66	66
Spring Branch	CO	4,005	2,053	2,024	51	51
Red Butte Canyon	UT	4,658	3,236	326	69	7
Lost Water Canyon	MT	3,658	1,470	1,470	40	40
Middle Canyon	ID	2,336	1,367	1,211	59	52
Harvey Monroe Hall	CA	3,832	1,226	1,226	32	32
Gibson Jack Creek	ID	2,316	1,247	1,170	54	51
Line Creek	WY	1,884	1,168	1,168	62	62
Finger Mesa	CO	3,194	1,094	1,094	34	34
Bald Mountain	NV	5,781	1,082	905	19	16
Pasture 45	NE	939	925	925	98	98
Blillo	NM	1,027	882	871	86	85
Meadow Canyon	ID	3,954	865	809	22	20
White Mountain	CA	1,848	994	675	54	37
Sentinel Meadow	CA	1,933	1,092	552	56	29
Devil's Garden	CA	800	795	762	99	95
Devil's Rock	CA	5,709	1,448	0	25	0
Cliff Lake	MT	2,347	633	620	27	26
Browse	UT	1,394	858	370	62	27
Monumental Creek	ID	755	658	557	87	74
Targhee Creek	ID	2,714	586	586	22	22

Extent and Disposition of Human Modified Rangeland

Since the 2000 RPA Rangeland Assessment (Mitchell 2000), advances in remote sensing and data availability for U.S. rangelands have enabled new analyses characterizing the decline of coterminous rangelands since the pre-settlement era in addition to quantifying the current extent and magnitude of fragmentation and human modified lands. Spatially explicit data describing human modified cover were recently created by analyzing 6000 sites across the coterminous United States and digitizing human modified cover from high-resolution aerial photography. These training areas were used to extrapolate the percent of human modified cover across the landscape using a consortium of geospatial data sources. Here, "human modification" refers to permanent conversion from rangeland to another land type and represents the landscape circa 2005. Modifications such as agricultural, residential, resource extraction, recreation and transportation, mixed use, and undeveloped were mapped. Phenomena such as the presence of exotic species are not sufficiently evaluated here but arguably can be labeled as a human modification. An in-depth analysis regarding the alteration or disappearance of rangeland vegetation types is beyond the scope of this report. However, this section does provide a synoptic overview regarding the wide-scale alteration of key rangeland vegetation types.

The extent of current and historic rangelands is identified using the data estimated by Reeves and Mitchell (2011). The estimated historical extent of rangelands in the coterminous United States identified from the NRI and FIA perspectives portrayed in Reeves and Mitchell (2011) is approximately 1.1 billion and 883 million acres, respectively (figure 10). These data have

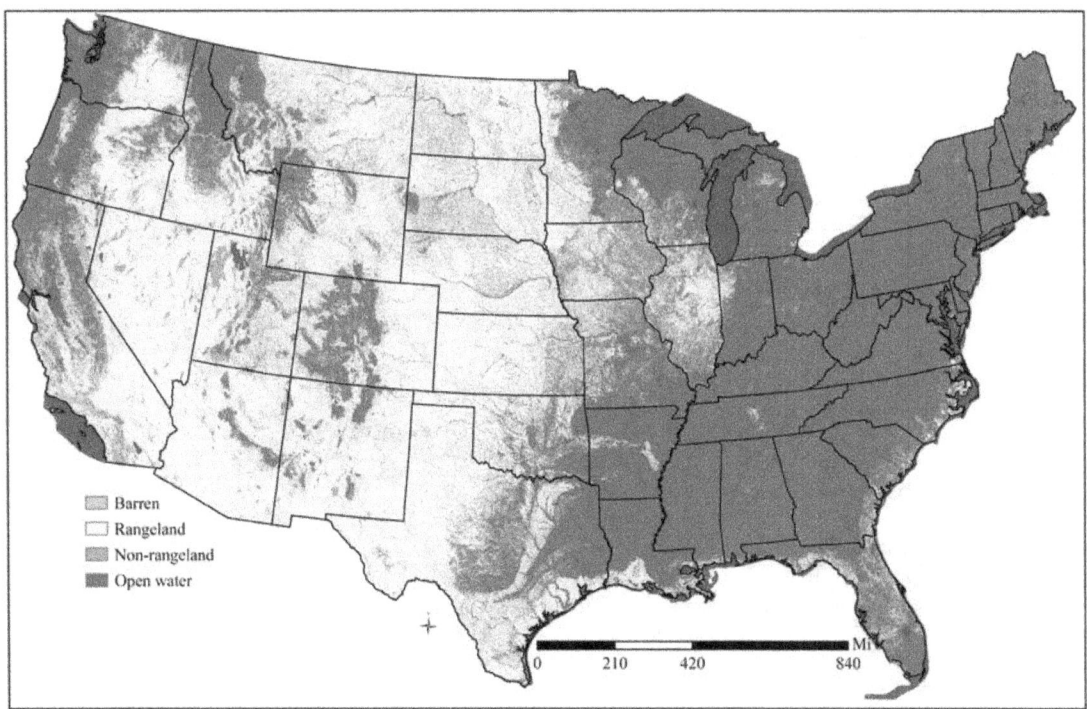

Figure 10—Postulated historic distribution of rangelands according to the NRCS (2009) definition; modeled after Reeves and Mitchell (2011).

been spatially intersected (overlain) with as-of-yet unpublished spatially explicit data depicting the percent of human modified rangelands (previously described). This process was also used to estimate the amount of residential development from 2010 to 2030. The resulting products are complete and consistent for the coterminous United States and are summarized in table 12.

Table 12—Evaluation of extent of human modified rangelands compared with historic distributions. In this study, "human modification" refers to permanent conversion from rangeland to another land use type. Only 17 western states are evaluated and data are as-of-yet unpublished.

State and Assessment Region (AR)	Historic rangeland (ac x 10³)	Rangeland lost (%)	Average distance (km) from ≥ 50 HMc[a]	Rangeland threatened by potential residential development 2030 (ac x 10³)[b]
WA	17,249	44	1.17	102
OR	34,488	15	4.61	80
CA	70,874	19	5.67	1,354
Pacific Coast AR	**122,611**	**21**	**3.82**	**1,536**
ID	29,763	20	4.71	77
NV	67,266	3	12.89	161
UT	38,748	7	9.39	166
AZ	66,974	5	12.61	364
MT	67,604	24	2.14	28
WY	49,306	8	3.18	13
CO	45,916	29	2.05	256
ND	43,214	71	0.17	29
SD	45,924	52	0.6	46
NE	47,538	56	0.64	74
KS	46,799	75	0.05	115
NM	68,636	9	7.93	137
Rocky Mountain AR	**617,688**	**30**	**4.70**	**1,466**
IL	20,247	87	0.01	188
WI	11,423	61	0.06	146
MO	15,027	69	0.02	132
IA	23,108	88	0.01	93
MN	21,708	84	0.07	116
North AR	**120,364**	**78**	**0.034**	**800**
OK	28,851	59	0.24	125
TX	128,547	36	2.57	1,129
FL	12,096	40	1.18	438
South AR	**140,643**	**67**	**0.466**	**1,567**
Coterminous U.S. total	**1,001,306**	**34**	**3.13**	**5,369**

[a] HMc is the percent of human modified rangeland.
[b] Estimates are derived from the SERGoM model (Buenemann 2010).

Overlaying maps depicting estimated human modification of western rangelands with this postulated historic rangeland distribution reveals that 34 percent of historical rangeland area has been lost due to land cover change associated with human land use (figure 11).

However, historic rangeland area and rangeland loss varies on a state-by-state basis (table 12). For both historic and current estimates of rangeland, Texas has the greatest rangeland area (table 12) but has lost 36 percent through conversion to other land types. Of all states with significant rangeland area, Iowa has lost the most on a proportional basis, followed closely by Illinois and Minnesota (table 12). Nevada has lost the smallest proportion of rangeland area and remains largely intact. The Pacific Coast Assessment Region exhibits the smallest proportion of rangelands (21 percent) that have been modified, while the North Assessment Region exhibits the highest proportion (78 percent).

Cropland agriculture is responsible for the majority of rangeland loss, resulting in a loss of 18 percent of the historic rangeland base (table 13). Residential land use contributes only about 6 percent to historic rangeland modification. Data depicting expected residential development by 2030 reveal that another 5 million acres of rangelands are expected to be converted (table 12) (Theobald 2005). Both Texas and Florida are expected to host over 1 million acres of new residential development by 2030 (figure 12).

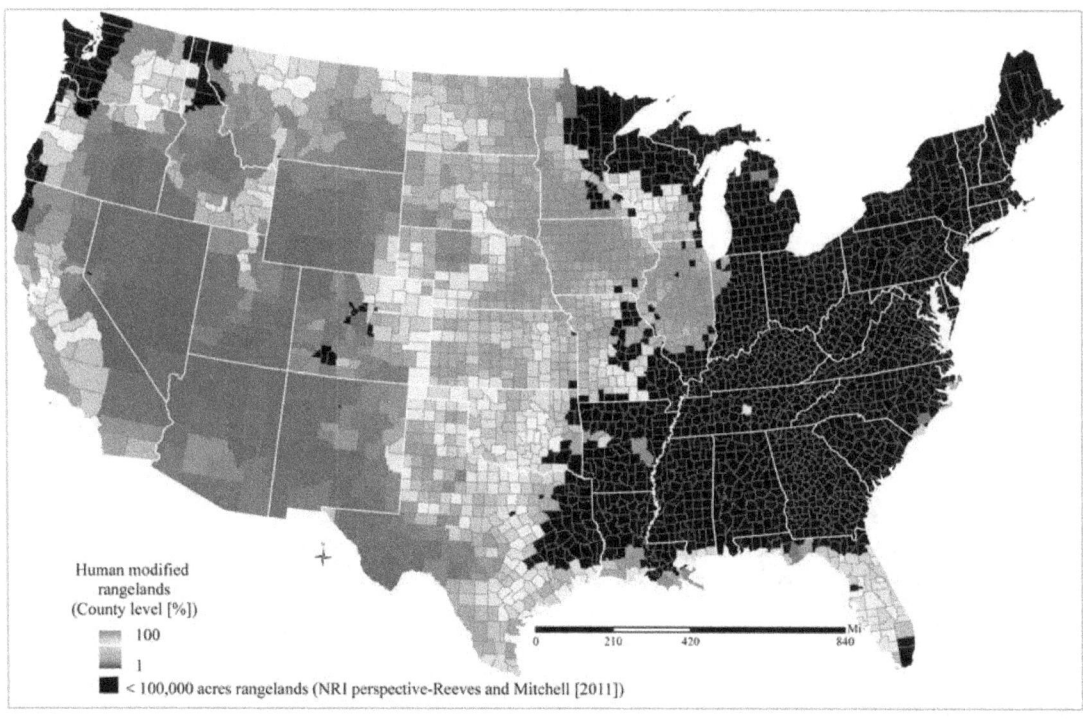

Figure 11—Estimated extent and magnitude of human modification on coterminous U.S. rangelands expressed as a percentage of an area.

Table 13—Quantification of proportion of land use classes to which rangelands have transitioned to. These land use types are those most responsible for the extent of human modification identified in this study. Only 17 western states are evaluated and data are as-of-yet unpublished.

Land use class	Modified rangeland area (Acres x 10^3)	Rangeland modified (% of historic area)
Residential	59,319	5.8
Mixed Use	6,244	0.6
Agriculture	183,228	18.0
Resource Extraction	74,936	7.4
Recreation	1,959	0.2
Transportation	1,968	0.2
Undeveloped	17,906	1.8
Total	**345,561**	**34.0**

Projected increase (%) in residential development in rangelands (2030)
91
1

Figure 12—Estimated increase in residential development represented as a percentage increase from present extent and magnitude of residential development. Projections are based on SERGoM model (Buenemann 2010).

Of particular interest from an ecological perspective is the proportion of human modification of each Ecological System and NVCS alliance. Table 14 depicts the estimated proportion of each Ecological System that has been converted to other uses. One caveat to the estimates of human modified rangelands is that the analysis described previously does not account for lands that are dominated by invasive species. In addition, the analysis does not always reflect the extent of pasturelands that are hard to detect from an aerial perspective and can rotate among land uses on a regular basis. Finally, oil and gas development since 2005 will not be

Table 14—Biophysical Settings (BPS) that are thought to have occupied >5 million acres and associated estimates of the proportion of lands that have been human modified. The human modification here does not sufficiently account for pasture lands or those lands dominated by invasive or non-native species.

BPS (described by ecological systems and NVCS Alliances)	Historic area	HMc[a] area	Proportion modified (HMc)
Northwestern Great Plains Mixedgrass Prairie	110,477	50,115	45
Inter-Mountain Basins Big Sagebrush Shrubland	6,522	6,874	10
Central Mixedgrass Prairie	64,535	40,530	63
Western Great Plains Shortgrass Prairie	63,399	28,532	45
Central Tallgrass Prairie	56,664	46,627	82
Northern Tallgrass Prairie	35,784	32,772	92
Inter-Mountain Basins Big Sagebrush Steppe	35,441	5,989	17
Inter-Mountain Basins Mixed Salt Desert Scrub	27,837	1,492	5
Western Great Plains Sand Prairie	26,701	10,540	39
Southeastern Great Plains Tallgrass Prairie	26,186	18,309	70
Apacherian-Chihuahuan Semi-Desert Grassland and Steppe	23,066	1,167	5
Inter-Mountain Basins Montane Sagebrush Steppe	20,692	1,280	6
Western Great Plains Floodplain Systems	18,765	8,205	44
Sonora-Mojave Creosotebush-White Bursage Desert Scrub	18,742	1,069	6
Sonoran Paloverde-Mixed Cacti Desert Scrub	17,370	1,345	8
Inter-Mountain Basins Big Sagebrush Shrubland - Wyoming Big Sagebrush	16,277	600	4
Mojave Mid-Elevation Mixed Desert Scrub	15,117	369	2
Western Great Plains Sandhill Steppe	14,669	4,724	32
North-Central Interior Oak Savanna	14,561	8,991	62
Colorado Plateau Pinyon-Juniper Woodland	12,056	218	2
Chihuahuan Loamy Plains Desert Grassland	10,028	954	10
Edwards Plateau Limestone Savanna and Woodland	9,622	1,782	19
Southern Blackland Tallgrass Prairie	9,615	6,445	67
Inter-Mountain Basins Greasewood Flat	9,480	1,247	13
Texas-Louisiana Coastal Prairie	9,058	6,842	76
Great Basin Xeric Mixed Sagebrush Shrubland	9,044	156	2
Tamaulipan Mixed Deciduous Thornscrub	8,523	3,358	39
California Lower Montane Blue Oak-Foothill Pine Woodland and Savanna	8,045	1,916	24
Inter-Mountain Basins Semi-Desert Shrub-Steppe	7,791	468	6
Columbia Plateau Low Sagebrush Steppe	7,736	594	8
Columbia Plateau Steppe and Grassland	6,828	1,959	29
Mogollon Chaparral	6,203	188	3
Great Basin Pinyon-Juniper Woodland	5,936	29	0
North American Warm Desert Sparsely Vegetated Systems	5,736	369	6
Sonora-Mojave Mixed Salt Desert Scrub	5,404	3,746	69
Inter-Mountain Basins Semi-Desert Grassland	5,341	507	9
Central Florida Pine Flatwoods	5,042	2,301	46
Edwards Plateau Limestone Shrubland	5,020	424	8
Inter-Mountain Basins Montane Riparian Systems	5,015	2,166	43

[a]HMc is human modified cover.

accounted for. Thus, some of the estimates of the proportion of human modification might appear lower than normal (as in the case of some tall grass prairie types). Of all rangeland types, the tall grass prairie systems appear to be the most converted. On average, Ecological Systems which occur in drier, less productive areas, have seen far less human modification.

The recent increase in visibility and concern (Hobbs and others 2008; Stokes and others 2006) regarding rangeland fragmentation provided impetus for research examining spatial extent and magnitude of the phenomena (for example, Leinwand and others 2010). Following is a spatially explicit, synoptic overview of fragmented rangelands using data that describe spatial patterns of rangeland vegetation and oil and gas development. Fragmentation is detrimental to natural landscapes due to factors such as loss of goods and services, decreased gene pools, and barriers to species that depend on rangelands for all or part of their life cycle.

At least two sources of data exist for characterizing fragmentation on coterminous United States rangelands, including Riitters (2010) and unpublished data derived from the human modification analysis. Here, both models of fragmentation are presented to facilitate a more complete understanding of the scope of fragmentation. Fragmentation, as quantified from the human modification analysis previously introduced represents the Euclidean distance from one human modified site to another (a site is "modified" when ≥50 percent of the area is modified by human activity) (table 12). Figure 13 indicates that the average distance between modified sites for coterminous U.S. rangelands is 1.77 miles. Agriculture accounts for the greatest amount of rangeland fragmentation.

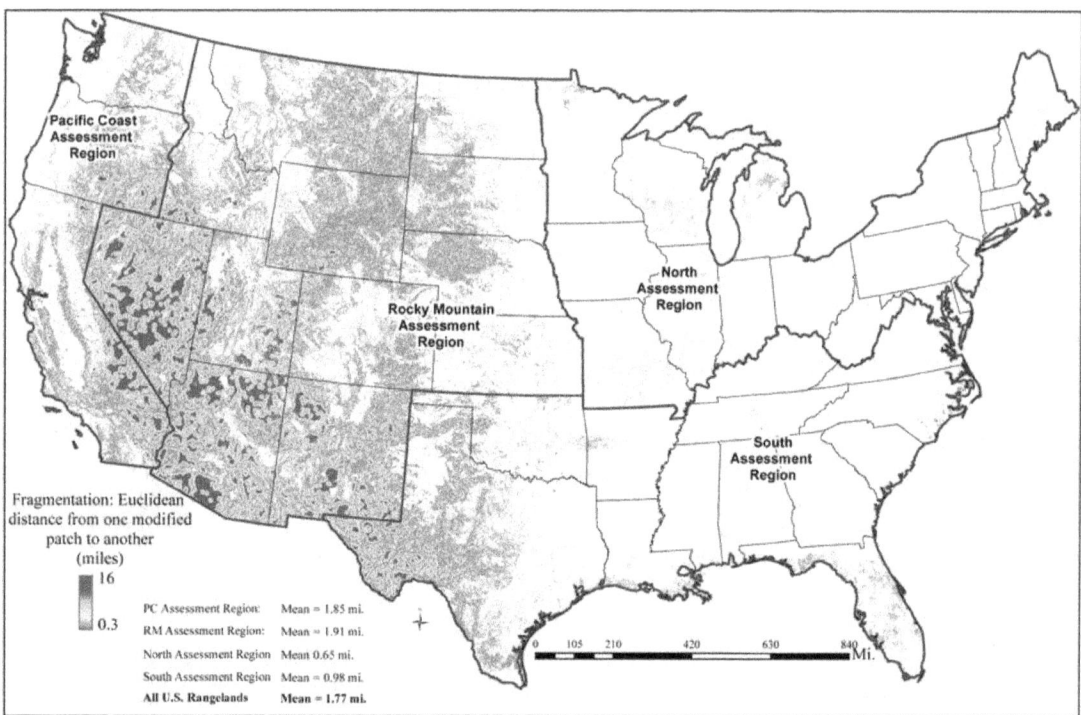

Figure 13—Estimated extent of rangeland fragmentation. Values represent the distance between "human modified sites"—"modified" means ≥50% of the area has been permanently changed due to human intervention.

An in-depth analysis of the density and morphological spatial patterns of grass and shrubland communities of the coterminous United States is presented in Riitters (2010). Here, these data were adapted to provide an index of rangeland fragmentation (figure 14). The index yields a relative value indicating the ratio of rangeland vegetation edge to the area of urban and agricultural landscapes. Higher values (warmer tones) indicate areas of rangeland vegetation that are relatively more fragmented. Figure 14 shows that Nevada and Arizona are the least fragmented states, while the most fragmented areas are those corresponding to high agricultural land use. Since the work of Riitters (2010) was performed on the National Land Cover Dataset (Vogelmann and others 2001), it will not appropriately characterize the extent of current fragmentation from oil and gas development. Thus, a separate analysis is required to describe the extent and configuration of oil and gas exploration.

Figure 15 depicts the estimated number of oil and gas wells without regard to current status (for example, active or inactive) circa 2009. In 2009, there were approximately 2.8 million oil and gas wells in the United States (including offshore sites) (www.whitestar.com) so accounting for the impact and footprint is important. Figure 15 depicts oil well density only for those counties exhibiting greater than 50,000 acres of rangelands. For reference, the Powder River Basin and Book Cliffs area (two areas that have experienced significant oil and gas development) are displayed in white. Quantifying fragmentation associated with oil and gas well pads is beyond this report, but the general scope of the issue can be seen in figure 16.

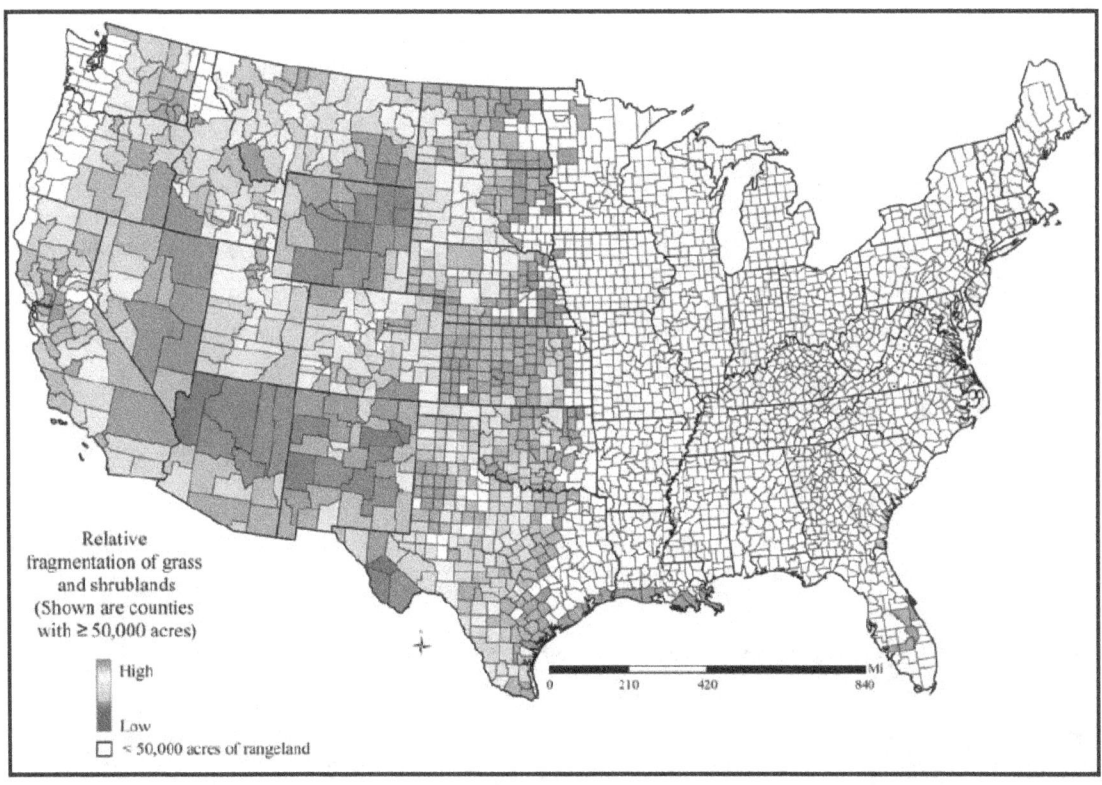

Figure 14—Relative fragmentation of grassland and shrubland vegetation in the coterminous United States. Fragmentation is estimated using data from Riitters (2010). Only counties with ≥50,000 acres of rangelands (from Reeves and Mitchell [2011]) are shown.

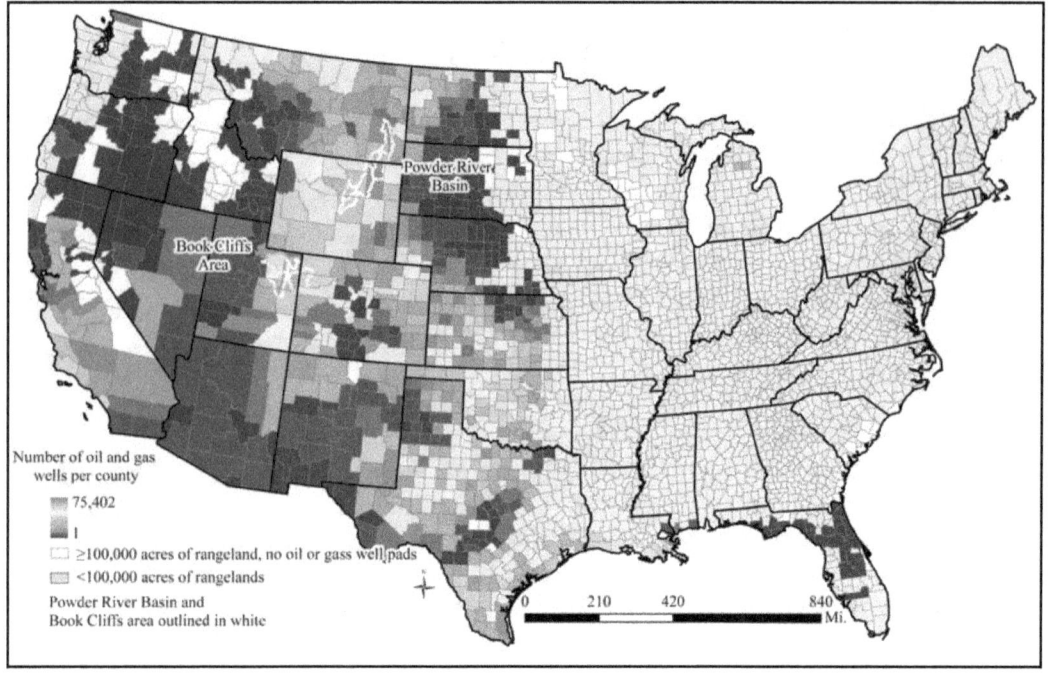

Figure 15—Number of oil and gas well pads per county estimated from data distributed by the Whitestar Corporation. Counties with ≥100,000 acres of rangelands with no oil wells in the database are depicted in white, while counties with ≤100,000 acres of rangelands are gray.

Figure 16—Estimated oil and gas well pad density. Where data are incomplete, states are shown in gray. The effect of even a modest number of well pads on rangeland patch size and fragmentation is evident in the air photo. Data source: www.whitestar.com.

The Conservation Reserve Program

While land enrolled in the Conservation Reserve Program (CRP) is not, by definition, range-land (it cannot usually be grazed by livestock or hayed except during certified emergencies), it may provide similar functions as rangelands and can impact the juxtaposition of rangelands across the landscape, therefore, it warrants discussion here. Both the 1989 and 2000 RPA Rangeland Assessments provided considerable detail regarding legislation and political situations leading to creation of the CRP. Enacted in 1985 as a provision of the Farm Bill, the Program is a cost share and rental payment program administered by the USDA Farm Service Agency (FSA) implemented to conserve highly erodible or environmentally sensitive farm-land and to improve agricultural commodity prices by reducing supply via conversion of crop-land to tame or native grasses, wildlife plantings, trees, filter strips, or riparian buffers (USDA FSA 2011; USDA NRCS 2011). Since 1985, the CRP has been amended considerably, most dealing with contract provisions. The 2008 Farm Bill stipulated that alfalfa is considered an agricultural commodity, which makes it eligible for the CRP process if it was cropped four of the previous six years (USDA ERS 2008). Also, for the first time, the bill allowed thinning to improve the condition of resources on lands containing windbreaks, shelterbelts, and wildlife corridors (USDA ERS 2008). Rents received by landowners are determined by the productivity of the soils in the area and average dry land crop cash rent equivalent (USDA ERS 2008), and rental rates may not exceed the FSA's maximum payment amount. In 2009, 766,400 CRP contracts were in place representing 34 million acres and an average rental payment of $51 per acre (table 15) (Barbarika 2009). The Rocky Mountain Assessment Region had the most CRP acres but exhibited the lowest average rent per acre, reflecting lower crop yields and reduced vegetation productivity pervasive in the arid western United States.

While the CRP program has had negative impacts such as use of non-native species (for example, *Agropyron cristatum* [crested wheatgrass] and *A. intermedium* [intermediate wheat-grass] for reseeding former cropland (Mitchell 2000), recent studies have demonstrated significant ecological and economic benefits of the CRP program. The CRP is estimated to provide $500 million per year in benefits from reduced erosion and $737 million per year in wildlife viewing and hunting benefits (Sullivan and others 2004) (www.ers.usda.gov/Publications/ AER834). In addition, the recent emphasis on biological carbon sequestration (Follett and Reed 2010) by rangelands emphasizes the potential of CRP lands seeded with rangeland vegetation to eliminate a significant quantity of atmospheric CO_2 (Jordan and others 2007). In

Table 15—Number of contracts, farms, acres enrolled, rental payments, and average rent by RPA Assessment Region (USDA 2009).

Assessment Region	Number of contracts	Number of farms	Acres enrolled	Rental payments (USD)	Average rent per acre
Alaska	82	62	28,691	1,082,417	38
Pacific Coast	17,295	7,697	2,234,593	115,617,061	52
Rocky Mountain	185,928	95,932	16,205,074	605,739,921	37
North	428,654	238,024	7,954,919	691,820,221	87
South	134,441	88,781	8,237,589	350,940,260	43
Total	**766,400**	**430,496**	**34,660,866**	**1,765,199,880**	**51**

addition, FSA estimates that CRP has decreased erosion by 440 million tons per year, sequestered over 17.6 million tons of carbon annually, and reduced nitrogen application by 681,000 tons. From a rangeland perspective, one of the greatest benefits from the CRP program is reduced fragmentation of landscapes, which enhances wildlife populations (USDA NRCS 2009) and ecological function (Skaggs and others 1994).

The ultimate fate of 34 million acres of land enrolled in the CRP program and associated benefits is difficult to predict and is dependent on such factors as the economics of crop production, agricultural policy, and values held by CRP participants (Heimlich 1995). Though new research indicating conversion of CRP lands to rangelands (or simply leaving rangeland vegetation in place after the contract expires) is sparse, previous research indicates that less than 20 percent of CRP lands will be maintained as grasslands (Heimlich and Kula 1990).

In addition to issues discussed by Mitchell (2000), two contemporary issues will likely influence the fate of CRP lands. First, is to address the extent to which CRP lands provide improved habitat or refuge for threatened or near-threatened species such as sage-grouse (*Centrocercus urophasianus*). Research suggests that sage-grouse populations are improved or maintained because of CRP lands (Schroeder and others 2006). Second, the quest and exploration for new sources of biofuels could remove lands from CRP but maintain them in permanent grass cover. About 17 million of the 34 million acres of CRP land (1998 data) (Adler and others 2009) may be available for biomass feedstock production (De La Torre Ugarte and others 2003). If native species are used, especially large statured warm season (C4 photosynthetic pathway) species such as switchgrass (*Panicum virgatum*), and technologies are developed to make biofuel production economically attractive, rangeland-like landscapes may increase in the future as CRP contracts expire.

In summary, CRP lands are providing multiple benefits and can function like rangelands and decrease fragmentation in landscapes dominated by rangeland vegetation. The extent to which rangelands will replace current CRP lands is subject to many economic, social, and political factors. On a positive note, regardless of the fate of post-contract CRP lands, the rangeland base will not be negatively affected since these lands are not currently classified as rangeland.

The Outlook for Extent of U.S. Rangelands

Here, we discuss how current processes may affect the rangeland base in the near future. Between 1982 and 2007, nearly 350,000 acres of non-Federal rangelands were lost annually (figure 6) to various land use changes. In the 2000 RPA report, Mitchell (2000) discussed the issue of consolidation, subdivision, and urbanization of rangelands. It appears that the process of consolidation has, at least temporarily, leveled off, but subdivision continues to expand. The average farm size has decreased from 431 acres in 1997 to 418 acres in 2007 (USDA NASS 2009). In addition, the percent of small farms has steadily increased over the same period (table 16). Economic and demographic influences will continue to change patterns of development across non-Federal rangelands. Changes in non-Federal rangelands are estimated in figure 17. In each RPA scenario (Wear 2011), rangelands decrease slowly over the next 50 years averaging losses from 116,000 to 175,000 acres per year, but overall changes in areal extent are small compared to the total rangeland base. In each scenario, the Pacific

Table 16—Average farm sizes estimates for the United States during 1997, 2002, and 2007.

Average farm size (acres)	1997	2002	2007
1 to 99	49.0	51.0	54.4
100 to 499	35.0	33.1	31.0
500 to 999	8.1	7.6	6.8
1000 to 1,999	4.6	4.7	4.2
>2000	3.4	3.7	3.6

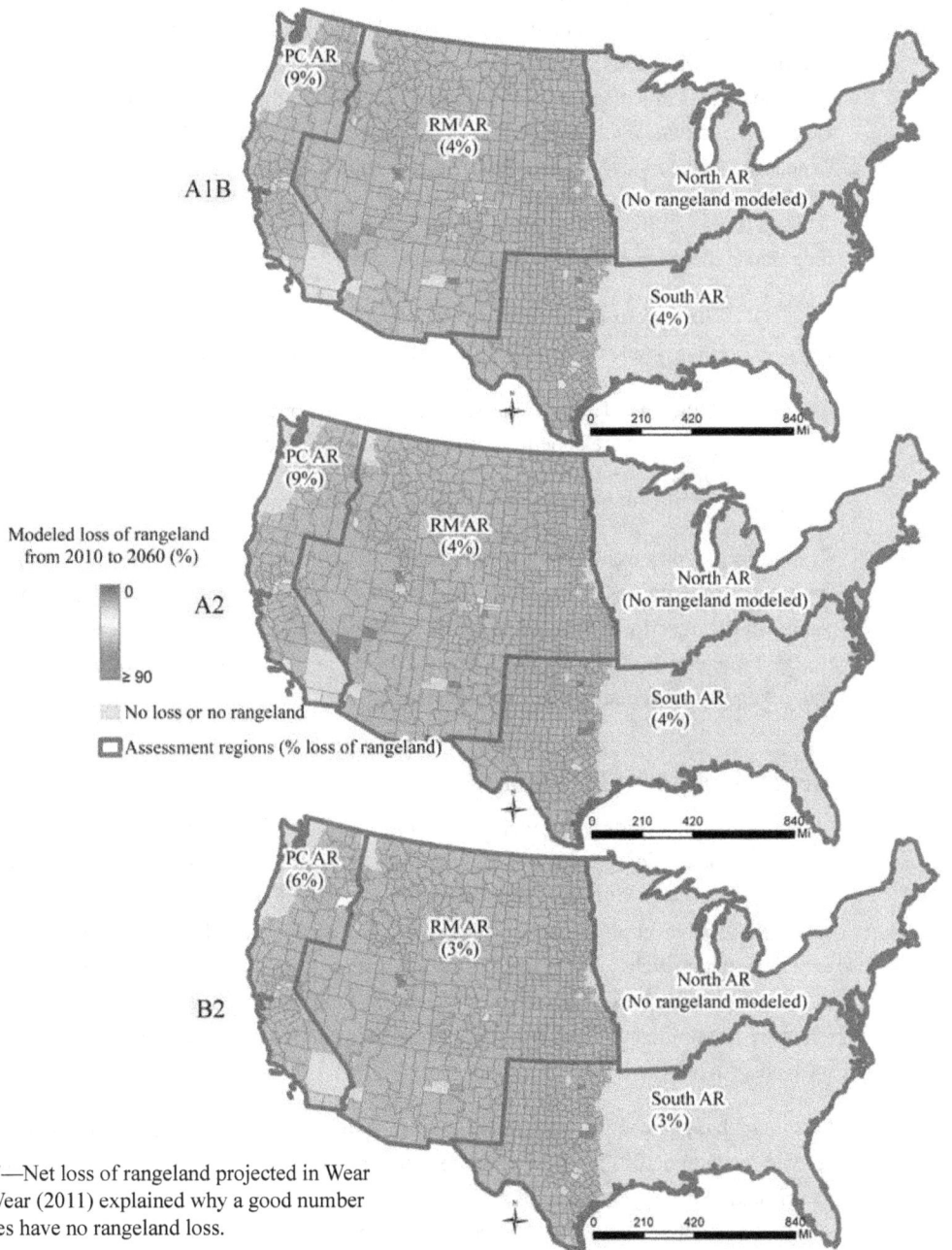

Figure 17—Net loss of rangeland projected in Wear (2011). Wear (2011) explained why a good number of counties have no rangeland loss.

Coast Assessment Region is projected to lose the most rangeland while the South and Rocky Mountain Regions are projected to experience smaller losses. Areas projected to experience the greatest loss are the Mojave Desert, particularly near Las Vegas, Nevada; the central Rocky Mountain Front; and eastern Texas near the transition from grasslands to forests and woodlands.

The extent of Federal rangelands will not likely decrease substantially in the future although a significant portion of lands have been transferred to non-Federal owners. For example, in Alaska alone, between 1999 and 2008 the BLM conveyed approximately 8.5 million acres (DOI 1999 and 2009) of lands to various groups, including Alaska Native Americans, via a variety of public laws, including the Alaska Native Claims Settlement Act and Alaska National Interest Lands Conservation Act (Karl, personal communication). Predicting losses and transfers of this magnitude in the future are beyond the scope of this report. While the extent of rangelands will probably not change dramatically in the future, it is reasonable to expect a slow decline (Mitchell 2000) and continued fragmentation, as indicated by figure 12.

At least three significant factors will potentially influence extent and fragmentation of U.S. rangelands that are noteworthy in this report:

1. The pattern of subdivision and urbanization of U.S. rangelands noted in the last Rangeland Assessment (Mitchell 2000) has continued over the last decade.

2. Rangeland decline due to recent surge in "sodbusting" or "new breakings" (Stubbs 2007) and the ephemeral nature of contractually conserved lands (such as CRP).

3. Significant increase in oil and gas development.

In summary, if past trends are good predictors, the overall rangeland extent should not change markedly in the future, especially on Federal lands. This expectation should not, however, vanquish the need for continued monitoring because the composition, function, and connectivity of rangelands could change substantially in the future even if the total extent and relative juxtaposition remain somewhat constant.

Global Rangeland Situation

Globally, rangelands provide livelihood to millions of people (Papanastasis 2009) in addition to a multitude of biological and social benefits. Cattle alone provide tens of billions of dollars to the world economy. In 2009, the United States generated roughly $32 billion worth of beef cattle production (http://www.ers.usda.gov/news/BSECoverage htm). Though not all livestock are raised exclusively on rangelands, current livestock production levels are not possible without the forage base that rangelands supply. The increasing societal pressures on rangelands are not limited to food and fiber; rangelands need to meet multiple demands simultaneously (Lund 2007).

From a global perspective, threats to rangelands include climate change, degradation, and land conversion (Lund 2007). Monitoring the extent and magnitude of these processes requires identification of rangelands to provide a spatial framework and baseline against which future assessments can be compared. Determining the exact amount and location of all rangelands globally is not only impossible, it is probably not needed. What is needed, however, is a common, consistently used definition of rangelands on which future assessments and monitoring can be based. Because no unified definition of rangelands exists, every estimate is subject to interpretation but is still useful for understanding the global scale of this land type. Satellite remote sensing can be used to determine the spatial arrangement of rangelands across the world because it is generally agreed upon that most shrublands and grasslands are rangelands (though debate exists over which species should be shrubs or trees). Figure 18 reveals the distribution of grasslands and shrublands throughout the world derived from the 2005 Moderate Resolution Imaging Spectroradiometer (MODIS) Global Land Cover Product (University of Maryland Classification) (Friedl and others 2002). Excluding Antarctica, there are roughly 52 billion acres of land in the world, of which rangelands occupy 47 percent (table 17).

Sere and Steinfeld (1996) estimated that roughly half of the world's rangelands are used for grazing livestock, and in areas such as the western United States and parts of Africa, wild herbivores account for much of the use. The relative amount of rangelands used for livestock

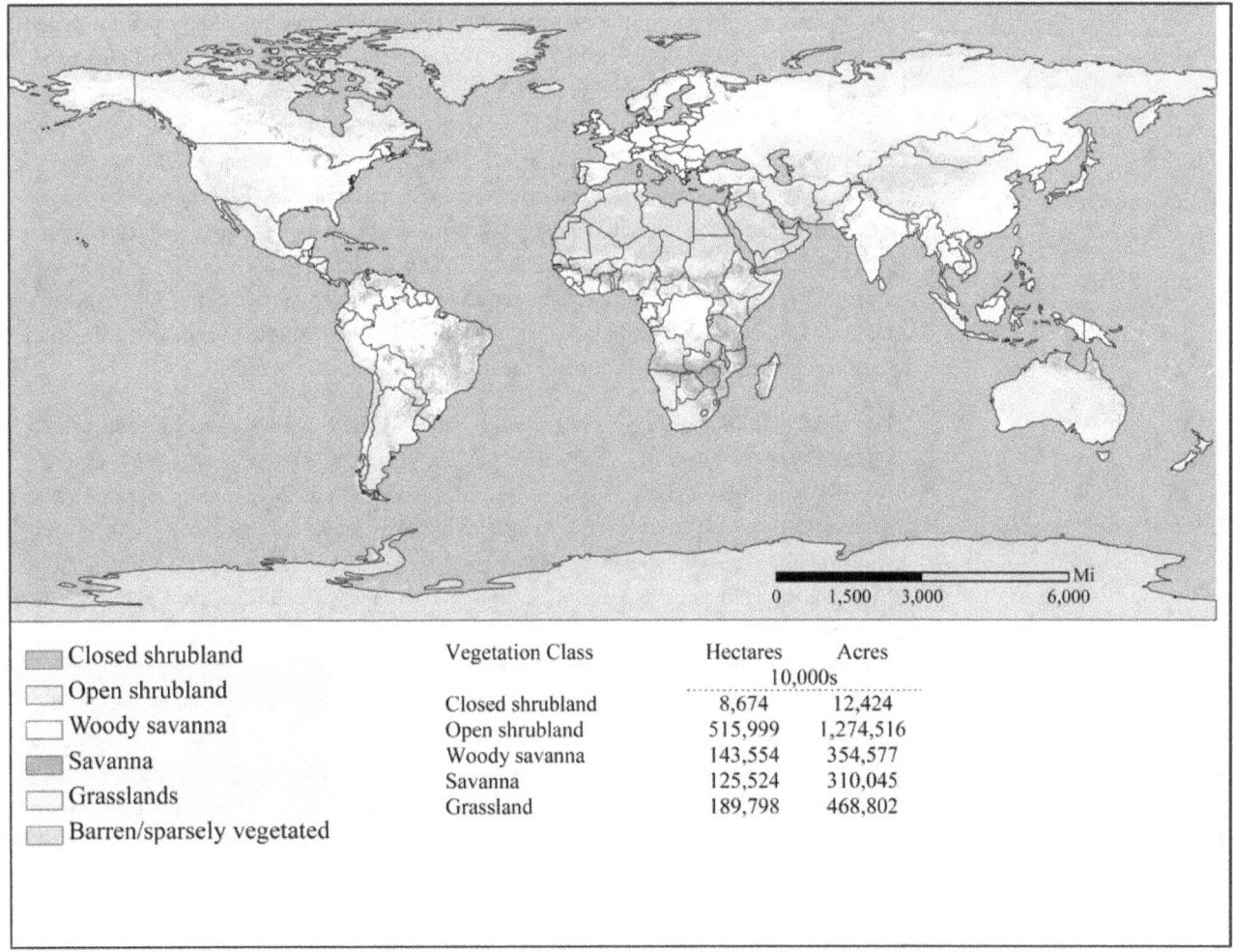

Vegetation Class	Hectares	Acres
	10,000s	
Closed shrubland	8,674	12,424
Open shrubland	515,999	1,274,516
Woody savanna	143,554	354,577
Savanna	125,524	310,045
Grassland	189,798	468,802

Legend:
- Closed shrubland
- Open shrubland
- Woody savanna
- Savanna
- Grasslands
- Barren/sparsely vegetated

Figure 18—Global distribution of grass, shrub, and savanna vegetation (Hansen 2000). Data Source: MODIS NPP collection 4.5, http://modis.gsfc nasa.gov/data/directbrod/index.php.

Table 17—These classes are considered rangelands for this report. Area estimates were derived from the 2005 MODIS Global Land Cover Product (University of Maryland Classification) (Friedl and Others 2002).

Land type (UMD classes)	Area (ac. x 10^3)	Percent of total land mass[a]
Closed Shrublands	214,243	0.413
Open Shrublands	12,745,163	24.562
Woody Savannas	3,545,772	6.833
Savannas3,100,446	5.975	
Grasslands	4,688,016	9.035
Total	**214,243**	**46.818**

[a] Excludes Antarctica and all significant inland water bodies.

grazing is likely to change in response to land use/land cover change, dietary preferences, and population trends. The United Nations Food and Agriculture Organization tracks land use/ land cover changes for four main groups: cropland, pasture, forest, and other. Rangelands are not explicitly accounted for. However, global pasturelands have shrunk by approximately 69 million acres (<1 percent of the extent in 1995) (figure 19) since 1995, largely at the expense of permanent agriculture expansion (figure 19). However, changes in the global rangeland base in the future are difficult to predict due to climate change and demographic patterns. Figure 20 demonstrates the projected increase in global population concluding with a mean estimate of roughly 10 billion people in 2060 (Naki□enovi□ and others 2000). Many of the fastest growing regions, or areas with current high population density, overlap with the world's rangelands, which will undoubtedly affect distribution, sustainability, degradation, and desertification of rangelands. Like the decade between 1990 and 2000, desertification and degradation are two of the most critical topics involving rangelands from an international per-spective. And, like the preceding decade, we still do not have spatially explicit information to verify the amount of desertification or the instability it causes (Mitchell 2000).

The formal definition of "*desertification*" provided by the United Nations Convention to Combat Desertification (http://www.unccd.int/) is "land degradation in arid, semi-arid, and dry sub-humid areas resulting from various factors, including climatic variations and human activities" (Reich and others 2001). Areas exhibiting a "very cold (boreal), hyper-arid or a humid" climate are not included in this definition. Significant debate exists over the causes and implications of perceived desertification. Two competing theories have been developed that explain vegetation dynamics. These are referred to as equilibrium and non-equilibrium dynamics, both of which can be used to explain the concept of rangeland degradation. Equilibrium theory, the older of the two, suggests that a vegetation community and condi-tion of a site follows a linear trajectory of successional states ending in a climax community in the absence of the disturbance. This view necessarily emphasizes grazing management as a determinant of both composition and degree of degradation. In contrast, non-equilibrium theory suggests livestock grazing has little effect on the productive capacity of a site, which is largely determined by rainfall (Behnke and Scoones 1993; Ellis 1994; Scoones 1994; Wessels and others 2007). An important concept in non-equilibrium theory is the potential for crossing ecological thresholds, beyond which, the site loses productive capacity and exhibits irrepa-rable changes in species composition, even when grazing is totally removed from the system (Behnke and Scoones 1993).

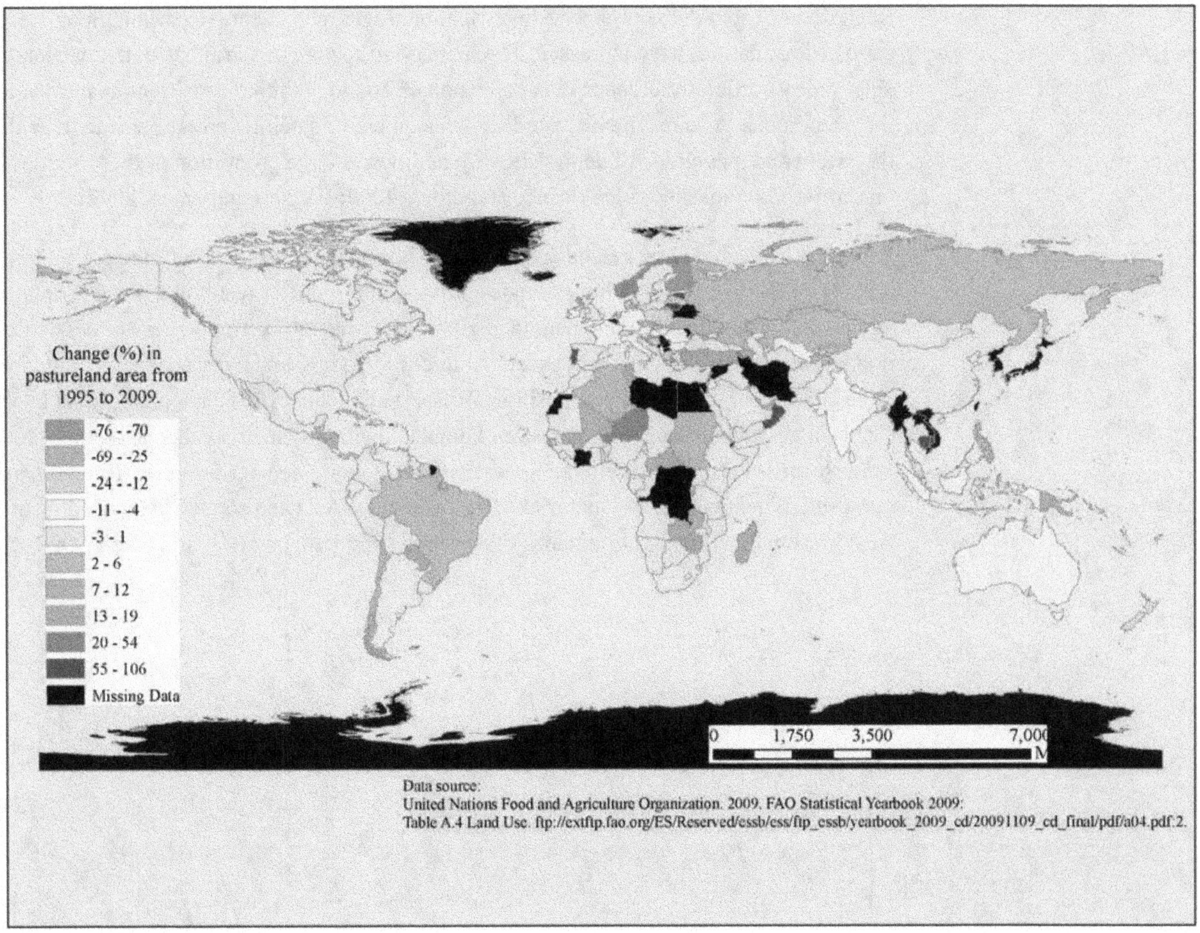

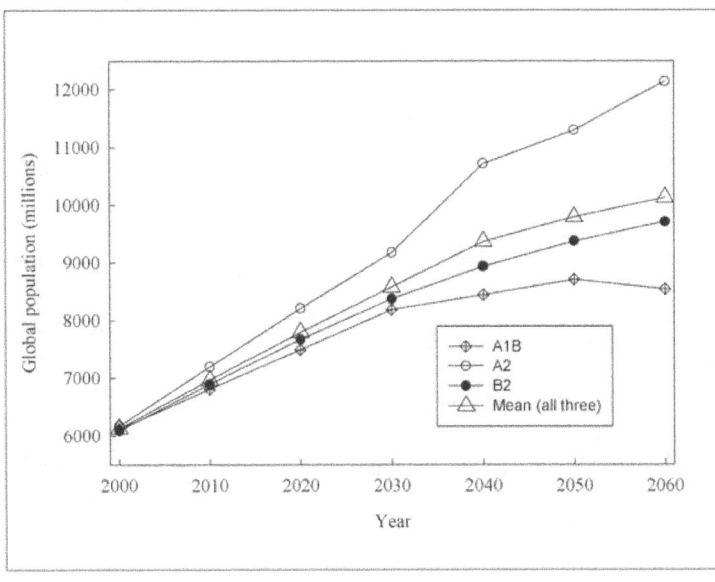

Figure 19—Percent of change globally in pastureland area from 1995 to 2009 (FAO 2009). Data source: United Nations Food and Agriculture Organization. 2009. FAO Statistical Yearbook 2009: Table A.4 Land Use, ftp://extftp fao.org/ES/Reserved/essb/ess/ ftp_essb/yearbook_2009_cd/20091109_cd_final/pdf/a04.pdf:2.

Figure 20—Global population growth projections according to the three IPCC storylines modified for RPA reporting process (Nakicenovic and others 2000).

Regardless of soundness of theory, investigation, focus, and debate regarding global desertification (degradation) have increased. The increase in focus and alarm has not, however, noticeably improved field-referenced data collection efforts to facilitate consistent quantification of the phenomena. As a result, most studies focus on use of satellite remote sensing to evaluate the extent and magnitude of degradation. In addition, a large proportion of these studies focus on semi-arid regions in Africa (Prince and others 2009; Wessels and others 2007).

Estimates of degraded rangeland vary from 1.7 billion acres (Brown 2002) to 8.1 billion acres (UNEP 1991). Still, other estimates provided in figure 21 result in a mean estimate of 44 percent of rangelands being degraded globally (Lund 2007). The process of desertification has affected every continent except Antarctica, leading to decreased productivity, irreparable changes in vegetation composition (Wessels and others 2007), altered nutrient cycles (Schlesinger and others 1990), and even faunal extinctions (Spottiswoode and others 2009). Primary areas currently experiencing desertification expressed as long-term decreases in rain use efficiency are sub-equatorial Africa, southeast Asia and south China, north-central Australia, and the Pampas grasslands of Argentina and Uruguay (Bai and others 2008).

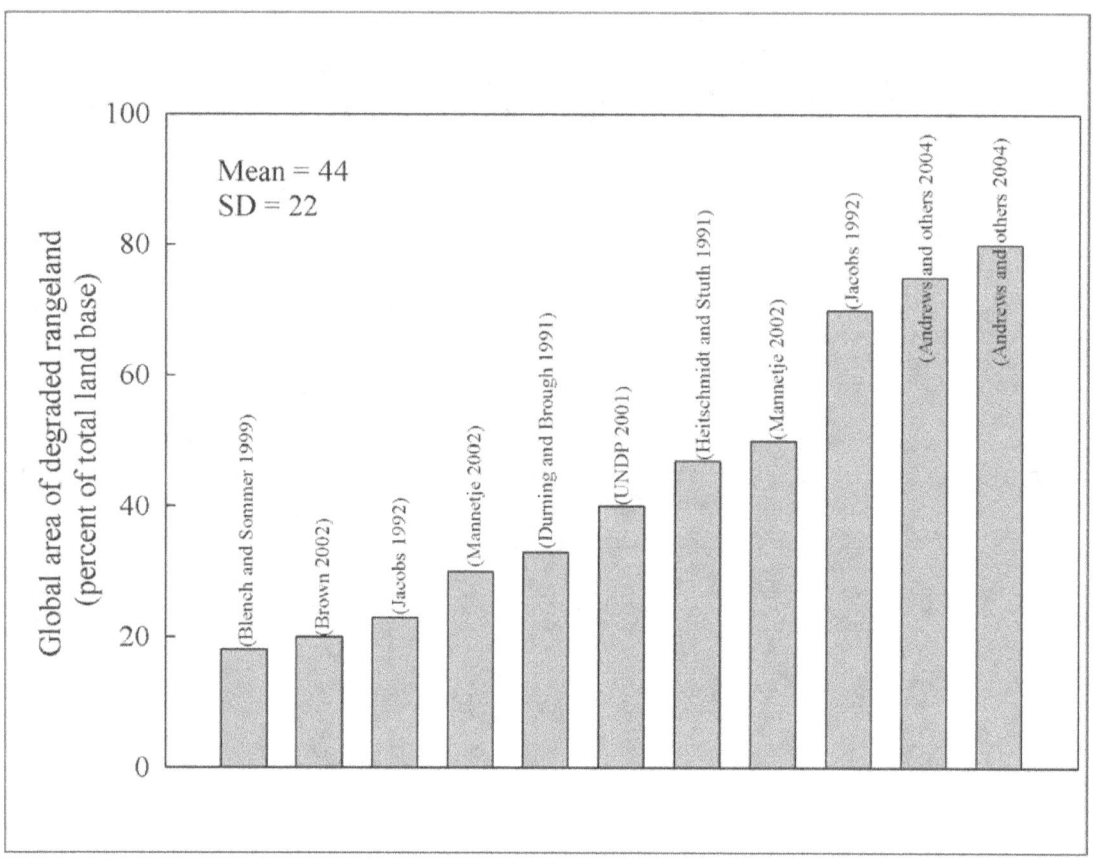

Figure 21—Estimated percent of global rangelands experiencing degradation (adapted from Lund [2007]).

Currently, two antithetical processes are acting to suggest a troubling trend. While desertification is acting to reduce productive capacity, global per capita beef consumption and production have increased sharply since 2000 (figure 22) (USDA ERS 2009). As countries around the world seek to increase standards of living and become more urbanized, meat consumption is likely to increase (Gale 2002). For example, since 1994, per capita consumption of beef in China has increased over 200 percent (USDA ERS 2009). If red meat consumption increases concomitantly with estimates of future global population, the extent of degradation will expand.

Summary

The different methods for quantifying rangeland area among, and even within, land management agencies make consistent accounting for U.S. rangelands impossible. This situation inspired new research (Reeves and Mitchell 2011) aimed at consistently and objectively quantifying rangeland area. The results of that work provide spatially explicit data that consistently describe the area of coterminous U.S. rangelands from the FIA and NRI perspectives. This research enables rangeland area estimates to be provided to an extent not previously possible.

Reeves and Mitchell (2011) estimated that rangelands occupy between 662 and 511 million acres. The USFS administers up to 47 million acres of rangelands while the BLM manages

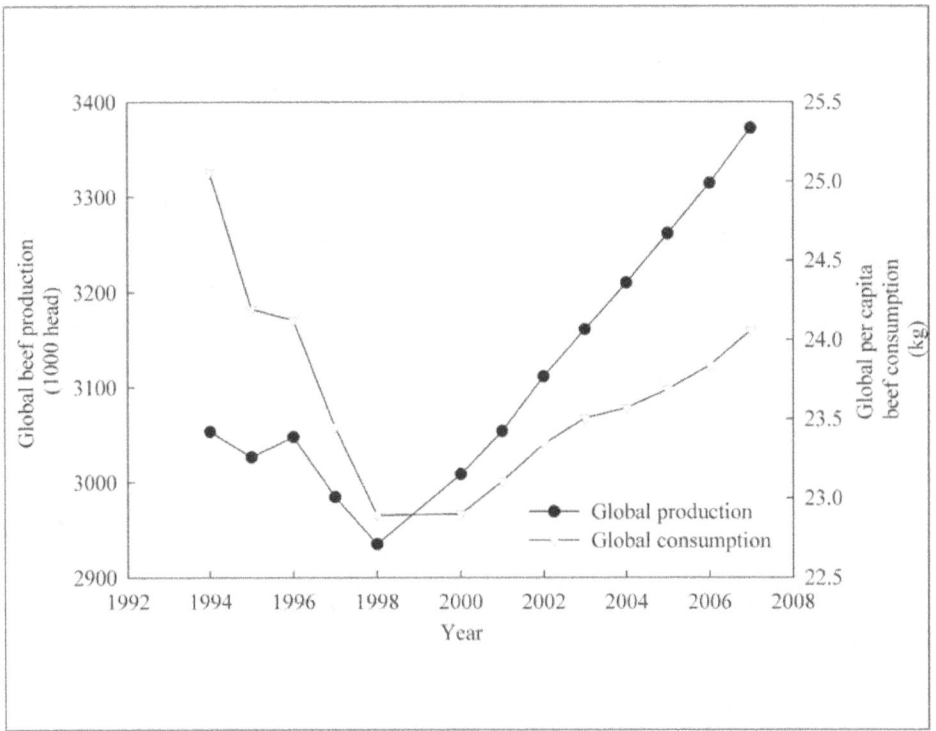

Figure 22—Global beef production and consumption from 1994 to 2007 (USDA ERS 2009).

up to 139 million acres. Rangelands account for nearly half of protected lands of the coterminous United States and up to 70 percent of the RNAs. Non-Federal rangelands account for 409 million acres and decreased at a rate of 350,000 acres per year between 1982 and 2007, though the rate of loss has recently leveled off.

In addition to discussing new estimates of rangeland area, this report provides spatially explicit analyses describing the extent and nature of human modified rangelands. Approximately 1.1 billion acres of rangelands existed during the pre-settlement era, of which 34 percent have been lost to human modification. Agriculture accounts for the greatest amount of rangeland conversion and significantly contributes to rangeland fragmentation. Fragmentation, as quantified here, represents the distance from one human modified site to another. The average distance between modified sites (a site is "modified" when ≥50 percent of the area is modified human activity) for coterminous U.S. rangelands is 1.77 miles.

Residential development is expected to convert another 5 million acres of rangelands by 2030. In addition, oil and gas development and new breakings (sodbusting) will probably continue to reduce the extent of non-Federal U.S. rangelands. In contrast, the extent of Federal rangelands is not expected to change dramatically in the future unless further land divestures by the BLM are realized or significant oil and gas exploration infrastructure such as roads, well pads, and similar structures are constructed and not reclaimed.

Unlike the situation in the United States, evaluating the status of trends of global rangelands is relatively difficult. There are about 24 billion acres of rangelands (from a remote sensing perspective), and although reductions in the rangeland base are difficult to estimate, since 1995 roughly 69 million acres of pastures have been usurped largely by expansion of agriculture. Both degradation and increased demands for goods and services will continue to impact the extent, composition, health, and productivity of rangeland ecosystems. Current estimates of rangeland degradation range from 20 to 73 percent of the rangeland base. Increased standard of living portends an increased demand for red meat. Global population is expected to reach 10 billion by 2060 and will create a situation where a decreased rangeland base (through further conversion to agricultural land) will be expected to supply more goods and services.

Chapter 3: Ecosystem Goods and Services

Introduction

Public perceptions of rangelands have been transforming since the importance of rangelands became apparent more than 130 years ago (Harris 1977). Among these dynamics in recent years is an increased focus on the relevance of ecosystem goods and services (EGS) as a reason for rangeland sustainability.

The concept of rangeland EGS is not new, although some elements concerning them are in their infancy, for example, quantifying and marketing carbon sequestration on a meaningful scale. Though the list is potentially large, this report focuses on EGS with national significance and for which sufficient information exists at that scale. Specifically, we report on trends in decadal productivity, forage supply, livestock production, and alternative energy.

Decadal Productivity Trends

In its most basic form, rangeland productivity can be described as the rate of change in biomass accumulation expressed on an area basis. Since primary production provides the foundation for all herbivory, it is a critical component to monitor on rangelands. Further, rangeland primary production is the subject of scrutiny for Criterion 3 (Maintenance of Productive Capacity on Rangelands) (Mitchell and others 1999) (http://sustainable. rangelands.org/pdf/Core_Indicators.pdf). A national assessment of rangeland productivity is difficult since no national standard for monitoring productivity at meaningful scales has been established. Nor have national monitoring programs been instigated that would enable estimation of rangeland production for U.S. rangelands from field-referenced plot data. The NRI program does, however, provide a set of approximately 10,000 plots (Herrick and others 2010) on which annual rangeland productivity can be estimated, but these data are only available on non-Federal rangelands and are not usually made available to scientists outside the NRCS to evaluate. For Federal lands, Joyce (1989) used authorized Animal Unit Months (AUMs) as a proxy for estimating productivity, though this process is only valid for lands within grazing allotments. Given the lack of data available for determining productivity for U.S. rangelands, ecosystem modeling, remote sensing (Fensholt and others 2006; Hunt and others 2004; Reeves and others 2006), or a combination of both (Jinguo and others 2006) can be used to estimate spatial and temporal trends across large areas.

This report focuses on annual estimates of net primary production (NPP) from the MODIS (Collection 4.5 data) vegetation product (Running and others 2004) from 2000 to 2009. The MODIS NPP product, expressed in units of kg Cm^2yr^{-1}, is available at a nominal resolution of 1 km^2 spatial resolution and has global coverage (MODIS NPP data are available at https:// lpdaac.usgs.gov/lpdaac/get_data/). This product can estimate landscape-level NPP but does not provide a framework for quantifying the proportion of aboveground production suitable for grazing, though assumptions can be made enabling reasonable estimates (see the "Forage Supply" section). The decadal analysis summarized below was created by first removing all areas in the coterminous United States exhibiting tree canopy cover greater than 10 percent.

This was done for two reasons. First, tree canopy cover obscures other vegetation beneath the canopy, and, therefore, NPP values derived from heavily forested areas will reflect the NPP of the trees, a poor depiction of rangeland vegetation. Second, a different technique was used in this report for estimating production (or forage) beneath tree canopies (see "Forage Supply").

The following evaluation of MODIS NPP on U.S. rangelands is based on as-of-yet unpublished data. The vegetation classes used to determine productivity were gleaned from the LANDFIRE Existing Vegetation Type product. There are approximately 134 thematic classes describing rangeland vegetation (vegetation dominated by herbs and/or shrubs) in the LANDFIRE Existing Vegetation Type product. These classes were condensed to 23 National Vegetation Classification System Groups and Macrogroups for reporting purposes and to reduce complexity (table 18). The crosswalk from NVCS Groups and Macrogroups to Ecological Systems is obviously subject to interpretation; table 18 communicates the implications of reported productivity estimates.

Table 18—Crosswalk between LANDFIRE Ecological Systems and Groups and Macrogroups from the National NVCS.

Existing vegetation type	NVCS Group or Macrogroup (collapsed classes for reporting)
Northern California Coastal Scrub	California Chaparral
California Maritime Chaparral	California Chaparral
California Mesic Chaparral	California Chaparral
California Xeric Serpentine Chaparral	California Chaparral
California Montane Woodland and Chaparral	California Chaparral
Southern California Coastal Scrub	California Chaparral
Mediterranean California Mesic Serpentine Woodland and Chaparral	California Chaparral
Southern California Dry-Mesic Chaparral	California Chaparral
Northern and Central California Dry-Mesic Chaparral	California Chaparral
California Northern Coastal Grassland	California Grassland & Meadow
California Central Valley and Southern Coastal Grassland	California Grassland & Meadow
California Annual Grassland	California Grassland & Meadow
Floridian Highlands Freshwater Marsh	Eastern North America Freshwater Wet Meadow, Riparian & Marsh
Acadian Salt Marsh and Estuary Systems	Eastern North America Freshwater Wet Meadow, Riparian & Marsh
Gulf and Atlantic Coastal Plain Tidal Marsh Systems	Eastern North America Freshwater Wet Meadow, Riparian & Marsh
Laurentian-Acadian Shrub-Herbaceous Wetland Systems	Eastern North America Freshwater Wet Meadow, Riparian & Marsh
Great Lakes Coastal Marsh Systems	Eastern North America Freshwater Wet Meadow, Riparian & Marsh
Central Interior and Appalachian Shrub-Herbaceous Wetland Systems	Eastern North America Freshwater Wet Meadow, Riparian & Marsh
Eastern Great Plains Wet Meadow-Prairie-Marsh	Eastern North America Freshwater Wet Meadow, Riparian & Marsh
North-Central Interior Oak Savanna	Eastern North American Grassland, Meadow & Shrubland
East Gulf Coastal Plain Savanna and Wet Prairie	Florida Peninsula Scrub & Herb
Florida Dry Prairie	Florida Peninsula Scrub & Herb
Northern Atlantic Coastal Plain Dune and Swale	Florida Peninsula Scrub & Herb
Texas-Louisiana Coastal Prairie	Florida Peninsula Scrub & Herb
Texas Saline Coastal Prairie	Florida Peninsula Scrub & Herb
Central and Upper Texas Coast Dune and Coastal Grassland	Florida Peninsula Scrub & Herb
Great Plains Prairie Pothole	Great Plains Mixedgrass Prairie & Shrubland
Western Great Plains Depressional Wetland Systems	Great Plains Mixedgrass Prairie & Shrubland
Western Great Plains Sand Prairie	Great Plains Mixedgrass Prairie & Shrubland
Central Mixedgrass Prairie	Great Plains Mixedgrass Prairie & Shrubland
Northwestern Great Plains Mixedgrass Prairie	Great Plains Mixedgrass Prairie & Shrubland
Western Great Plains Foothill and Piedmont Grassland	Great Plains Mixedgrass Prairie & Shrubland

(continued)

Table 18—(Continued).

Existing vegetation type	NVCS Group or Macrogroup (collapsed classes for reporting)
Western Great Plains Shortgrass Prairie	Great Plains Shortgrass Prairie & Shrubland
North-Central Interior Sand and Gravel Tallgrass Prairie	Great Plains Tallgrass Prairie & Shrubland
Northern Tallgrass Prairie	Great Plains Tallgrass Prairie & Shrubland
Texas Blackland Tallgrass Prairie	Great Plains Tallgrass Prairie & Shrubland
Eastern Great Plains Tallgrass Aspen Parkland	Great Plains Tallgrass Prairie & Shrubland
Central Tallgrass Prairie	Great Plains Tallgrass Prairie & Shrubland
Modified/Managed Northern Tall Grassland	Great Plains Tallgrass Prairie & Shrubland
Western Great Plains Tallgrass Prairie	Great Plains Tallgrass Prairie & Shrubland
Modified/Managed Southern Tall Grassland	Great Plains Tallgrass Prairie & Shrubland
Edwards Plateau Limestone Savanna and Woodland	Great Plains Tallgrass Prairie & Shrubland
Southeastern Great Plains Tallgrass Prairie	Great Plains Tallgrass Prairie & Shrubland
Great Basin Pinyon-Juniper Woodland	Intermountain Singleleaf Pinyon - Western Juniper Woodland
Inter-Mountain Basins Juniper Savanna	Intermountain Singleleaf Pinyon - Western Juniper Woodland
Chihuahuan Succulent Desert Scrub	North American Warm Desert Scrub & Grassland
Sonora-Mojave Mixed Salt Desert Scrub	North American Warm Desert Scrub & Grassland
Chihuahuan Mixed Desert and Thornscrub	North American Warm Desert Scrub & Grassland
Apacherian-Chihuahuan Mesquite Upland Scrub	North American Warm Desert Scrub & Grassland
Chihuahuan Stabilized Coppice Dune and Sand Flat Scrub	North American Warm Desert Scrub & Grassland
Chihuahuan-Sonoran Desert Bottomland and Swale Grassland	North American Warm Desert Scrub & Grassland
Chihuahuan Sandy Plains Semi-Desert Grassland	North American Warm Desert Scrub & Grassland
Apacherian-Chihuahuan Semi-Desert Grassland and Steppe	North American Warm Desert Scrub & Grassland
Chihuahuan Gypsophilous Grassland and Steppe	North American Warm Desert Scrub & Grassland
Chihuahuan Creosotebush Desert Scrub	North American Warm Desert Scrub & Grassland
Sonoran Mid-Elevation Desert Scrub	North American Warm Desert Scrub & Grassland
Mojave Mid-Elevation Mixed Desert Scrub	North American Warm Desert Scrub & Grassland
Chihuahuan Mixed Salt Desert Scrub	North American Warm Desert Scrub & Grassland
Chihuahuan Loamy Plains Desert Grassland	North American Warm Desert Scrub & Grassland
Great Basin Xeric Mixed Sagebrush Shrubland	North American Warm Desert Scrub & Grassland
Colorado Plateau Blackbrush-Mormon-tea Shrubland	North American Warm Desert Scrub & Grassland
Sonora-Mojave Creosotebush-White Bursage Desert Scrub	North American Warm Desert Scrub & Grassland
Sonoran Paloverde-Mixed Cacti Desert Scrub	North American Warm Desert Scrub & Grassland
Sonoran Granite Outcrop Desert Scrub	North American Warm Desert Scrub & Grassland
Western Great Plains Dry Bur Oak Forest and Woodland	Northern Great Plains Woodland
North Pacific Montane Grassland	Rocky Mountain-Vancouverian Mesic Grass & Forb Meadow
Rocky Mountain Subalpine-Montane Mesic Meadow	Rocky Mountain-Vancouverian Mesic Grass & Forb Meadow
Northern Rocky Mountain Subalpine-Upper Montane Grassland	Rocky Mountain-Vancouverian Mesic Grass & Forb Meadow
Southern Rocky Mountain Montane-Subalpine Grassland	Rocky Mountain-Vancouverian Mesic Grass & Forb Meadow
Western Great Plains Sparsely Vegetated Systems	Sparsely Vegetated
Inter-Mountain Basins Sparsely Vegetated Systems	Sparsely Vegetated
North American Warm Desert Sparsely Vegetated Systems	Sparsely Vegetated
Pacific Coastal Marsh Systems	Undifferentiated herb dominated
South Texas Sand Sheet Grassland	Undifferentiated herb dominated
South Texas Lomas	Undifferentiated herb dominated
South Texas Dune and Coastal Grassland	Undifferentiated herb dominated
Tamaulipan Savanna Grassland	Undifferentiated herb dominated
Tamaulipan Mixed Deciduous Thornscrub	Undifferentiated Shrub
Edwards Plateau Limestone Shrubland	Undifferentiated Shrub
Tamaulipan Calcareous Thornscrub	Undifferentiated Shrub
Western Great Plains Wooded Draw and Ravine	Vancouverian & Rocky Mountain Grassland & Shrubland
Northern Rocky Mountain Montane-Foothill Deciduous Shrubland	Vancouverian & Rocky Mountain Grassland & Shrubland
Quercus gambelii Shrubland Alliance	Vancouverian & Rocky Mountain Grassland & Shrubland
Northwestern Great Plains Shrubland	Vancouverian & Rocky Mountain Grassland & Shrubland
Northern Rocky Mountain Lower Montane-Foothill-Valley Grassland	Vancouverian & Rocky Mountain Grassland & Shrubland

(continued)

Table 18—(Continued).

Existing vegetation type	NVCS Group or Macrogroup (collapsed classes for reporting)
Rocky Mountain Gambel Oak-Mixed Montane Shrubland	Vancouverian & Rocky Mountain Grassland & Shrubland
Northern Rocky Mountain Subalpine Deciduous Shrubland	Vancouverian & Rocky Mountain Grassland & Shrubland
Rocky Mountain Lower Montane-Foothill Shrubland	Vancouverian & Rocky Mountain Grassland & Shrubland
Quercus havardii Shrubland Alliance	Vancouverian & Rocky Mountain Grassland & Shrubland
Artemisia tridentata ssp. vaseyana Shrubland Alliance	Vancouverian & Rocky Mountain Grassland & Shrubland
Quercus turbinella Shrubland Alliance	Vancouverian & Rocky Mountain Grassland & Shrubland
Columbia Basin Palouse Prairie	Vancouverian & Rocky Mountain Grassland & Shrubland
Sonora-Mojave Semi-Desert Chaparral	Western North America Interior Sclerophyllous Chaparral Shrubland
Arctostaphylos patula Shrubland Alliance	Western North America Interior Sclerophyllous Chaparral Shrubland
Mogollon Chaparral	Western North America Interior Sclerophyllous Chaparral Shrubland
Great Basin Semi-Desert Chaparral	Western North America Interior Sclerophyllous Chaparral Shrubland
Madrean Oriental Chaparral	Western North America Interior Sclerophyllous Chaparral Shrubland
North Pacific Montane Shrubland	Western North American Alpine Scrub, Forb Meadow & Grassland
North Pacific Dry and Mesic Alpine Dwarf-Shrubland or Fell-field or Meadow	Western North American Alpine Scrub, Forb Meadow & Grassland
Rocky Mountain Alpine Turf	Western North American Alpine Scrub, Forb Meadow & Grassland
Rocky Mountain Alpine Dwarf-Shrubland	Western North American Alpine Scrub, Forb Meadow & Grassland
Introduced Upland Vegetation-Perennial Grassland and Forbland	Western North American Cool Semi-Desert Scrub & Grassland
Western Great Plains Sandhill Steppe	Western North American Cool Semi-Desert Scrub & Grassland
Columbia Basin Foothill and Canyon Dry Grassland	Western North American Cool Semi-Desert Scrub & Grassland
Columbia Plateau Scabland Shrubland	Western North American Cool Semi-Desert Scrub & Grassland
Introduced Upland Vegetation-Annual Grassland	Western North American Cool Semi-Desert Scrub & Grassland
Inter-Mountain Basins Montane Sagebrush Steppe	Western North American Cool Semi-Desert Scrub & Grassland
Wyoming Basins Dwarf Sagebrush Shrubland and Steppe	Western North American Cool Semi-Desert Scrub & Grassland
Columbia Plateau Steppe and Grassland	Western North American Cool Semi-Desert Scrub & Grassland
Inter-Mountain Basins Big Sagebrush Steppe	Western North American Cool Semi-Desert Scrub & Grassland
Columbia Plateau Low Sagebrush Steppe	Western North American Cool Semi-Desert Scrub & Grassland
Colorado Plateau Mixed Low Sagebrush Shrubland	Western North American Cool Semi-Desert Scrub & Grassland
Inter-Mountain Basins Semi-Desert Shrub-Steppe	Western North American Cool Semi-Desert Scrub & Grassland
Inter-Mountain Basins Big Sagebrush Shrubland	Western North American Cool Semi-Desert Scrub & Grassland
Introduced Upland Vegetation-Annual and Biennial Forbland	Western North American Cool Semi-Desert Scrub & Grassland
Inter-Mountain Basins Semi-Desert Grassland	Western North American Cool Semi-Desert Scrub & Grassland
Inter-Mountain Basins Greasewood Flat	Western North American Cool Semi-Desert Scrub & Grassland
Coleogyne ramosissima Shrubland Alliance	Western North American Cool Semi-Desert Scrub & Grassland
Inter-Mountain Basins Mixed Salt Desert Scrub	Western North American Cool Semi-Desert Scrub & Grassland
Inter-Mountain Basins Mat Saltbush Shrubland	Western North American Cool Semi-Desert Scrub & Grassland
Southern Colorado Plateau Sand Shrubland	Western North American Cool Semi-Desert Scrub & Grassland
Inter-Mountain Basins Curl-leaf Mountain Mahogany Woodland and Shrubland	Western North American Scrub Woodland & Shrubland
California Coastal Live Oak Woodland and Savanna	Western North American Warm Temperate Forest
Central and Southern California Mixed Evergreen Woodland	Western North American Warm Temperate Forest
Southern California Oak Woodland and Savanna	Western North American Warm Temperate Forest
California Central Valley Mixed Oak Savanna	Western North American Warm Temperate Forest
Mediterranean California Mixed Oak Woodland	Western North American Warm Temperate Forest
Southern Rocky Mountain Pinyon-Juniper Woodland	Western North American Warm Temperate Forest
Southern Rocky Mountain Juniper Woodland and Savanna	Western North American Warm Temperate Forest
Madrean Pinyon-Juniper Woodland	Western North American Warm Temperate Forest
Madrean Juniper Savanna	Western North American Warm Temperate Forest
Madrean Encinal	Western North American Warm Temperate Forest
Tamaulipan Mesquite Upland Scrub	Western North American Warm Temperate Scrub Woodland & Shrubland
Western Great Plains Mesquite Woodland and Shrubland	Western North American Warm Temperate Scrub Woodland & Shrubland

The most productive systems occur in coastal California (generally chaparral types), Florida Peninsula and Scrub Vegetation, Eastern North American Grassland Meadow and Shrubland, Western North American Warm Temperate Forest, and Great Plains Tallgrass Prairie and Shrubland (table 19). Figure 23 depicts the spatial patterns of rangeland productivity across the coterminous United States. From 2000 to 2009, U.S. rangelands averaged approximately 4300 pounds per acre (SD = 2700) (0.218 kg Cm^2yr^{-1}, SD = 0.137). This value includes above- and belowground vegetative structures as well as areas with shrubs, succulents, herbs, and, in some cases, trees due to the pixel resolution of the MODIS NPP product. Therefore, caution must be used in interpreting the values reported here as they cannot be reliably compared with aboveground *herbaceous* productivity from previous studies. Likewise, U.S. rangelands exhibited a mean coefficient of variation of around 16 percent (table 19). Regions with the highest variability generally occur in more xeric regions such as the southwestern United States and the southern Great Plains presumably in response to inter-annual variability in precipitation (Reeves and others 2006; Zhao and Running 2010) (figure 24). Some localized areas experienced decadal average coefficient of variability of over 100 percent.

Table 19—Biomass (lbs ac^{-1}) estimated from MODIS NPP (Running and others 2004) for NVCS Groups or Macrogroups.

Vegetation class (Group or Macrogroup-NVCS)	NPP[a] Lbs ac^{-1} yr^{-1} (kg C m^{-2} yr^{-1})	CV[b] %
California Chaparral	6,586 (0.74)	10.78
California Grassland & Meadow	6,319 (0.71)	11.31
Florida Peninsula Scrub & Herb	6,141 (0.69)	9.34
Eastern North America Freshwater Wet Meadow, Riparian & Marsh	5,162 (0.58)	10.24
Western North American Warm Temperate Forest	4,450 (0.5)	16.28
Eastern North American Grassland, Meadow & Shrubland	4,005 (0.45)	10.16
Undifferentiated herb dominated	4,005 (0.45)	14.54
Great Plains Tallgrass Prairie & Shrubland	3,560 (0.4)	16.3
Northern Great Plains Woodland	3,560 (0.4)	17.28
Rocky Mountain-Vancouverian Mesic Grass & Forb Meadow	3,382 (0.38)	12.07
Undifferentiated Shrub	3,382 (0.38)	21.16
Western North American Warm Temperate Scrub Woodland & Shrubland	3,115 (0.35)	22.56
Great Plains Mixedgrass Prairie & Shrubland	2,848 (0.32)	17.79
Vancouverian & Rocky Mountain Grassland & Shrubland	2,314 (0.26)	14.57
Western North American Scrub Woodland & Shrubland	2,136 (0.24)	12.06
Great Plains Shortgrass Prairie & Shrubland	2,047 (0.23)	24.58
Western North American Alpine Scrub, Forb Meadow & Grassland	1,958 (0.22)	13
Western North America Interior Sclerophyllous Chaparral Shrubland	1,869 (0.21)	18.18
Intermountain Singleleaf Pinyon - Western Juniper Woodland	1,513 (0.17)	14.12
Western North American Cool Semi-Desert Scrub & Grassland	1,513 (0.17)	15.79
North American Warm Desert Scrub & Grassland	1,246 (0.14)	23
Sparseley Vegetated	1,246 (0.14)	17.68
Average[c]	**0.37 (+/- .18)**	**15.5**

[a] Represents average NPP (above-ground) of all vegetation life forms within the NVCS class based on the MODIS NPP vegetation product.
[b] CV is coefficient of variation and represents the amount of inter-annual variability of NPP from 2000 to 2009 in each vegetation class evaluated.
[c] These values must not be assumed to represent all rangelands and instead represent only the Groups or Macrogroups evaluated in the table. In addition, these values represent total aboveground NPP from a satellite perspective.

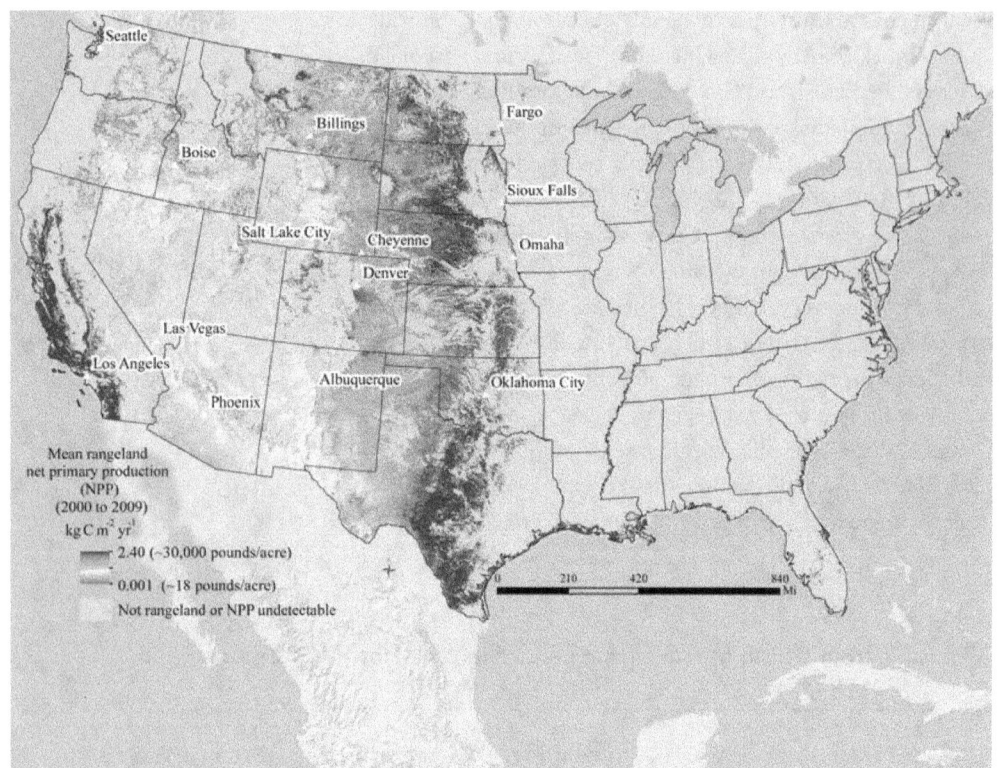

Figure 23—Mean annual rangeland net primary production (NPP) from 2000 to 2009. Here, NPP values represent both above and below-ground production. Only patches comprised of rangelands occupying ≥198 contiguous acres are shown, thus eliminating many rangeland patches of the eastern United States (Zhao 2010).

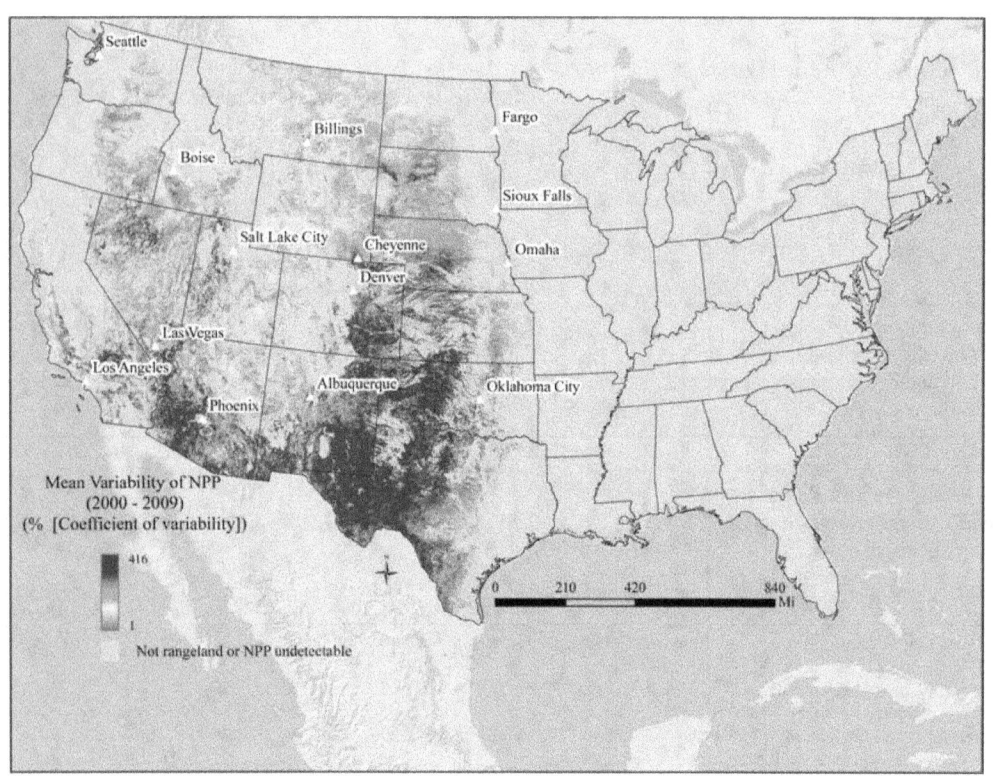

Figure 24—Mean annual coefficient of variability (CV) of rangeland net primary production (NPP) from 2000 to 2009 shown as a percentage. Here, the CV values represent both above and below-ground production. Only areas comprised of rangelands occupying ≥198 contiguous acres are shown, thus eliminating many rangeland patches of the eastern United States (Zhao 2010). Data Source: MODIS NPP collection 4.5, http://modis.gsfc nasa.gov/data/directbrod/index.php.

The vegetation types exhibiting the greatest variation were Great Plains Shortgrass Prairie and Shrubland, North American Warm Desert Scrub and Grassland, and Western North American Warm Temperate Scrub Woodland and Shrubland. Rangeland vegetation exhibiting the highest average productivity tends to have the lowest variability among years (figure 25) reflecting greater stability (less inter-annual variation) in precipitation and moisture conditions. This phenomenon is expressed as an increasing rangeland productivity gradient extending from the Rocky Mountains eastward, as demonstrated in figure 23.

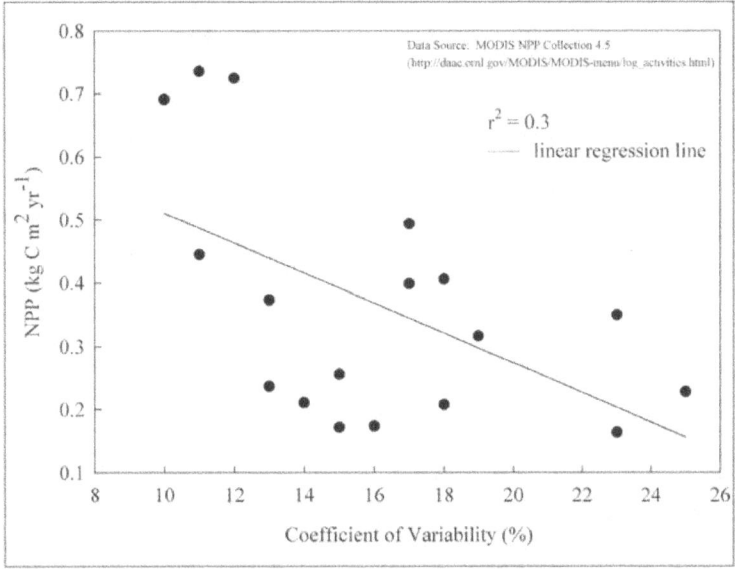

Figure 25—Relationship between mean rangeland vegetation productivity derived from the MODIS NPP products from 2000 to 2009 and coefficient of variation. More productive areas generally yield less variability, tending to produce more reliable forage abundance.

Overall, from 2000 to 2009, U.S. rangelands have exhibited a weakly positive, albeit insignificant, trend in productivity ($r^2 = 0.1$, $P<0.37$) (figure 26). However, the Rocky Mountain Assessment Region exhibited a stronger increasing trend ($r^2 = 0.38$, $P<0.06$) from 2000 to 2009 than other assessment regions (figure 27). The increase in productivity in the region needs to be interpreted with caution and could be produced by a number of factors. Determining the exact cause of the increase is beyond the scope of this report and requires more research. Nevertheless, the region experienced a pulse of increased productivity over the time period examined.

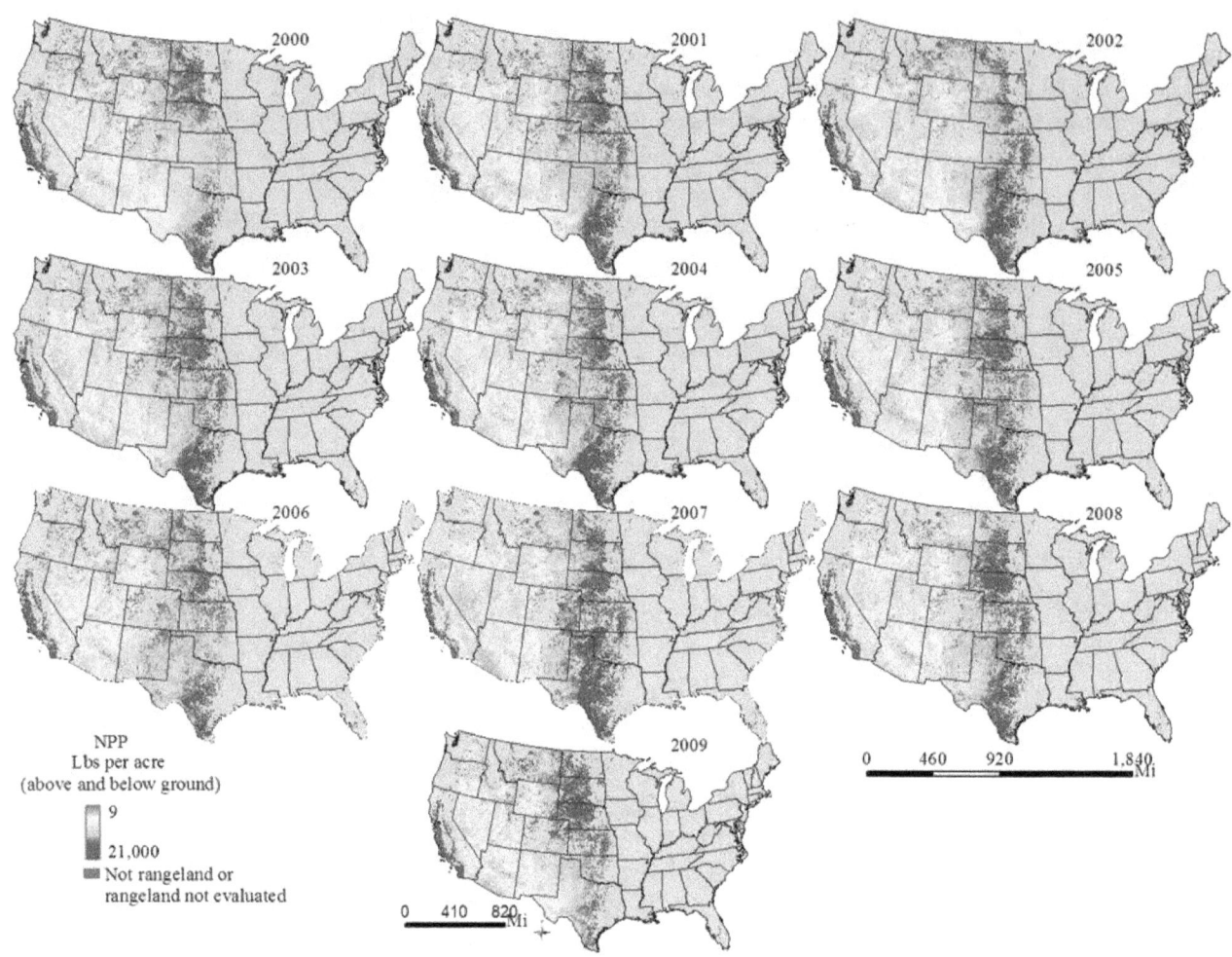

NPP
Lbs per acre
(above and below ground)

9
21,000
Not rangeland or
rangeland not evaluated

Figure 26—The estimated net primary production from 2000 to 2009 derived from 1-km MODIS NPP Collection 4.5 data, http://modis. gsfc nasa.gov/data/directbrod/index.php.

Forage Supply

The 1989 RPA Rangeland Assessment (Joyce 1989) extensively evaluated the forage supply and generally concluded that the amount of forage available for herbivory is a difficult metric to quantify. In addition, it was concluded that the forage supply would likely be sufficient to support the growing demand for red meat. We concur with that assessment based on the following crude but comprehensive method of accounting for the available forage in the coterminous United States. Estimates of forage derived from pastures are added to the previous section's analysis of rangeland productivity, thus addressing the issue of overall forage supply. The true forage supply not only includes all grazing lands (figure 28) but also various feedstuffs, such as corn, oats, and barley (figure 28). The amount of grazeable crop residues or cereal grains is not quantified, therefore, the resultant estimates derived here could underestimate the total available forage in the coterminous United States.

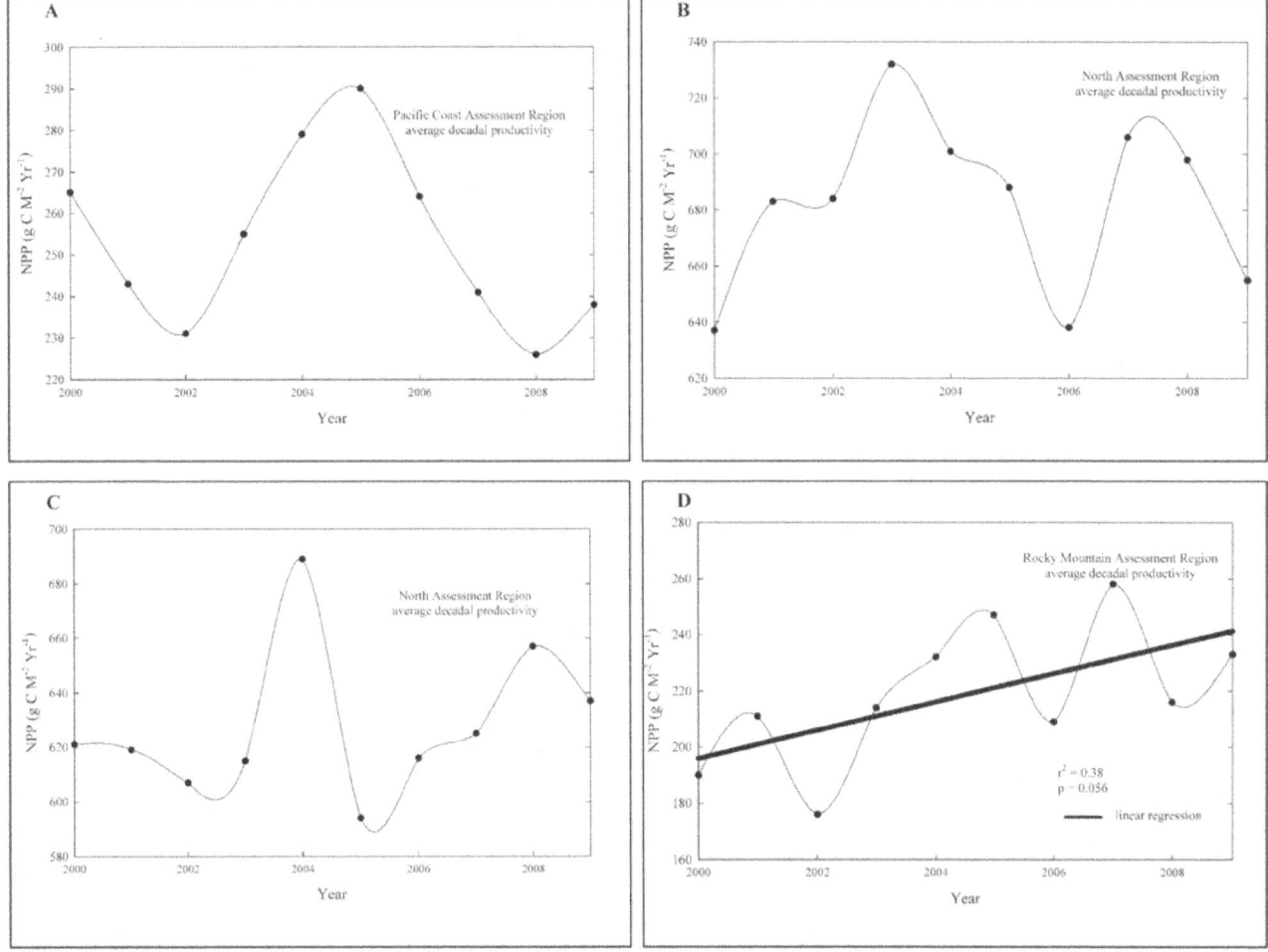

Figure 27—Time series of net primary production from the MODIS sensor from 2000 to 2009 for each of the RPA Assessment Regions. Only the Rocky Mountain Assessment Region exhibited a significant (p = 0.056) positive increase in vegetation productivity over the last decade.

Using 10-year mean MODIS NPP, rangeland area identified by Reeves and Mitchell (2011), and the pasture areas and forested areas identified in the LANDFIRE Existing Vegetation Type, it is possible to conservatively estimate the total average annual forage supply using a series of assumptions. The assumptions used to convert average annual MODIS NPP from $KgCm^2yr^{-1}$ to above ground biomass (forage) are:

- Biomass is comprised of approximately 50 percent carbon.

- The root to shoot ratio on average ranges from 50 to 70 percent across vegetation types.

- Only 80 percent of the aboveground biomass in wildland settings, where herbs and shrubs dominate, is available forage (a gross estimate).

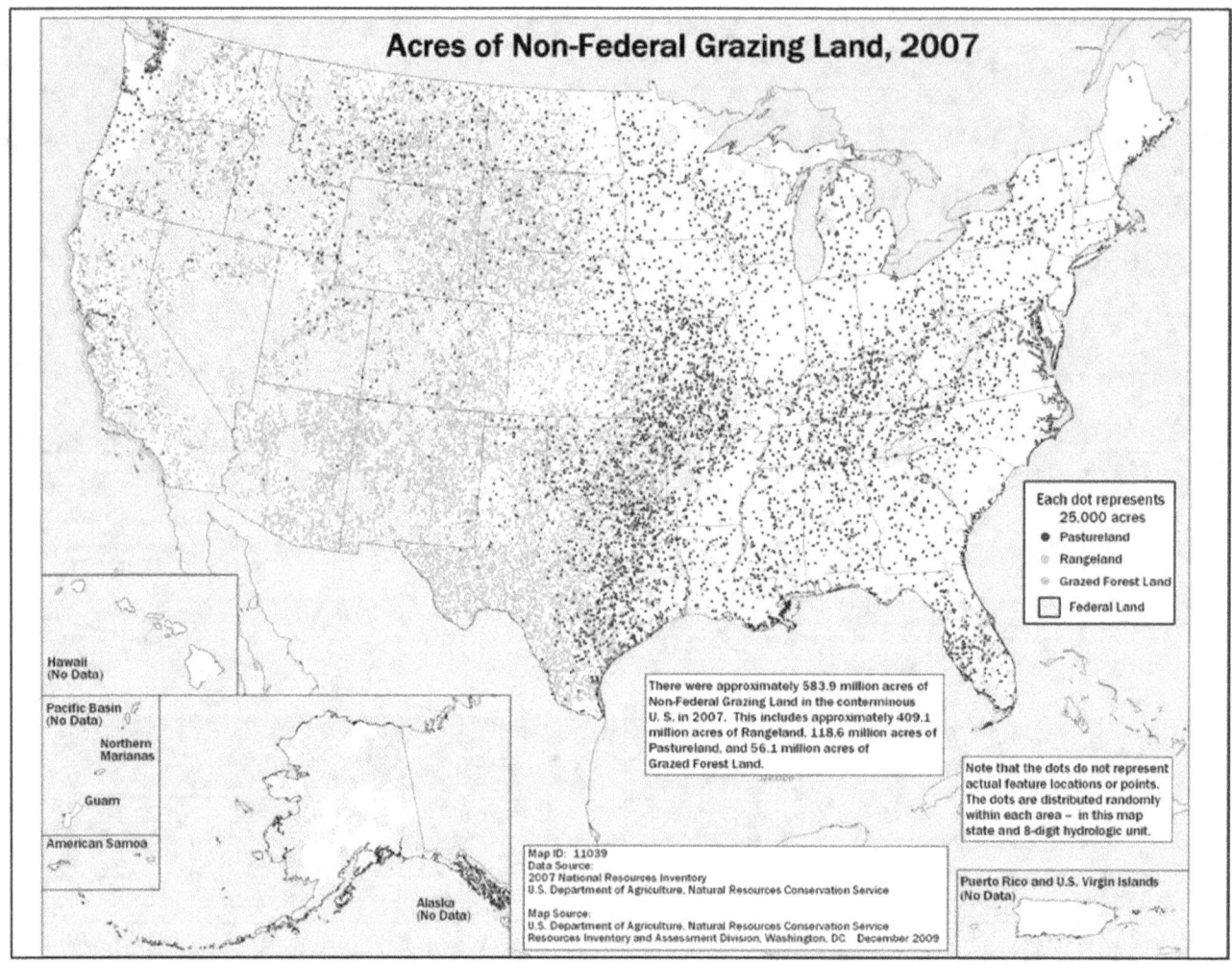

Figure 28—Estimated 2007 distribution of non-Federal grazing lands in the coterminous United States (USDA 2009).

This figure varies by ecosystem and the herbivore that is using the range (for example, a shrub field will generally be less useable for a herd of cattle than for goats or deer). In some vegetation types, this assumption of available vegetation is higher than one might expect. To account for this and to provide a conservative estimate of forage at the national level, we further assume that the estimates of forage derived using the methods presented here are overestimated by 30 percent.

Using the MODIS NPP data (data processing discussed in "Decadal Productivity Trends" section) and the assumptions to convert NPP to biomass, overall forage supply in the coterminous United States was estimated at roughly 1.9 to 2.6 trillion pounds of grazeable pasture, rangeland forage, and forage beneath tree canopies (table 20).

Table 20—Coarse estimate of annual forage supply (from rangelands, forests, and pastures) across the coterminous United States estimated from MODIS NPP and a set of necessary assumptions.

Root:Shoot ratio assumption	Forage from rangelands[a]	Forage from pasturelands[b]	Forage from forest lands[c]	Annual total forage estimate	AUM capacity[d]
	- - - - - - - - - - - - - - - Aboveground biomass (100,000's lbs)- - - - - - - - - - - - - - -				
70/30	13,787,185	11,030,733	1,419,000	26,236,918	3,363,707,435
50/50	9,847,989	7,879,095	1,419,000	19,146,084	2,454,626,153

[a]Assumes that 80% of aboveground NPP will be allocated to available forage–forage that is palatable and reachable.
[b]Assumes that 100% of aboveground NPP will be allocated to available forage–forage that is palatable and reachable.
[c]No below-ground allocation needed since (Gaines and others 1954) estimated above-ground forage yield.
[d]Assumes monthly forage requirement of 780 lbs dry matter month[-1] (Scarnecchia 1985).

Based on the remote sensing approach described here, pasture forage is conservatively estimated to average 4000 pounds per acre nationwide. At these levels, every one million acres of pasture lost correspond to 5.1 million AUMs or approximately 427,000 cattle per year assuming they are grazed continuously (not always the case). These analyses assume that all estimated forage is available, palatable, and nutritionally acceptable, which is a reasonable assumption for average pasture conditions since most pastures are managed to provide forage of some kind.

While most pasture lands in the southern United States are used on an annual basis, only a small fraction of grazeable forest land is used (Joyce 1989) and therefore might represent a relatively untapped reservoir of forage. Accurately estimating the amount of grazeable forage beneath forested canopies is beyond the capacity of this report. However, Gaines and others (1954) estimated that in the southeastern United States, longleaf pine (*Pinus palustris*) stands exhibited forage production that varied from 430 to 1000 pounds per acre depending on canopy closure. Using a conservative assumption that half of the lower end of this value (215 pounds per acre) can represent average forage production per acre for forested stands of the United States, it is possible to coarsely estimate a forage supply beneath forested stands. The Existing Vegetation Cover from the LANDFIRE vegetation product suite reveals an estimate of 660 million acres of lands with ≥10 percent tree cover. When combined with the conservative estimate of 215 pounds per acre of forage beneath forest canopies, yield is estimated at 71 million tons of forage. Not all of the forage is useable or palatable for all classes of herbivores, but this provides a conservative, defensible estimate of gross forage amount.

Even if the total forage supply, as quantified here, is over-estimated by 30 percent, the forage in the United States—minus crop residues and agriculturally developed feedstuffs for energy (for example, wheat, barley, and sorghum), protein (for example, cotton meal and sunflower meal), and roughages (for example, silages and wheat bran)—should support approximately 143 to 196 million animal units per year or 1.7 to 2.4 billion AUMs (table 21).

Table 21—Estimates of animal capacity based on forage calculations from MODIS NPP and other GIS data products. A variety of species are chosen to give the reader a rough idea of how many animals can be supported by the estimated forage yield from rangeland, pasture, and forage beneath forested canopies. Agricultural feedstuffs such as corn, oats, and barley are not included in the available forage calculations.

Species	Assumed average weight (lbs)	AUM conversion	Animals[a]	
			# for a year (100,000's)	# for a month (100,000's)
Cow	1,000	1	2,046	24,546
Horse	1,100	1	2,046	24,546
Elk[b]	600	1.5	3,068	36,819
Mule deer[b]	125	4.5	9,205	110,458
Sheep	120	5	10,228	122,731
Goat	120	5	10,228	122,731
Pronghorn antelope	90	6	12,273	147,278

[a]Estimates assume that all other habitat requirements are met and only consider forage as a limiting resource. The numbers are conservatively based on the lower root:shoot ratio estimate of 50% from table 20. In addition, these numbers are offered only as a general guide.
[b]While these AUM conversions have been used in the past (USDA SCS 1988), more careful computations for mule deer and elk would require knowledge of herd composition and the age of offspring. The numbers only represent mature animals and the "average" forage requirements.

The conversions presented in table 21 are not straightforward (Van Tassel and others 1995) and many factors, beyond those presented here, must be considered at a local level. It should be noted that these forage calculations do not take into consideration areas dominated by transitional rangelands identified in Reeves and Mitchell (2011). In some regions, transitional rangelands represent large reservoirs of forage suitable for herbivory, but from a national perspective, the relative contribution to the forage base is small. Though these estimates are debatable, and the assumptions used to make these calculations do not apply to all situations, they yield insight to the magnitude of available forage in the United States for grazing or browsing herbivores.

Livestock Production

Vegetation production ultimately controls the *capacity* of the land to support herbivory, but from a commodity perspective, livestock production is one of the best measured indicators of goods and services. Joyce (1989) described historical trends in cattle, sheep, horses, and goats from the mid-1800s until 1986 while Mitchell (2000) provided historical context through 1995. In this report, where possible, trends from the mid-1990s to roughly 2009 are the focus.

Cattle and Sheep Numbers

The United States has the largest fed-cattle industry in the world and is the world's largest producer of beef (http://www.ers.usda.gov/Briefing/Cattle/). Beef production tends to follow a rather predictable cycle that is characterized by a series of peaks and troughs in herd size and production that typically last from 8 to 12 years (Mitchell 2000). The 2000 Range

Assessment highlighted a prediction by the Economic Research Service (ERS) that by 2007, a peak of roughly 103 million head would be reached. In fact, numbers have not been that high since a peak in U.S. cattle production in 1982 of approximately 104 million animals (USDA NASS 2009). Table 22 indicates that the cattle numbers between 2002 and 2007 remained within 1.4 percent of the estimated 10-year average of approximately 96.6 million. Table 23 illustrates the distribution of cattle circa 2007 and the loss in cattle population since 1997. The coterminous United States lost approximately 2.6 million cattle between 1997 and 2007 (USDA NASS 2009) but losses were distributed asymmetrically. The North Assessment Region lost nearly 26 percent while the Pacific Coast Assessment Region gained 10 percent. In 2007, the South Assessment Region had the most cattle at approximately 34.1 million animals (table 23). The South Assessment Region, however, includes Texas and Oklahoma, which combined, comprise 56 percent of the cattle population in that region. Nebraska and Kansas each yield greater than 80 cattle per square mile, while Texas, which contained approximately 13.7 million cattle, only has 52 cattle per square mile (USDA NASS 2009). As indicated in Mitchell (2000), the situation with sheep numbers is completely different than with cattle.

Since 1997, sheep numbers have declined by approximately 26 percent reflecting the trend that has been in place since roughly the late 1930s when nearly 50 million sheep were present. In the United States, sheep numbers have declined by roughly 200,000 animals per year since 1997 and were estimated at only 5.8 million animals in 2007. Jones (2004) provided an excellent overview of the U.S. sheep industry and an analysis of the main factors linked to the steady decline. Chief among these factors are:

1. Lamb consumption is very low compared with other meats. Per capita sheep consumption has dropped by approximately 35 percent since 1975 (estimated from Jones [2004]).

2. Synthetic fabrics have decreased dependence on wool production.

3. Overall poor marketing of the U.S. sheep meat industry (imports have risen nearly 500 percent since 1975 (estimated from Jones [2004])

4. Disease and predator losses continue to raise domestic production costs.

Although these factors have greatly decreased the U.S. sheep population, ranch diversification and re-kindled awareness of lamb and mutton through increased imports offer hope for the future of the U.S. sheep industry.

Table 22—Stock numbers from the NASS Agricultural Census. Bison were not counted in the 1997 Agricultural Census.

Year	Goats	Cattle	Horses	Sheep	Bison
1997	2,251,613	98,989,244	3,020,117	7,821,885	N/A
2002	3,780,466	95,497,994	3,644,278	6,341,799	231,008
2007	4,412,529	96,347,858	4,028,827	5,819,162	198,234

Table 23—Cattle population and distribution in the coterminous United States and RPA Assessment Regions in 2007 and change since 1997.

State (Assessment Region)	Cattle Population (2007)	Gain/(loss) (%) (1997 to 2007)	Cattle per mi^{-2}	Gain/(loss)[a] since 1997
(Pacific Northwest AR)				
California	5,498,025	7	35	376,092
Oregon	1,389,189	(10)	14	(133,562)
Washington	1,088,846	(11)	16	(122,504)
Pacific Northwest Total	**7,976,060**	**10**	**24.8**	**120,026**
(Rocky Mountain AR)				
Kansas	6,669,163	3	81	231,324
Nebraska	6,576,950	(2)	85	(153,203)
South Dakota	3,687,728	(1)	48	(22,901)
Colorado	2,745,253	(19)	26	(516,840)
Montana	2,589,679	-0.002	18	(5,932)
Idaho	2,236,147	17	27	373,508
North Dakota	1,811,523	(0.001)	26	(1,753)
New Mexico	1,525,976	(12)	13	(178,487)
Wyoming	1,311,799	(27)	13	(349,101)
Arizona	1,000,038	13	9	133,252
Utah	843,474	(8)	10	(63,482)
Nevada	441,629	(17)	4	(74,481)
Rocky Mountain Total	**31,439,359**	**0**	**26.9**	**(628,096)**
(North AR)				
Missouri	4,292,702	(1)	61	(60,512)
Iowa	3,982,344	7	71	264,950
Wisconsin	3,373,923	(4)	60	(123,552)
Minnesota	2,395,217	(0.002)	28	(4,400)
Pennsylvania	1,609,147	(5)	35	(81,217)
New York	1,443,297	(3)	30	(36,274)
Ohio	1,272,402	(5)	31	(64,735)
Illinois	1,231,105	(23)	22	(281,793)
Michigan	1,048,206	(0.003)	18	(2,924)
Indiana	875,350	(20)	24	(173,973)
West Virginia	411,028	(7)	17	(29,863)
Vermont	264,823	(15)	28	(39,816)
Maryland	190,504	(36)	20	(68,327)
Maine	88,191	(19)	3	(16,461)
Connecticut	50,213	(36)	10	(18,138)
Massachusetts	46,852	(37)	6	(17,510)
New Jersey	38,198	(53)	5	(20,285)
New Hampshire	36,880	(28)	4	(10,279)
Delaware	20,994	(34)	10	(7,125)
Rhode Island	5,085	(28)	5	(1,439)
North Total	**22,676,461**	**(26)**	**34.3**	**(793,673)**
(South AR)				
Texas	13,709,543	(6)	52	(794,901)
Oklahoma	5,391,337	0.002	77	12,387
Kentucky	2,395,455	(3)	59	(81,494)
Tennessee	2,122,018	(4)	50	(91,701)
Arkansas	1,802,653	1	34	18,462
Florida	1,711,011	(9)	31	(147,244)
Virginia	1,566,217	(9)	39	(136,458)
Alabama	1,187,171	(30)	23	(359,228)
Georgia	1,117,087	(15)	19	(172,341)
Mississippi	987,342	(21)	21	(208,497)
Louisiana	878,664	(6)	19	(51,450)
North Carolina	820,182	(17)	17	(139,648)
South Carolina	400,996	(20)	13	(78,762)
South Total	**34,089,676**	**(1)**	**40.2**	**(2,230,875)**
U.S. Total	**96,181,556**	**(7)**	**32**	**(3,532,618)**

[a] Cannot sum values for each state to derive totals for each AR.

Grazing on Federal Lands

While numerous state, local, and Federal agencies permit grazing on public lands, USFS and BLM administer the largest holdings of grazeable lands (figure 8). Permitted use on BLM and NFS lands is generally reported as AUMs. The traditional definition of an AUM is biomass of forage consumed by a 1000-lb cow with a suckling calf in one month, tantamount to 780-lb dry weight (Mitchell 2000). The BLM still uses this standard for evaluating forage supply, but for billing purposes a modified AUM concept is used. Both the USFS and BLM have modified the classical AUM definition for billing, making it more closely aligned with "Head Months" (HMs). HMs can be conceptualized as the number of animals per month without regard for breed or size differences due to the difficulty in tracking the size, breed, and species of all animals needed to make appropriate AUM calculations (for example, a 1200-lb cow will consume more than an 800-lb cow of the same breed). However, tracking these characteristics on public lands would be exceedingly difficult and costly.

During the 1980s and 1990s, permitted livestock use fluctuated within 10 percent of 10 million AUMs. During the last decade, however, permitted livestock grazing on BLM lands has decreased by 12 percent and was at a decadal low in 2004 (table 24) (BLM 2000 to 2009). The average annual permitted use decreased to approximately 7.9 million AUMs compared with approximately 10 million AUMs over the last two decades (Mitchell 2000). In comparison, permitted use on NFS lands has fluctuated within 19 percent of 7.6 million AUMs between 2000 and 2008 (table 25) (USDA FS 2000 to 2008).

Table 24—Livestock use from 2000 to 2009 on BLM lands expresses as AUMs.

Year	Cattle, yearlings, and buffalo	Horses and burros	Sheep and goats	Total
2000	8,890,057	55,253	892,278	9,837,588
2001	7,335,444	50,987	725,577	8,112,008
2002	7,111,592	48,778	712,149	7,872,819
2003	6,035,807	43,390	639,257	6,718,454
2004	5,930,432	44,023	620,503	6,594,958
2005	6,105,170	48,312	645,117	6,798,599
2006	6,825,124	48,357	662,931	7,536,412
2007	7,862,879	51,182	678,724	8,592,785
2008	7,858,634	51,726	682,059	8,592,419
2009	7,890,953	51,089	697,135	8,639,177
Average	7,184,609	49,310	695,573	7,929,522
SD	923,961	3,403	72,633	986,988

Table 25—Livestock use and non-use from 2000 to 2008 on NFS lands expressed as number of animals, head months, and AUMs.

Year	Action	Cattle (1,000s)			Horses and burros (1,000s)			Sheep and goats (1,000s)			Total (1,000s)		
		n[a]	HM[b]	AUM[c]	n	HM	AUM	n	HM	AUM	n	HM	AUM
2000	Permitted	1,295.4	6,759.0	8,538.6	10.4	43.6	52.5	1,036.8	3,083.1	880.8	2,342.5	9,885.7	9,471.8
2000	Authorized	1,234.3	5,712.4	7,205.5	6.3	32.8	39.3	949.0	2,516.3	718.4	2,189.6	8,261.5	7,963.2
2001	Permitted	1,355.8	7,065.2	8,905.5	9.9	43.3	51.5	1,068.3	2,433.9	925.4	2,433.9	10,365.4	9,882.4
2001	Authorized	1,219.4	5,540.5	5,381.5	7.4	38.7	37.5	954.1	2,678.6	684.7	2,180.9	6,658.4	6,103.7
2002	Permitted	1,311.4	6,940.3	8,736.6	8.7	38.1	45.0	1,050.9	3,124.0	893.7	2,371.1	10,102.4	9,675.3
2002	Authorized	1,068.8	4,580.7	5,826.7	5.7	27.5	32.2	909.4	2,201.2	630.1	1,983.9	6,809.4	6,489.0
2003	Permitted	1,286.6	6,405.8	8,114.1	8.9	37.8	43.9	1,072.9	2,876.4	829.7	2,368.3	9,320.0	8,987.8
2003	Authorized	983.1	4,084.7	5,209.3	5.4	27.6	32.5	740.6	1,823.9	521.7	1,729.1	5,936.2	5,763.5
2004	Permitted	1,187.5	5,797.5	7,348.3	8.1	31.3	37.0	983.9	2,624.0	764.1	2,179.5	8,452.8	8,149.3
2004	Authorized	990.4	3,914.4	4,992.8	5.4	23.1	27.7	759.3	1,846.6	531.1	1,755.1	5,784.1	5,551.7
2005	Permitted	1,343.9	6,646.4	8,406.1	9.4	41.3	48.8	1,048.2	2,744.9	783.7	2,401.5	9,432.6	9,238.6
2005	Authorized	1,173.3	4,738.4	6,025.8	6.5	32.6	38.4	882.0	2,035.8	574.3	2,061.8	6,806.8	6,638.5
2006	Permitted	1,254.0	5,668.9	7,202.0	5.6	50.6	61.7	950.8	2,451.8	705.8	2,215.8	8,205.3	8,013.5
2006	Authorized	1,045.9	4,105.9	5,215.3	5.2	26.4	31.6	690.6	1,637.8	467.5	1,746.5	5,801.0	5,754.9
2007	Permitted	1,255.5	5,828.4	7,324.5	5.3	25.4	29.8	926.5	2,556.9	727.5	2,187.3	8,410.8	8,081.8
2007	Authorized	1,078.0	4,293.8	5,454.0	6.4	28.4	34.0	744.9	1,786.1	506.3	1,829.2	6,110.1	5,994.2
2008	Permitted	1,266.9	5,882.8	7,482.5	5.3	24.9	29.8	932.4	2,567.2	730.6	2,213.5	8,505.9	8,252.3
2008	Authorized	1,176.1	4,789.0	6,099.8	5.6	26.5	31.7	812.6	1,981.0	563.0	1,991.6	6,796.6	6,694.5

[a]n indicates the number of animals in a given category.
[b]HM is head months defined as "The time in *months* that livestock spend on National Forest System land." This is the measurement used for billing purposes. (USFS 2000-2008, grazing statistical summaries).
[c]AUM here is defined by the USFS as "The amount of *forage* required by a 1,000-pound cow, or the equivalent for 1 month" (USFS 2000-2008, grazing statistical summaries).

Mere examination of permitted livestock use does not yield a complete representation of the public land grazing situation. Permitted use is the maximum amount of AUMs permitted to be utilized under a grazing permit, grazing agreement, livestock use permit, or other permitting document. USFS uses authorized use to track the amount of livestock authorized to graze on Federal lands for the current grazing year. Actual use, employed by the BLM, is the amount of AUMs that are actually utilized on Federal lands for the current grazing year. In some cases, where the BLM does not collect actual use data, billed use is a surrogate measure for actual use. Billed use (billed use refers to authorized and "active" types of uses, non-use, unauthorized use, etc., are not included in billed use) is the total amount of AUMs that were billed for a specific grazing permit (lease, etc.) for a specific grazing fee year. Authorized use and actual use can differ substantially from permitted use for a number of reasons, including weather conditions, rangeland readiness, allowable use, and permittee needs. Quantifying the non-use of permitted AUMs on National Forest System lands has been a topic of discussion in both Joyce (1989) and Mitchell (2000). Both Joyce (1989) and Mitchell (2000) defined non-use as 1–authorized AUMs/permitted AUMs, where authorized use was the sum of all paid permits contained in annual authorizations and permitted use was the sum of all animals permitted to graze, both expressed as AUMs (Mitchell 2000). Over the last 30 years, the percentage of non-use on sheep allotments has fluctuated between 18 and 37 percent (Mitchell 2000) (figure 29). Compared with the 1980s and 1990s, however, the most recent decadal data suggest a slight increase in proportion of non-use. Between 1977 and 1994, the average non-use by sheep and cattle was approximately 14 and 20 percent, respectively; those numbers both rose to approximately 28 percent from 2000 to 2008, each suggesting a slightly positive trend in non-use.

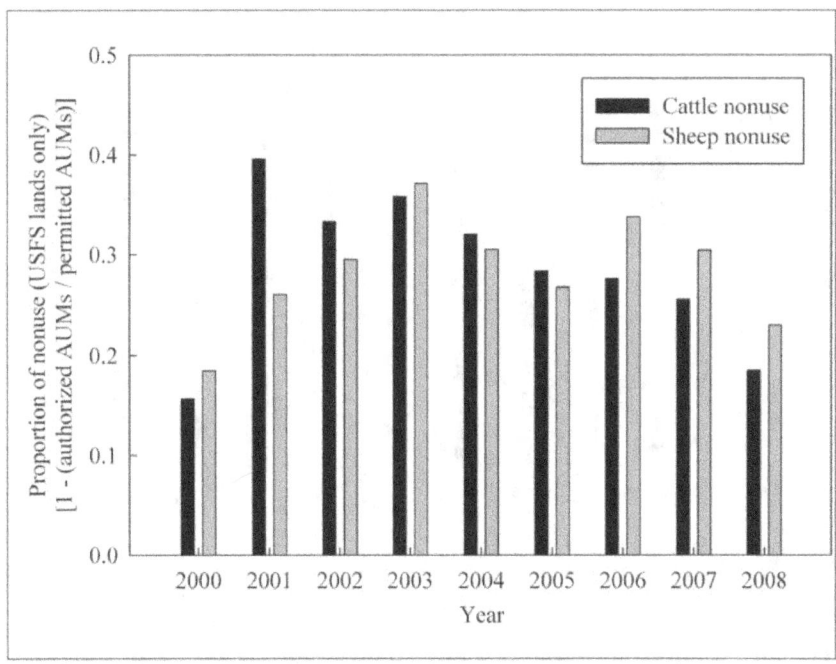

Figure 29—Percent nonuse ([1-(authorized AUMs/permitted AUMs)]) of grazing allotments administered by the USFS.

Livestock grazing on Federal lands generates revenue on an annual basis, which is a function of either the authorized AUMs for BLM lands or HMs for NFS lands multiplied by the national grazing fee. The national livestock grazing fee has varied only 15 percent of $1.54 over the last 22 years (Cooley, personal communication). The estimated average annual gross receipts from grazing activities on NFS lands is approximately $9.1 million, while the estimated annual gross receipts from grazing activity on BLM lands is $11.8 million (figure 30). Most of the money received from grazing on Federal lands comes from the western United States. The dollar figures presented here should only be used as a general guide and may not represent exact figures as local conditions and frequency of database updates produce slightly different numbers.

Other Livestock

Table 22 exemplifies several noteworthy trends that have manifested over the last decade. Horses have increased approximately 33 percent, while goats have increased by 96 percent. The trend in domestic goat production emulates the global trend. Since 1985, goat numbers have increased globally from 500 million to over 900 million (FAO 2009, http://faostat fao. org/). Many reasons can be attributed to the increase, the most notable of which suggest changing dietary preferences and ethnic influences on meat production (Solaiman 2007). In

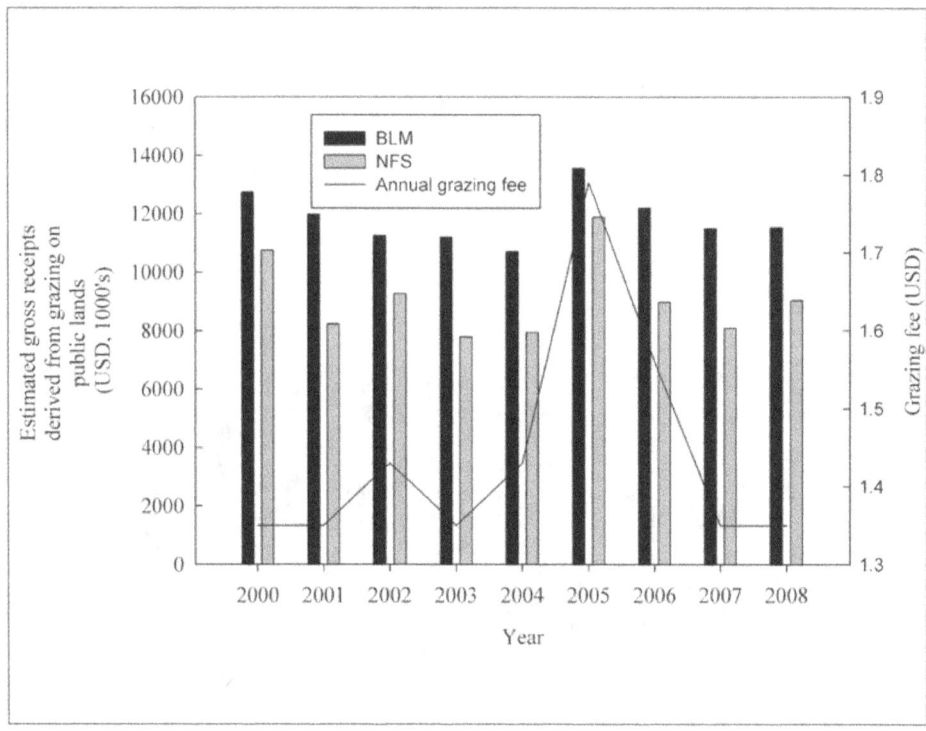

Figure 30—Estimated gross receipts from public lands cattle grazing on USFS and BLM allotments (Cooley 2010; USFS 2000 to 2008).

the United States, goats are also gaining popularity due to efficient conversion of feed. In addition, goats are valuable as holistic vegetation management tools (Luginbuhl and others 2000). The distribution of goats in the coterminous United States is shown in figure 31. As noted by Mitchell (2000), most horses owned in the United States are used for recreational purposes. The distribution of horses is fairly even across the coterminous United States (figure 32). Both goat and horse numbers have increased substantially since the 2000 RPA Assessment (table 22).

Bison numbers on private lands is estimated at about 200,000 animals (USDA NASS 2009), which, combined with animals on public lands, yields an estimate of approximately 220,000 bison. Since the last assessment, however, the number of bison has decreased. However, this decrease in bison numbers is not likely a reliable indicator of future trends. The USDA Census of Agriculture does not account for bison calf recruitment. Increased consumer demand and record meat prices have effectively drawn down the U.S. herd since 2002 (Matheson, personal communication). Bison numbers are greatest on the Northern Great Plains, particularly, South Dakota, which, in 2007, hosted approximately 38,000 bison on private lands alone (figure 33) (USDA NASS 2009).

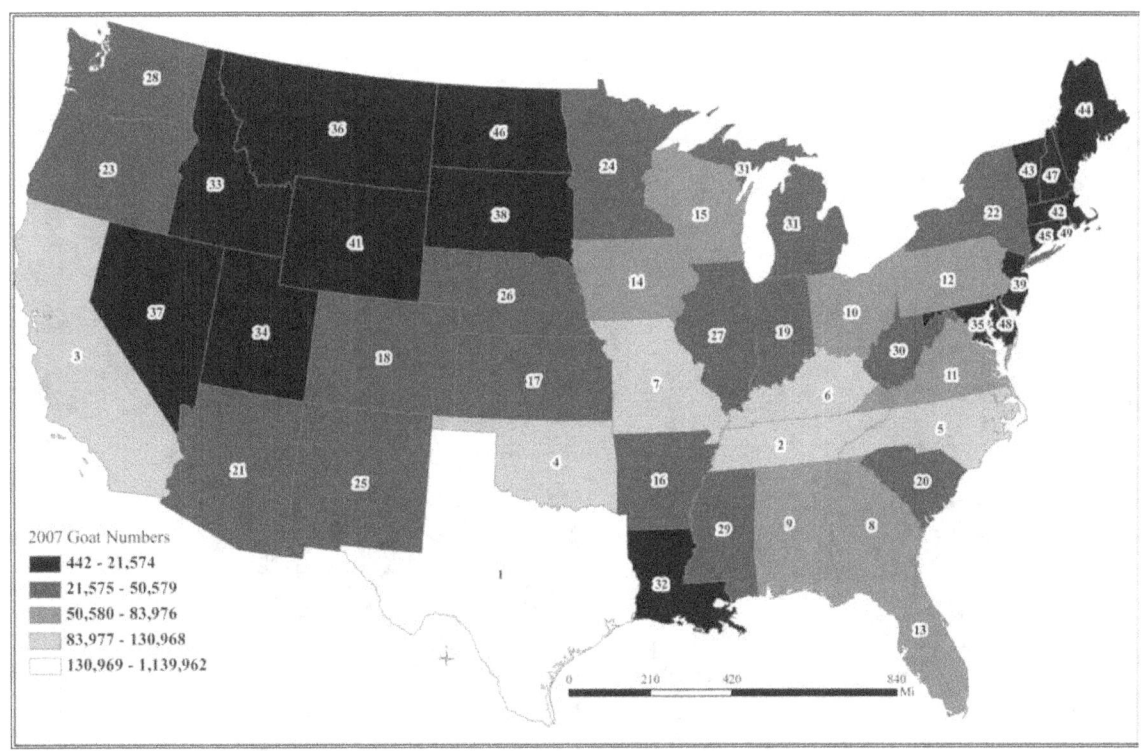

Figure 31—Estimated 2007 distribution of goats in the coterminous United States (USDA, NASS 2010). Data Source: USDA Census of Agriculture (2007).

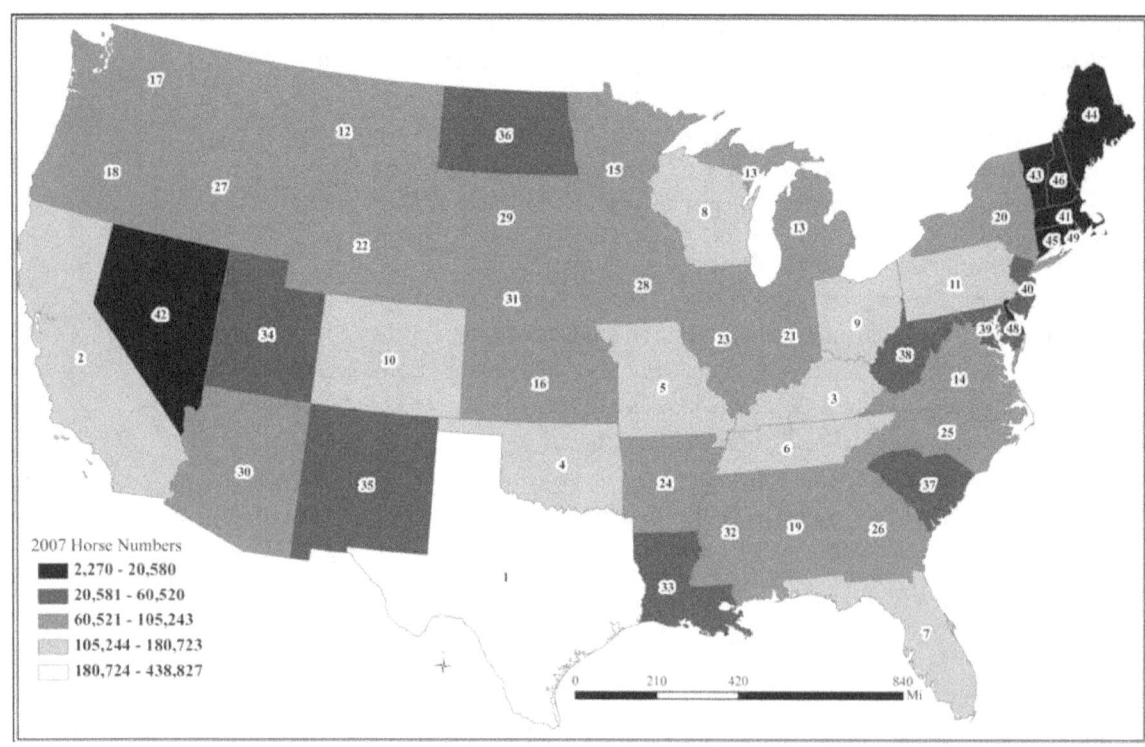

Figure 32—Estimated 2007 distribution of horses in the coterminous United States (USDA, NASS 2010). Data Source: USDA Census of Agriculture (2007).

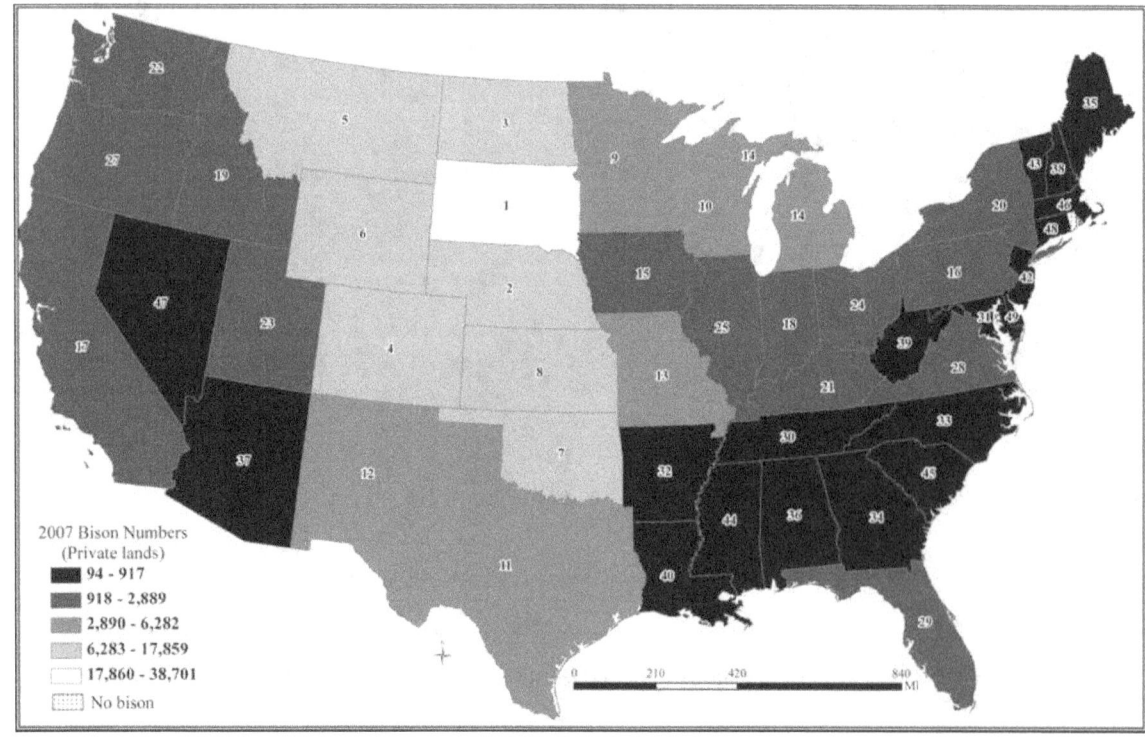

Figure 33—Estimated 2007 distribution of bison in the coterminous United States (USDA, NASS 2010). Data Source: USDA Census of Agriculture (2007).

Livestock Appropriation of Forage

Quantifying the amount of forage across the landscape is not the only metric needed to determine the relationship between forage supply and demand. Forage use across the landscape is asymmetrical, and understanding the distribution of forage and herbivores yields unique perspective regarding quantity and juxtaposition of herbivory and appropriation of net primary production to livestock. Such an analysis provides information on where thresholds might be crossed in the future, beyond which rangeland forage may not be sufficient for sustaining a given stocking rate.

Nearly 36 percent of global population depends on approximately $904 billion per year in dryland ecosystem goods and services that cover 41 percent of the terrestrial surface (Costanza and others 1997; MEA 2005). This dependence on rangelands for goods and services and the inherent susceptibility of rangelands to degradation, characterized as a reduction of vegetation canopy cover and accelerated soil erosion (Lepers and others 2005; MEA 2005), require monitoring of land degradation. Causes of degradation are not always clear and may be due to interactions between stressors. Examples of stressors are extreme climatic events and land management practices such as livestock grazing and El Niño and La Niña events that have three- to seven-year return intervals (Holmgren and Scheffer 2001; Holmgren and others 2006; Washington-Allen and others 2006). The goal of the current livestock appropriation study was to develop spatially explicit data describing the relationship between forage availability and forage demand. While the study described in this section is not a degradation monitor, per se, it does yield insight to the sustainability of livestock appropriation of NPP through space and time and where thresholds might be crossed, beyond which a given level of grazing may not be possible in the future.

To gain insight to this problem, research was conducted to quantify the proportion of aboveground biomass allocated to domestic livestock herbivory. Cattle and sheep are the main herbivores used for the analysis, which obviously falls short of a census that would include deer, elk, antelope, horses, goats (in some areas), bison, and other ungulates. Information regarding numbers and spatial distribution of wildlife and less abundant livestock are scant and difficult to interpret. Additionally, in 2007, bison and horses (combined) only represented 4,227,061 animals requiring only 4.3 percent of the forage needed by cattle, sheep, and goats. In localized situations, horses and bison may have a significant impact on the forage supply, but from a regional or national perspective, bison and horses have a small influence. As a result and according to data availability, forage demand for sheep, goats, and cattle are reported here. In this section, we focus on livestock numbers available from the National Agricultural Statistics Survey (NASS) and evaluate the estimated amount of NPP allocated to these livestock. Here, noteworthy results of the forage appropriation study are reported on, but limiting methodological details which will be available in a forthcoming peer-reviewed publication.

Spatially explicit data describing livestock numbers and available forage are needed to quantify livestock appropriation of NPP. Since spatially explicit, field-referenced data describing forage availability at regional or national scales are non-existent, remote sensing was used to estimate forage availability. To correspond to availability of other data, remote sensing time series analysis of forage quantity from 2000 to 2009 (figure 26) (see the "Forage Availability" section) was created. These data included estimations of NPP from the MODIS sensor, which has collected data globally at varying spatial resolutions from year 2000 to present day. The NPP data were converted to available forage as previously described in the "Forage Availability" section.

In contrast to forage availability, forage demand is reasonably well known at the state and county levels. The cattle and sheep numbers used for this study were derived from the NASS annual survey and bi-decadal censuses to create a time series from 2000 to 2009. The census and survey numbers from NASS, however, depict total numbers of livestock and therefore do not sufficiently separate animals fed in feedlots from those raised on rangelands. Given that most ranch calendars show grazing for 3 to 6 months during the growing season, animal numbers were converted to forage demand from rangelands by reducing the overall annual forage demand by 50 percent (6 months out of 12). This technique represents a conservative estimate of average forage demand from rangelands. Figure 34 shows the forage demand for cattle at the county-level in western U.S. rangelands, while figure 35 shows livestock (sheep, goats, and cattle) forage demand from 2000 to 2009 at the state level. After accounting for forage demand and forage availability, estimates of aboveground biomass appropriated to sheep, cattle, and goats were calculated as:

$$LAAGB = FA - FD \qquad \text{[formula 1]}$$

where LAAGB is livestock appropriation of aboveground biomass, FA is forage availability, and FD is forage demand.

Patterns of Forage Availability and Demand

The spatial pattern of forage availability shows an increasing gradient from west to east with lower production values in southwestern Arizona, southeastern California, west Texas, south-central Wyoming, and Nevada (figure 26). The greatest levels of productivity occur along the eastern edge of the rangeland extent and in California. In general, livestock forage demand appears to follow an increasing gradient from east to west and from north to south for a six-month grazing period from 2000 to 2009 (figure 35). From 2003 to 2009, the Rocky Mountain states of Colorado and Wyoming hosted fewer livestock compared with 2000 (figure 35)—a pattern shared by other states in the region.

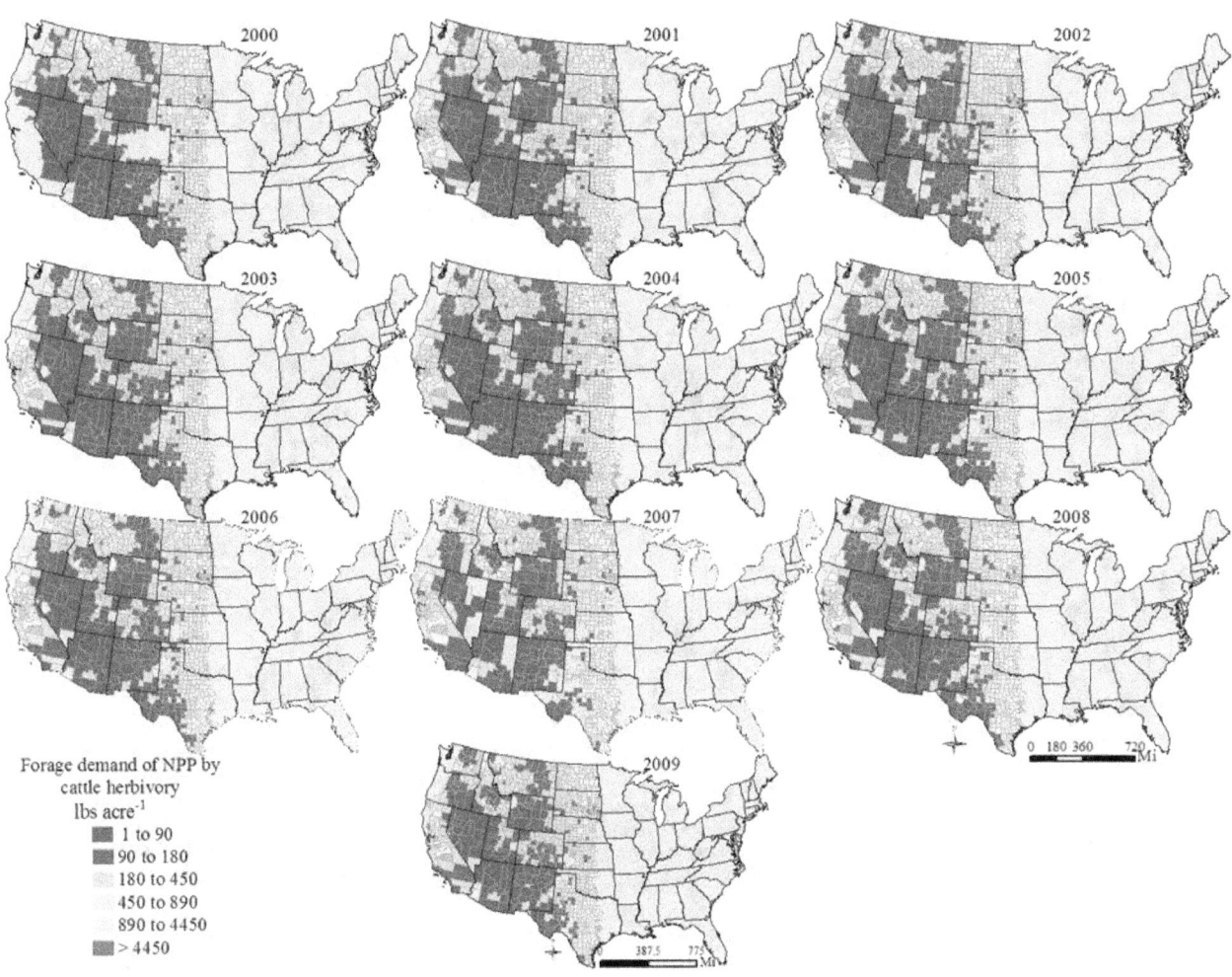

Figure 34—County-level cattle forage demand in western U.S. rangelands from 2000 to 2009 estimated from the USDA Census of Agriculture. County level data are not consistently available for goats and sheep.

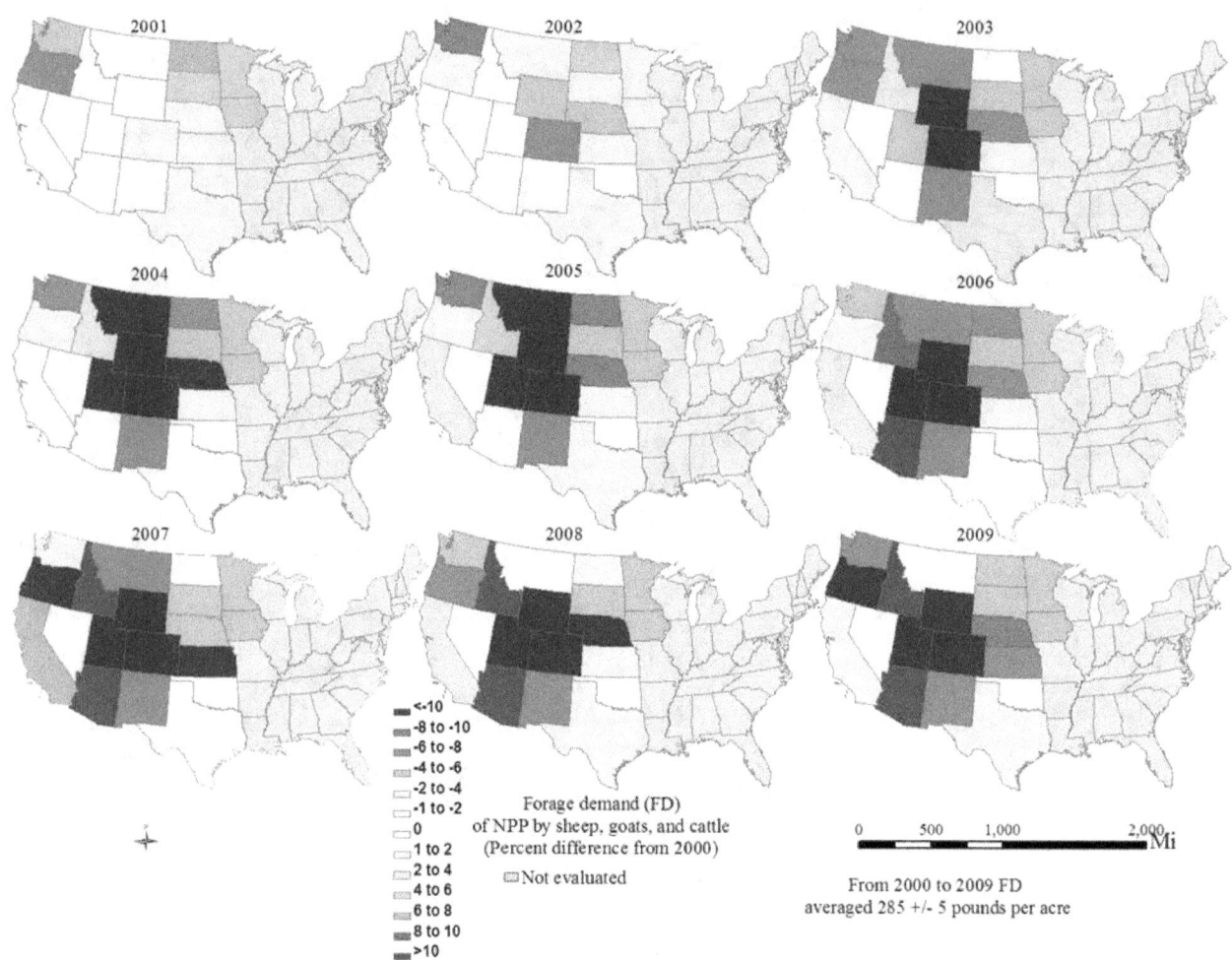

Figure 35—State-level livestock forage demand (cattle, goats, and sheep) in western U.S. rangelands from 2000 to 2009 estimated from the USDA Census of Agriculture.

Analyzing the relationship using formula 1 revealed an assessment of livestock impacts at the national level (figures 36 and 37). Using formula 1, we characterize areas where FD>FA as hotspots. Likewise, areas where FD = FA are warm spots and areas where FD<FA as coolspots. From 2000 to 2009, approximately 11 million acres of rangelands appear to have unsustainable forage demands (hotspots), while 590 million acres show sustainable trends (coolspots, FA>FD). New Mexico showed the least amount of hotspots (hotspots, FA<FD) and Texas showed the most (table 26). Table 27 shows the proportion of hotspots and coolspots in states with large rangeland area from 2000 to 2009.

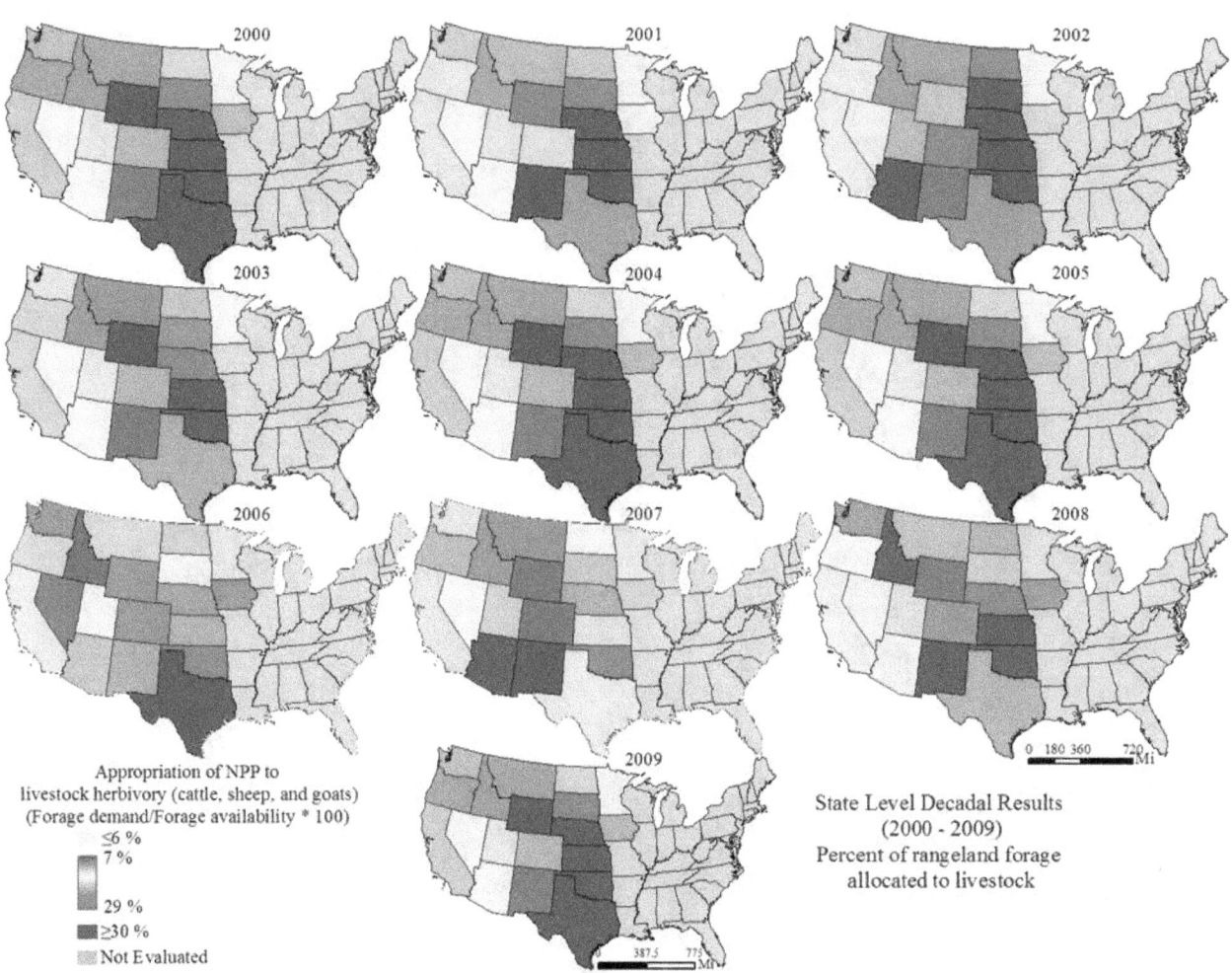

Figure 36—Appropriation of above-ground biomass to grazing livestock at the state level from western U.S. rangelands from 2000 to 2009. In this analysis (including all the assumptions and missing data), a mean value of 144 g m^{-2} yr^{-1} suggests that from 2000 to 2009, on average, U.S. rangelands are running a surplus of about 1280 (±818) lbs ac^{-1} of forage based on the assumptions outlined in the "Forage Availability" section.

This national-scale analysis examining the relationship between forage demand and forage availability indicates that most regions with significant rangeland area harbor sustainable numbers of livestock and suitable quantities of forage. On average, rangelands appear to be running a surplus of 1280±818 pounds per acre. This finding is corroborated by the analysis of overall forage found in table 20, which suggests, from a national perspective, the potential for an increase in animal units of approximately 30 to 50 percent. These analyses, however, do not consider local rangeland conditions, political or environmental implications, or the impact of feedlots or pastures on forage availability. These factors need to be considered when examining the coarse-scale results reported here.

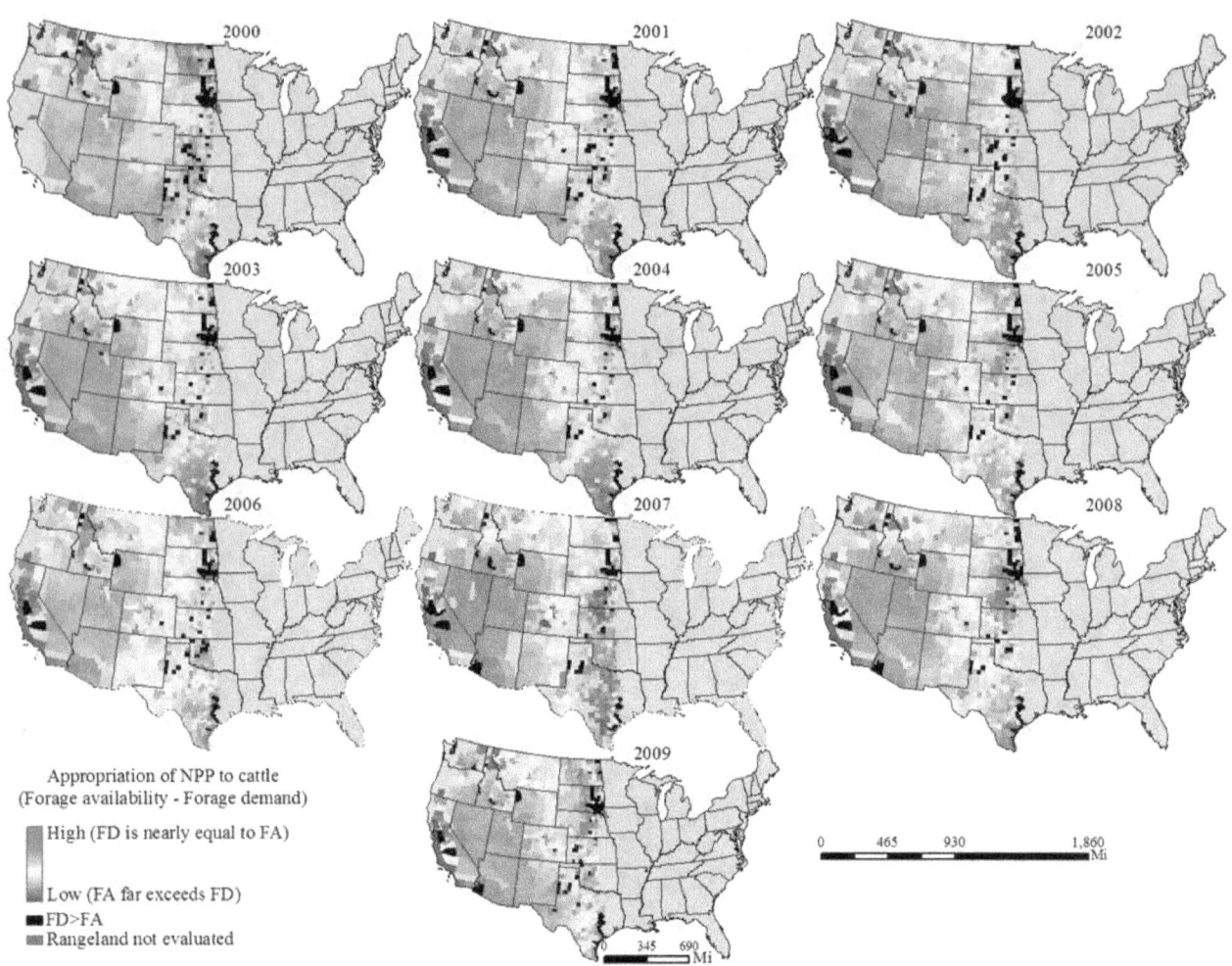

Figure 37—Appropriation of above-ground biomass to grazing livestock at the county level from western U.S. rangelands from 2000 to 2009.

Table 26—Breakdown of forage appropriated from U.S. rangelands to livestock at the county and state assessment levels. Analysis represents average forage availability (FA) and forage demand (FD) from 2000 to 2009.

State	Forage appropriated to cattle Area effected (*County*-level assessment)				Forage appropriated to livestock Area effected (*State*-level assessment)			
	Hotspots (FD>FA)	Coolspots (FD<FA)	Hotspots (FD>FA)	Coolspots (FD<FA)	Hotspots (FD>FA)	Coolspots (FD<FA)	Hotspots (FD>FA)	Coolspots (FD<FA)
	- - - - - - - % - - - - - - - - -		- - - - - - Ac (10³) - - - - - -		- - - - - - - - - % - - - - - - - -		- - - - - - Ac (10³) - - - - - -	
Arizona	1.90	98.10	1,008	52,004	0.03	99.97	18.23	52,994
California	6.97	93.03	2,488	33,204	0.49	99.51	175.83	35,517
Colorado	1.41	98.59	423	29,536	0.01	99.99	1.56	29,958
Idaho	5.67	94.33	1,246	20,715	0.02	99.98	4.46	21,956
Kansas	7.22	92.78	954	12,252	0.19	99.81	25.53	13,180
Montana	0.49	99.51	239	48,105	0.00	100.00	1.92	48,343
Nebraska	1.29	98.71	342	26,238	0.02	99.98	4.67	26,576
Nevada	0.01	99.99	6	57,309	0.00	100.00	0.86	57,314
New Mexico	0.00	100.00	1	59,617	0.00	100.00	0.79	59,618
North Dakota	0.26	99.74	35	13,526	0.03	99.97	4.04	13,558
Oklahoma	6.36	93.64	848	12,482	0.67	99.33	88.81	13,241
Oregon	0.02	99.98	6	24,823	0.00	100.00	0.34	24,829
South Dakota	2.36	97.64	626	25,884	0.02	99.98	6.08	26,504
Texas	2.81	97.19	2,651	91,716	0.06	99.94	60.37	94,306
Utah	0.49	99.51	143	29,016	0.01	99.99	3.11	29,155
Washington	1.19	98.81	96	7,962	0.01	99.99	0.77	8,056
Wyoming	0.24	99.76	112	45,659	0.00	100.0	0.55	45,771
Total			**11,224**	**590,048**			**398**	**600,876**

Table 27—Time series analysis of forage appropriated from U.S. rangelands to livestock at the county and state assessment levels.

	2000	2001	2002	2003	2004	2005	2006	2007	2008	2009	Mean
County-level cattle appropriation											
Hotspots (FD>FA)	1.97	1.93	2.32	1.56	1.16	1.14	1.82	1.79	1.82	1.88	**1.74**
Cool spots (FD<FA)	98.03	98.07	97.68	98.44	98.84	98.86	98.18	98.21	98.18	98.12	**98.26**
State-level livestock appropriation											
Hotspots (FD>FA)	0.26	0.03	0.08	0.02	0.00	0.01	0.04	0.08	0.04	0.03	**0.06**
Cool spots (FD<FA)	99.74	99.97	99.92	99.98	100.00	99.99	99.96	99.92	99.96	99.97	**99.94**

Climate Change and Rangelands

Other reports supporting the 2010 RPA Assessment have placed considerable emphasis on examining the potential effects of climate change using a suite of scenarios representing a range of hypothesized global social and economic situations. The purpose of scenarios in the RPA Assessment (USDA FS 2012) is to characterize the common demographic, socio-economic, and technological driving forces underlying changes in resource condition and to evaluate the sensitivity of resource trends to a feasible future range of these driving forces. These scenarios closely mimic those of the Fourth Intergovernmental Panel on Climate Change (IPCC) assessment (Meehl and others 2007) and assume that different socioeconomic conditions produce varying amounts of greenhouse gas emissions that are assumed to affect Earth's climate, as simulated using a host of Global Circulation Models (GCMs). These climate data, produced during the Fourth IPCC assessment, were subsequently spatially downscaled (Coulson and others 2010a, 2010b) to a resolution 0.083 degrees (nominally 4.96 miles [8 km] resolution). These future climate possibilities can be used to estimate trends in rangeland goods and services in response to climate change.

Climate change will impact U.S. rangelands through manipulation of major drivers of vegetation growth and distribution such as temperature and precipitation (figure 38). Changes in these climatological components will be distributed asymmetrically, and some rangeland vegetation may respond favorably while some will perform poorly. Expected impacts on rangeland vegetation are difficult to characterize owed to uncertainty, regional variability, poorly understood vegetation dynamics, and complicated interactions and feedbacks. Understanding these complicated dynamics requires ecosystem models capable of simulating rangeland ecosystem behavior while considering multiple processes and stressors.

Complex Interactions

Precipitation and temperature have been reliable predictors of extent and ordination of plant groups (for example, cool-season C3 and warm-season C4 species) (Epstein and others 1997; Knapp and others 2001; Paruelo and Lauenroth 1996) across the landscape. Changes in these drivers have clear and well understood implications for vegetation. However, rising CO_2 levels may complicate these relationships in the future. For instance, warmer and drier conditions should favor C4 grasses (Knapp and others 2001; Winslow and others 2003) so, short and tallgrass prairies may stand to benefit, but rising CO_2 should favor C3 species (Morgan and others 2004, 2007; Polley and others 2003, 2006; Reich and others 2001). Increased CO_2 improves water use efficiency due to decreased time for which leaf stomates must remain open to acquire a suitable amount of CO_2, but there are limits beyond which increased CO_2 does not enhance water relations. Further complicating these relationships are changing temperature and precipitation regimes. Increased variation, intensity, and changes in the timing of precipitation can also influence species composition and productivity of U.S. rangelands. For example, as springtime temperatures increase in the Great Basin, the extent and magnitude of cheatgrass (*Bromus tectorum*) may increase as it becomes an even stronger competitor by using available moisture earlier in the season.

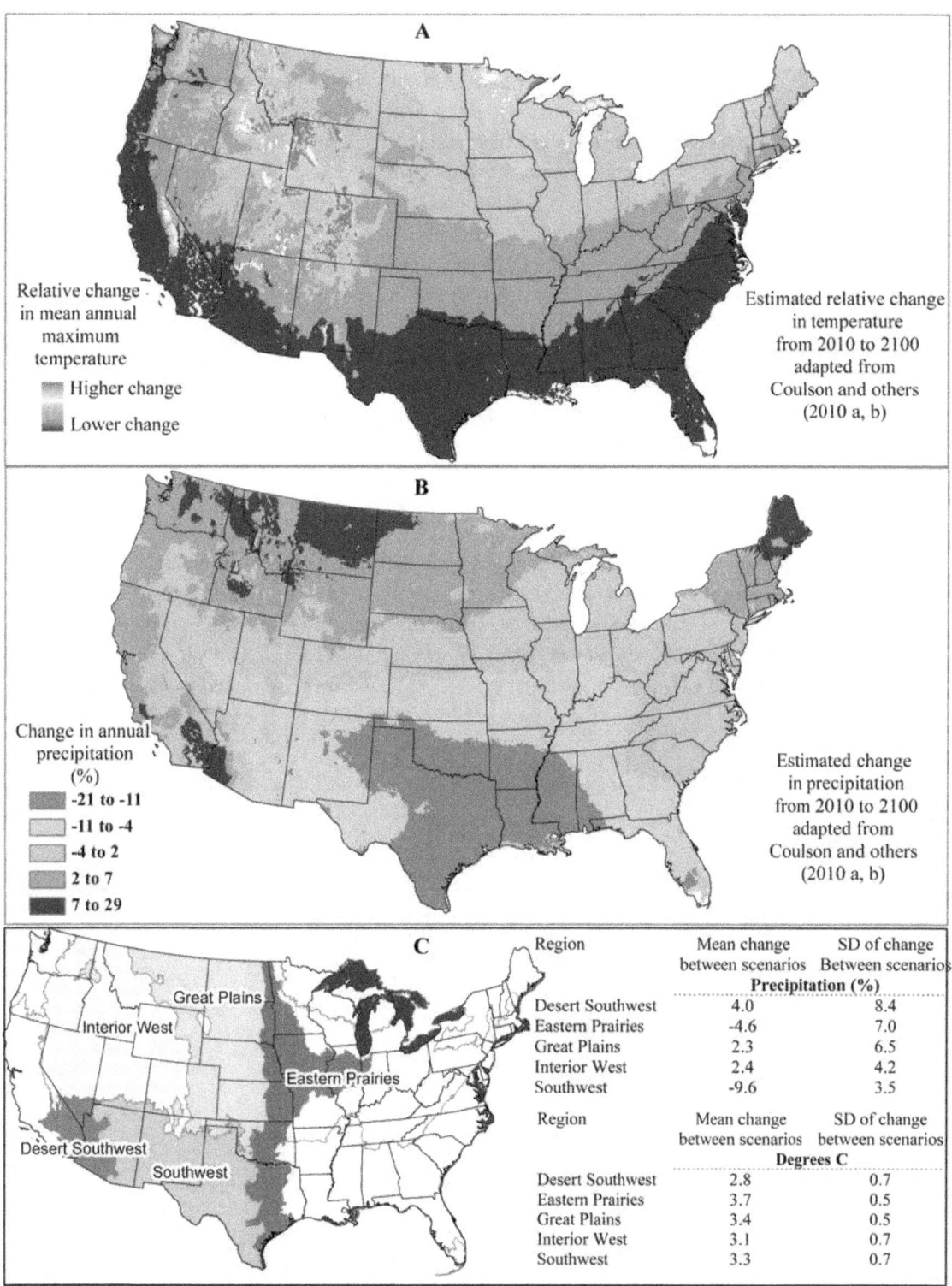

Figure 38— Estimated normalized change in mean maximum temperature (A) and percent change in precipitation (B) from the period of 2010 to 2100 based on three SRES scenarios (A1B, A2, and B2). Warmer tones in (A) indicate a greater increase in temperature relative to present conditions. Regional averages indicate the asymmetrical nature of expected change (C). Underlying data were created by Coulson and others (2010a, 2010b).

As seen in figure 38, northern latitudes are expected to warm in all scenarios while maintaining or increasing precipitation. This combination of factors should enhance productivity on northern and high-altitude rangelands through lengthened growing season. However, if temperatures continue to rise as suggested in all scenarios (figure 39), gains in production owed to increased growing season length and precipitation could be offset due to decreased moisture availability at some time in the future, especially in the southwestern United States. The situation is just the opposite in the southwestern United States where increases in temperature are coupled with decreased precipitation. If this situation unfolds as climate projections suggest, rangeland productivity should decrease and only the most drought-tolerant species such as desert shrubs and succulents will prevail. Rangeland production will likely fall substantially under these conditions and desert and semi-desert grasslands in the region may retreat to new areas, perhaps at higher elevations or where microclimates permit growth and reproduction. However, predicting the re-ordination of species assemblages and plant functional groups is probably more difficult than evaluating the effects of changing climates on productivity.

Implications for Managers

Understanding what changing climates mean for future management strategies is difficult. There are a few possible effects, however, that are likely to influence management decisions in the future. Although increased CO_2 generally increases rangeland productivity, it can decrease leaf nitrogen content (plants do not need to invest more in photosynthetic capacity if acquiring CO_2 is easier), which decreases protein content (fewer chloroplasts and less leaf

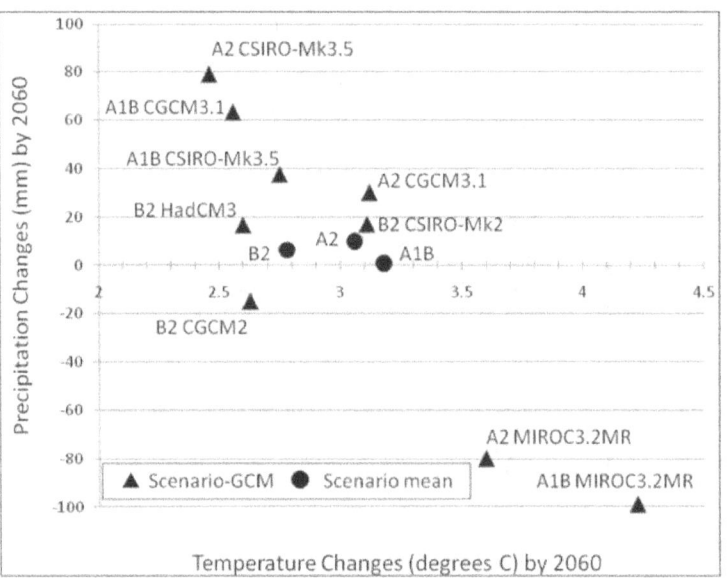

Figure 39—Ordination of estimated future climates based on three SRES scenarios (A1B, A2, B2). Underlying data were created by Coulson and others (2010a, 2010b)

nitrogen content) and therefore nutritional value. This implies stocking rates and grazing systems will need to be adjusted accordingly so that animal performance and rangeland health are not adversely impacted. Similarly, increasing temperatures have been shown to increase cell wall constituents while decreasing soluble sugars; the combination of which reduces digestibility and forage quality. For example, Minson and McLeod (1970) found a 1 percent decrease in digestibility per 2 °F increase in temperature along a latitudinal gradient from south to north. Changing species composition may also impact forage quality as higher CO_2 seems to favor C3 over C4 plants, and C3 plants often have higher forage digestibility (Wilson and Brown 1983). Recent experimental results, however, confound this generality and found that needle-and-thread (*Hesperostipa comata*) and fringed sage (*Artemisia frigida*) (both are C3 species but have low forage value) strongly increased production under increased CO_2 scenarios on a shortgrass steppe. Management strategies aimed at adapting to changing species composition should include increased use of alternative livestock such as goats, which readily utilize species that are generally unpalatable for cattle. Additionally, Federal land managers and land owners may need to consider utilization or promotion of a new suite of rangeland goods and services that could thrive under a more drought prone environment.

Warmer temperatures will likely result in increased fire frequency and intensity, potentially creating more favorable conditions for invasive species such as cheatgrass, which would likely decrease overall forage quality and biodiversity. Thus, management schemes must be flexible and sensitive to changes in species composition and productivity resulting from climate change. Changes are likely to manifest in unexpected ways and effects may be revealed subtly, suggesting that rigorous and comprehensive monitoring strategies could be needed.

Alternative Energy

Energy is fundamental to sustainable development because it is a critical component of any solution for mitigating the increasing challenges of food and water shortages, disease, poverty, and climate change (Serageldin 1999). The Twentieth Century was characterized by abundant, low-cost energy derived from fossil fuels. By the end of the century, fossil fuels accounted for 90 percent of global primary energy consumption, with about 40 percent being derived from crude oil (Smil 2000). The remaining 10 percent of energy demand was met almost exclusively by hydropower and nuclear sources while renewable energy, including solar and wind, provided less than 1 percent (Duncan 2001).

Energy production in the United States at the end of the Twentieth Century was similar to the global picture (Black and Veatch 2008). Fossil fuels—coal, oil, and natural gas—provided more than 85 percent of all the energy used in the United States. Today, they still account for nearly two-thirds of our electricity supply and almost all of our transportation fuels.

There is broad agreement that more diverse sources of energy are needed in order for the United States and other developed countries to progress toward energy independence (Resources for the Future 2005). While energy independence remains elusive, moving toward it will involve greater use of nuclear, biomass, solar, wind, and geothermal resources (Rahman 2003). Furthermore, while world energy demand is expected to increase 45 percent by 2030 (mainly due to strong economic growth in China, India, and other developing countries), these countries are generally less able to exploit renewable energy sources than developed nations (IEA 2008). Consequently, developed nations, notably the United States, are expected to lead the shift toward renewable energy.

We emphasize the importance of western rangelands for providing future energy production, focusing on three "dual-use" energy technologies—unconventional natural gas, biomass or biofuels, and wind energy sources (in other words, those that do not preclude the simultaneous use of land for other purposes, including grazing) (Pimentel and others 1994). While solar energy yields more potential than all other sources, its development generally precludes other land uses, so it is necessarily excluded from this report. However, this does not mean that there are fewer "effects" due to development of wind, biomass, and unconventional natural gas. Indeed, oil and gas well heads, windmills, and harvest areas (in the case of biofuels) have unavoidable negative effects but can be developed in such a fashion that allows other land uses to occur.

Western rangelands hold significant potential for developing an unconventional, domestic fuels industry due to substantial oil and gas reserves, renewable biofuel opportunities, and significant wind energy sources (Black and Veatch 2008). Moreover, increased development of these energy sources is likely because their exploitation relies on well-established technologies. It should be noted at the outset that all energy sources, both renewable and non-renewable, are subject to environmental and economic constraints, solutions to which will rely upon both economic and political driving forces (Chow and others 2003).

Unconventional Natural Gas Production

Natural gas derived from hydrocarbon-rich shale formations (plays) is a relatively clean fuel compared to oil or coal and is a key component of energy development for electricity and heating. In December 2010, the U.S. Energy Information Administration projected domestic supplies of natural gas from coal beds and shale by 2035 to dramatically exceed their previous projection, from 480 trillion cubic feet to 827 trillion cubic feet (http://www.eia. doe.gov/forecasts/aeo/executive_summary.cfm). Support for these estimates is strengthened by observing the increased efforts of major producers to develop unconventional natural gas (Kuuskraa and others 2007). Presently, natural gas provides about 22 percent of the Nation's energy sources, and it is estimated that current recoverable resources could supply natural gas for the next 90 years (GWPC 2009).

Gas plays are widely distributed in the United States. Major plays under rangeland ecosystems are located in Montana, Wyoming, North Dakota, Colorado, New Mexico, Kansas, Oklahoma, and Texas (figure 40). These natural gas production sites are a substantial contributor to the U.S. strategy for moving toward energy independence. Natural gas is also a cleaner-burning fuel for power generation compared to coal (table 28) (EIA 2010).

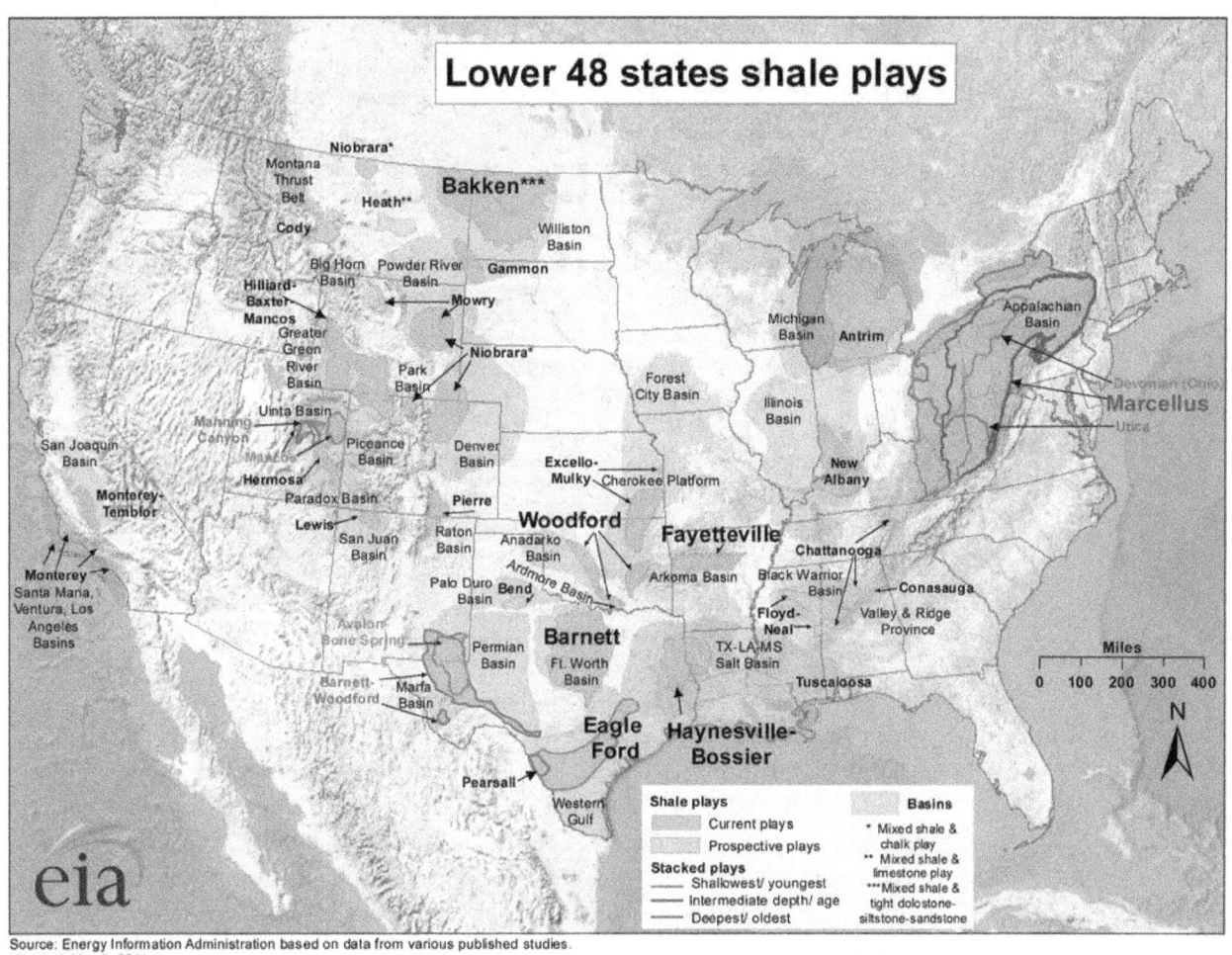

Figure 40—Major shale plays in the contiguous 48 states. This figure is derived from the Energy Information Administration emanating from a variety of studies.

Table 28—Fossil fuel emission levels of various pollutants from natural gas, oil, and coal (EIA 2010).

Pollutant	Natural gas	Oil	Coal
	- - (lbs per billion Btu of energy input) - -		
Carbon dioxide	117,000	164,000	208,000
Carbon monoxide	40	33	208
Nitrogen oxides	92	448	457
Sulfur dioxide	1	1,122	2,591
Particulates	7	84	2,744
Mercury	0.000	0.007	0.016

Development of unconventional natural gas plays presents unique challenges. Federal statutes, including such legislation as the Clean Water Act, Safe Drinking Water Act, Clean Air Act, and National Environmental Policy Act, provide the regulatory basis for development. State and local agencies also have inputs into wellhead development and operations. Key issues include permitting of wells, water management, air emissions, wildlife impacts, and noise attenuation (Lyon and Anderson 2003; Rice and Bullock 2000; Sawyer and others 2006).

Research involving the use of enhanced gas recovery technologies to inject CO_2 into coalbed methane sites shows promise to reduce CO_2 emission from power production. The approach is comprised of a closed CO_2-cycle process whereby waste CO_2 generated by natural gas power plants is injected back into coalbed methane reservoirs to provide even more methane-based natural gas (Gunter and others 1997).

Sustaining rangeland ecosystem services in areas of natural gas development will likely rely upon the energy industry's ability to balance the economics of exploration and production with environmental compliance requirements. Evolving practices that are facilitating this balance are: horizontal drilling, hydraulic fracturing, reduced water demand, and efforts to reduce the surface disturbance of well siting and associated road networks.

Wind Energy

Wind-powered electricity production has increased by 25 percent annually in the United States since 2000 (Bird and others 2005). Current capacity of wind generated power in the United States is 40,180 MW, but China produces more wind energy than any other country and grew its production output by 75 percent in 2010 (WWEA 2011). Despite the dramatic increases, wind energy accounted for less than 1 percent of total electricity generation in the United States in 2007 (NRC 2007). The rangeland-rich state of Texas is the leading producer of electricity from wind power.

The greatest potential for increasing electricity production from wind exists both off-shore and on-shore in western states dominated by rangeland ecosystems (figure 41). Projections of future wind power vary widely. The U.S. Department of Energy (2005) determined that the United States could potentially produce up to 20 percent of its electricity demand by 2030, a 17-fold increase in wind power capacity to 300 GW, with improved turbine technology, significant changes in transmission, and expanded markets. More than 20 states now require electricity suppliers to include a small fraction of their supply from renewable energy sources, with proportions characteristically increasing over time. This, along with other factors, has created conditions for steady growth in wind power, even if the ambitious goal of 20 percent has not yet been reached.

The advantages of wind-energy facilities are that they are driven by a persistent energy source and emit no pollutants. Nevertheless, the expansion of such facilities can create adverse environmental effects. The construction and maintenance of wind-energy facilities alter ecosystems through habitat destruction and increase fatalities of birds and bats through collision with the turbine blades (Curry 2009). The long-term impacts on bird and bat populations depend upon multiple factors, including abundance, longevity, reproductive rates,

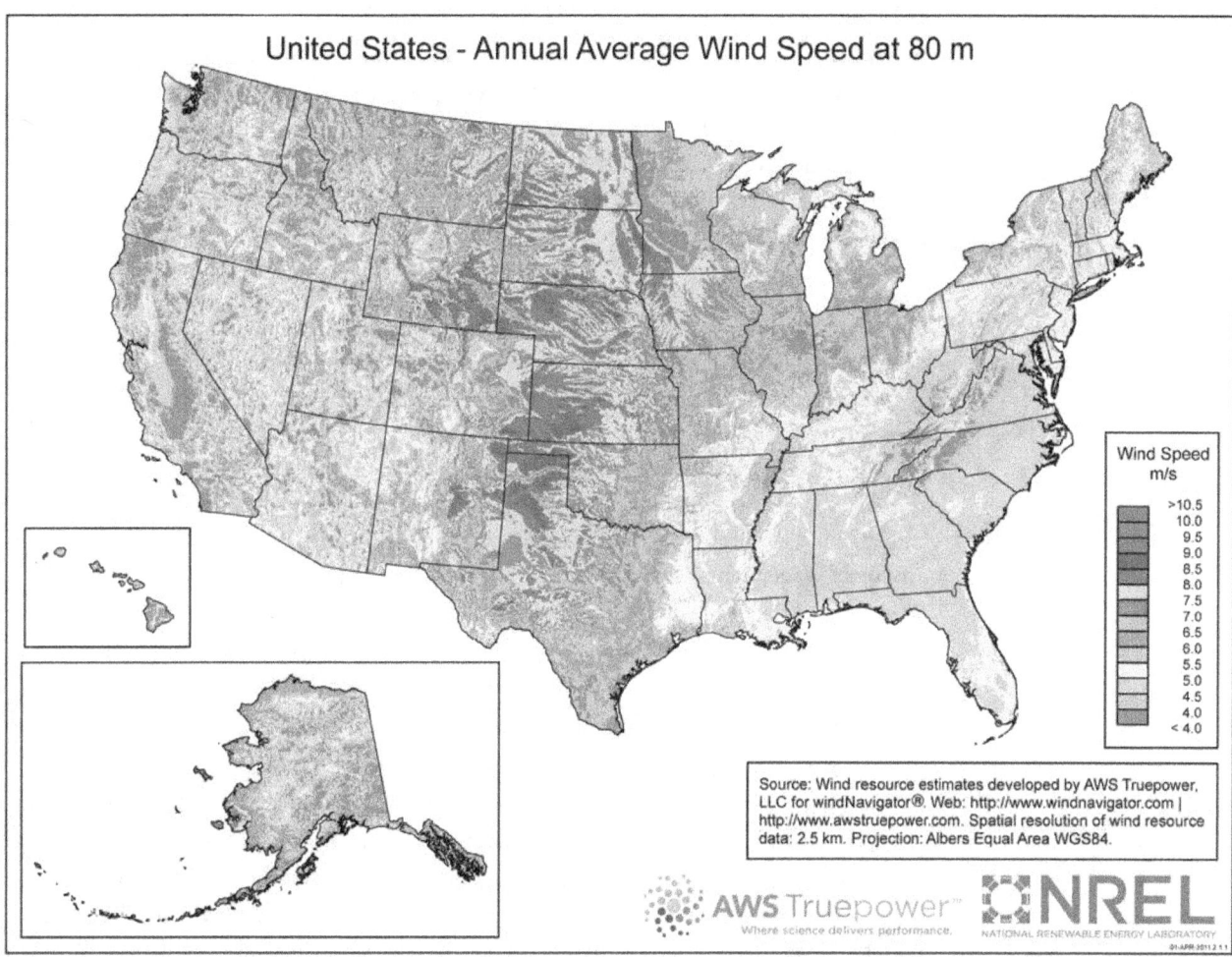

Figure 41—Annual average wind speed in the United States (wind resource estimates developed by AWS Truepower, LLC for wind Navigator available at: https://www.windnavigator.com and http://www.awstruepower.com.

and behavioral characteristics of affected species (Kunz and others 2007). Impacts on birds in the western United States is likely to be greatest for raptors because their migratory paths include ridges upon which wind turbines are most frequently placed (Erickson and others 2001).

In addition to impacts of wind-energy generation on various species, effects to humans include diminished aesthetic quality of the landscape, elevated noise, shadow flicker, and electromagnetic interference (Krohn and Damborg 1999). One further consideration is that, while developing wind energy will benefit society at large, the environmental and social costs of such developments are borne by local landowners and communities located near wind farms. The need for new transmission lines to connect wind farms to the Nation's power grid also has social and economic implications costs to rural communities and landowners (Denholm 2006).

Biofuel

Biomass potentially provides an abundant carbon-neutral, or even carbon-negative, resource for producing energy (Mathews 2008). Progress in producing energy from biomass, particularly cellulosic biomass, rests with progress in biotechnology, genetics, biochemistry, and engineering (Ragauskas and others 2006). The U.S. Department of Energy has investigated achieving the goal of replacing 30 percent of oil used for transportation with biofuels—a program called the "Billion Ton Study" (Perlack and others 2005). Achieving such a goal will not be easy but might be feasible (Parikka 2004).

Switchgrass (*Panicum virgatum L.*) has attracted considerable attention for biofuel production due to its considerable energy production potential with lower fertilizer and fossil fuel inputs on marginal croplands than corn (Walsh and others 2003). However, there are concerns over conversion of large swaths of native rangelands to biofuel monocultures (Fargione and others 2008). Possible effects include increased agrichemical pollution, loss of diverse forage resources, and loss of landscape and associated biological diversity (Bies 2006; Cook and others 1991; Groom and others 2008). Biological obstacles also exist to the commercial economic production of switchgrass for biofuels, although advances in genetic engineering and plant breeding show potential to mitigate obstacles to some extent (Sanderson and others 2006). In the Midwest, the highest potential for switchgrass production is concentrated in the tallgrass prairie region, but it extends throughout the central and eastern United States (McLaughlin and Kszoz 2005).

Dedicated energy crops, like switchgrass, can be cost effectively produced on land unsuited for row crops, while still providing erosion control for agricultural set-aside lands (Milbrandt 2005) (figures 42 and 43). Mixed native grasslands can produce significant biomass, especially in tall grass prairies where biomass can exceed 8100 pounds per acre (10 tons per hectare) (Kucera and others 1967). Tilman and others (2006) reported that biofuel derived from low-input, high-diversity mixtures of native species provided more usable energy, greater greenhouse gas reductions, and less agrichemical pollution than corn-based ethanol or soybean biodiesel. In addition, this approach would avoid the loss of biodiversity due to conversion of existing multi-species grasslands to biofuel monocultures partly because native species mixtures can grow on agriculturally degraded lands. Production of biofuel from existing rangelands may, therefore, offer ranchers new income generating opportunities but would likely also result in tradeoffs with existing livestock and wildlife operations.

Summary

During the last decade, a concerted effort to quantify EGS has been made. Only a subset of the total list of EGS has been discussed in this report. Most bio-centric ecosystem goods and services derived from rangelands are linked to productivity. Overall, from 2000 to 2009, primary productivity on coterminous U.S. rangelands has remained relatively constant but more xeric regions have experienced wide inter-annual variability, presumably due to oscillations in precipitation. The Rocky Mountain Assessment Region experienced an increase in productivity averaging approximately 44 pounds per acre per year of aboveground production. The productivity of U.S. rangelands is directly linked to the overall forage supply.

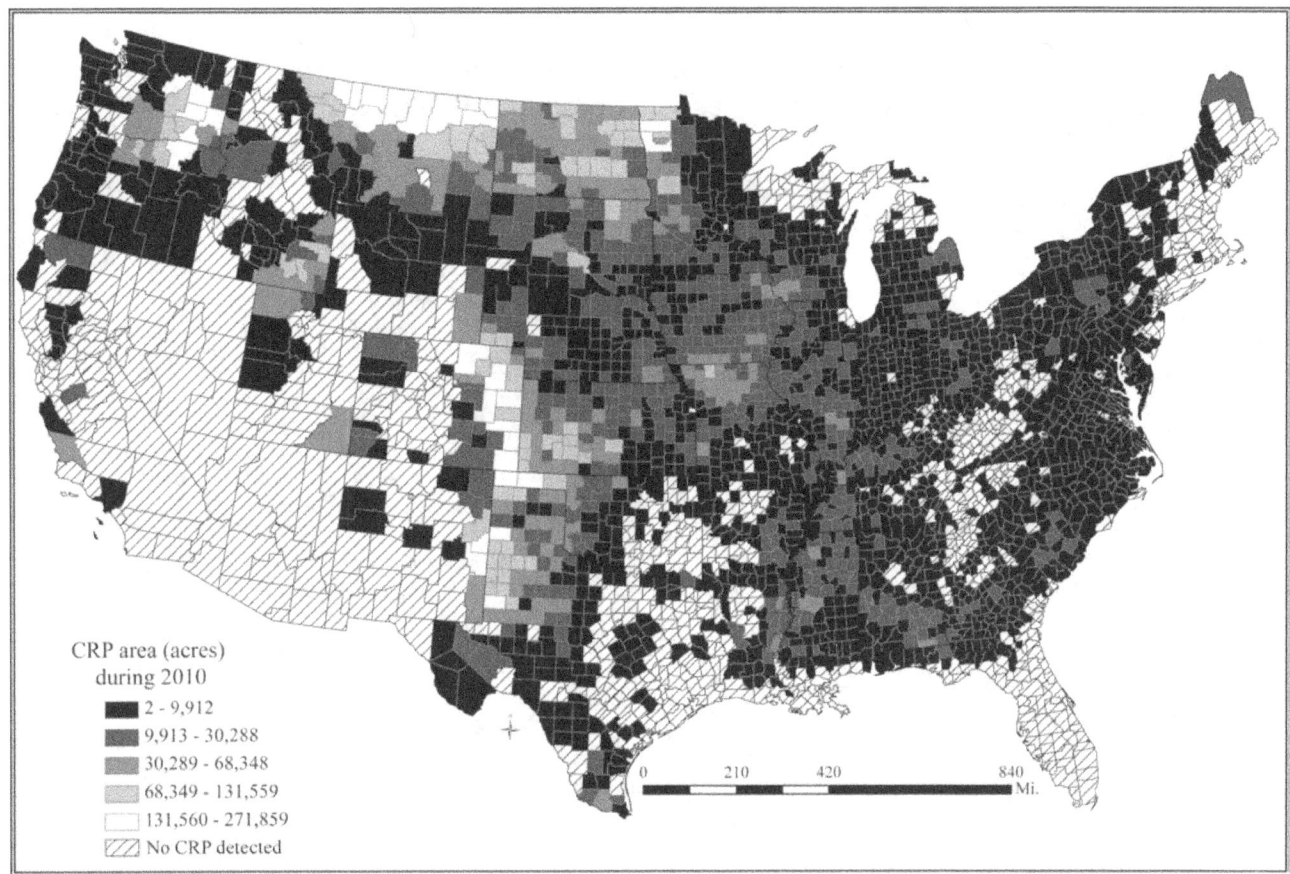

Figure 42—Area of land under CRP circa 2010.

From a national perspective, there appears to be a moderate surplus of forage during an average year considering current livestock levels. Using remote sensing and a series of assumptions, the total estimated forage supply should support approximately 143 to 196 million animal units per year or 1.7 to 2.4 billion AUMs. This estimate does not account for agricultural feedstuffs, crop residues, or feedlots. While vegetation production ultimately controls the capacity of the land to support herbivory, livestock production is one of the best measured indicators of rangeland EGS.

Overall, livestock numbers have remained relatively constant from 2000 to 2009. Cattle production has remained within 1.4 percent of the estimated 10 year average of 96.6 million head. At 80 cattle per square mile, both Kansas and Nebraska have the highest cattle densities in the United States, while the South Assessment Region contains the most cattle and the North Assessment Region contains the least. Sheep numbers have continued to decline by about 200,000 animals per year since 1997 and are now estimated at fewer than 6 million animals, a decline of over 800 percent since peak numbers in the 1930s. Sheep and cattle are the largest animal class in terms of numbers, but since 2000, several significant trends in numbers of other livestock classes have been revealed.

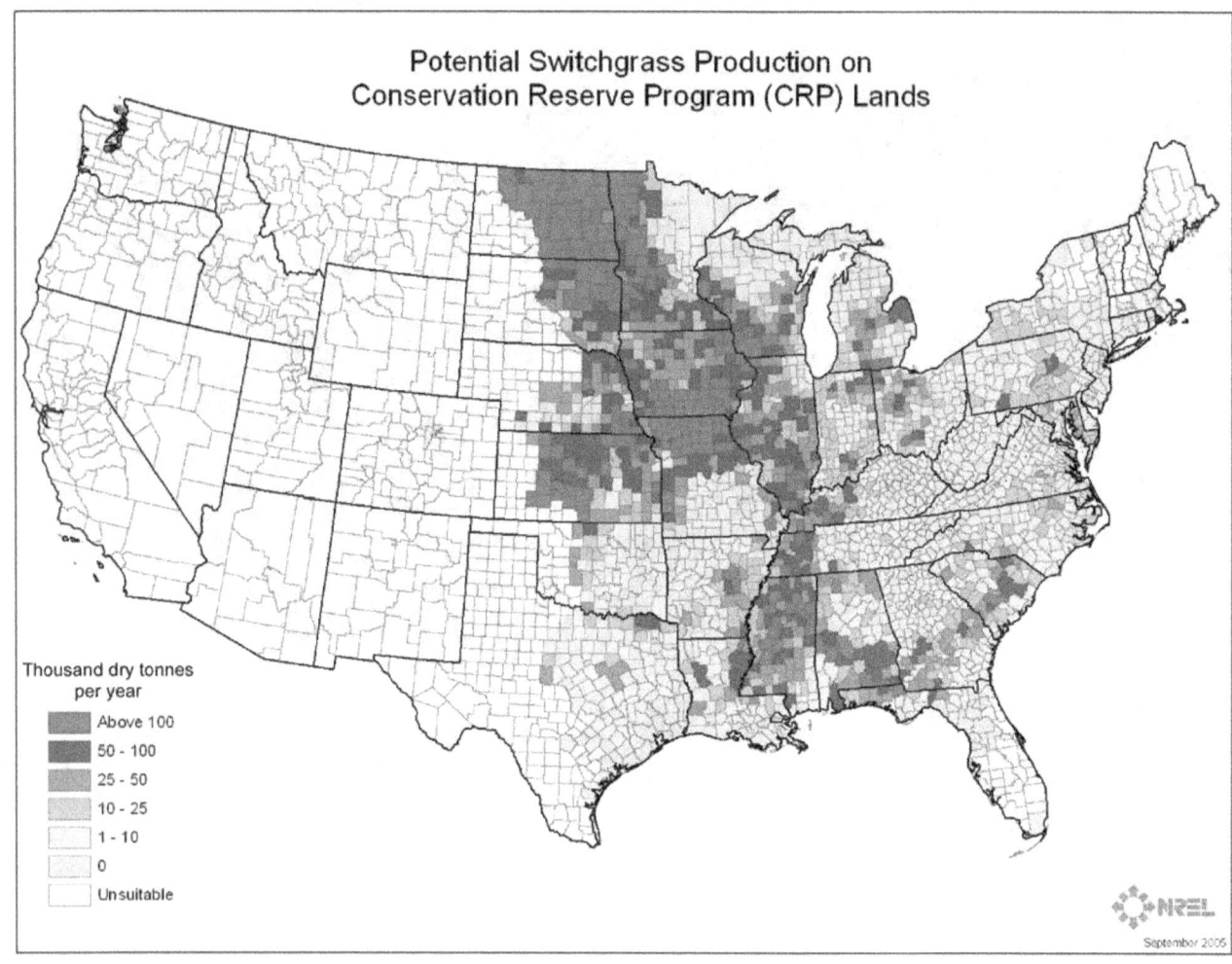

Figure 43—Potential switchgrass (*Panicum virgatum* L.) production on CRP lands estimated from the Oak Ridge Energy Crop County Level Database, December 20, 1996 version. CRP area estimates came from the USDA Farm Service Agency, County CRP signup 26 information July 2003.

Since 2000, horses have increased approximately 33 percent, while goats have increased by 96 percent emulating a significant increase of roughly 300 million goats worldwide since 1985. As a niche market, bison have also increased in numbers to approximately 230,000 animals nationwide.

Grazing on Federal lands remains a critical service provided by the BLM and USFS as annual average gross receipts (grazing fee multiplied by AUMs) from grazing yields about $21 million per year. The grazing fee has averaged $1.42 (SD = $0.14) since 2000. The total livestock levels on BLM lands have varied within 12 percent of 7.9 million animals since 2000, while grazing on NFS lands has remained within 19 percent of 7.6 million AUMs between 2000 and 2008. Merely evaluating livestock numbers does not tell the whole story because livestock are distributed asymmetrically across the landscape and in some cases can exceed the capacity of the land to sustain them. In light of this fact, this 2010 RPA Rangeland Assessment contained a description of the estimated appropriation of net primary production to livestock.

Overall, most rangeland areas produce far more forage than is utilized by livestock. From 2000 to 2009, approximately 2 percent of coterminous U.S. rangelands appear to have unsustainable forage demands (where forage demand exceeds forage availability) at the county level, while 98 percent show a sustainable situation. On average from 2000 to 2009, Texas yielded the greatest area of unsustainable forage demands while New Mexico exhibited the least. This appropriation assessment, however, will require further analysis in the future, especially with regard to the number of feedlots in each county, which may skew the results reported here. Though analyses of goods and services provided by rangelands often focus on livestock numbers, the recent emphasis on reducing greenhouse gas emissions has sparked a quest for understanding the potential for cleaner energy.

At the end of the Twentieth Century, coal, oil, and natural gas provided more than 85 percent of all the energy used in the United States. There is broad agreement that more diverse sources of energy are needed for the United States and other developed countries to lead the way toward more reliance on renewable energy. Rangelands are uniquely qualified to provide access to cleaner energy sources because they are often comprised of broad, windswept plains receiving a relatively high proportion of solar radiation. The remoteness and juxtaposition of rangelands make them prime candidates for developing cleaner energy sources such as wind, sun, and natural gas.

Though natural gas is not always seen as a viable cleaner energy source, in terms of pollutant discharge, it is 30 percent cleaner than oil and 45 percent cleaner than coal. Natural gas provides about 22 percent of the Nation's energy, and it is estimated that current recoverable resources could supply natural gas for the next 90 years. Many of the most productive, unconventional natural gas plays are located on western rangelands. Sustaining rangeland ecosystem services in areas of natural gas development will rely upon society's ability to balance the economics of energy exploration and production with environmental considerations and public demand.

In concert with increased emphasis on natural gas production, wind power generation has increased 25 percent per year since 2000 but has still comprised less than 1 percent of total electricity generation in the United States in 2007. Most wind generation facilities occur in relatively open, windswept areas and Texas currently leads the Nation in wind power generation. The U.S. Department of Energy estimates that by 2030 wind power could deliver up to 20 percent of total energy needs. For this to happen, a dramatic increase in generation, storage, distribution, and transmission infrastructure on U.S. rangelands is required. Despite being a very clean source of energy, wind power will not come without environmental cost, and the potential effects of wind power generation on a large scale are unknown and need further study.

Power generation from biofuels has received considerable attention recently. The U.S. Department of Energy has investigated the goal of replacing 30 percent of oil used for transportation with biofuels, which will not be easy but could be feasible. Rangelands hold significant promise for the development of biofuels, particularly in the more productive areas, including the tallgrass prairie region. In particular, switchgrass has received much attention as a species requiring less fossil fuel and fertilizer inputs than row crops, while often yielding 8000 pounds per acre or more. While switchgrass and other native tallgrass prairie species could provide a sustainable supply of easily harvested biomass, there are concerns over conversion of large swaths of native rangelands to biofuel monocultures, including increased agrichemical pollution, loss of diverse forage resources, and loss of landscape and associated biological diversity. Perhaps the most appropriate solution will include innovative methods of rejuvenating degraded rangelands to increase the output of EGS while harvesting the resultant biomass from a variety of rangeland ecosystems, including rejuvenated areas and sites dominated by invasive mesquite, juniper, and other brush species. Ultimately, the development of cleaner energy sources will involve significant use of U.S. rangelands, and more research is needed to quantify tradeoffs between power generation, other EGS, and environmental concerns.

Chapter 4: Rangeland Health

Introduction

Rangeland health can be defined as "the degree to which the integrity of soil and the ecological processes of rangeland ecosystems are sustained" (NRC 1994). The concept of rangeland health has evolved greatly since inception and was originally focused on comparison of current vegetation composition to a climax plant community postulated to represent a site-specific equilibrium state (Dyksterhuis 1949; Joyce and others 2000). Assessment of rangeland health using this more traditional theory is hindered by an inherent difficulty of determining reference conditions (Herrick and others 2010).

More recent research has offered a competing theory of non-equilibrium rangeland dynamics, first espoused by Westoby and others (1989), represented by steady states bounded by ecological thresholds, beyond which new states exist. At the same time, ecologists began to argue that ecosystem stress should be described by metrics other than merely vegetation composition (Rapport and others 1985). Rangeland health is currently characterized using a variety of both qualitative and quantitative indicators (Herrick and others 2010) describing multiple facets of ecosystem integrity such as erosion, percent bare ground, species composition, and annual production (Pellant and others 2005). There is critical need for information describing types, patterns, and severity of rangeland degradation to support policy and management (McPeak 2003) and identify ecosystem processes requiring restoration (Geist and Lambin 2004; Herrick and others 2010). Mitchell (2000) identified that these scientific advances had not yet been incorporated into national datasets of rangeland condition. Unfortunately, with the exception of the NRI, the situation has improved little since 2000. In addition, aside from the NRI, data sets of rangeland condition are still not homogenized in a manner permitting comparisons between data collected by multiple agencies, though efforts are being made to standardize protocols (for example, Herrick and others 2010). Further, unlike the BLM and NRCS, the USFS currently has no agency-wide data collection mandate permitting consistent evaluation of rangeland health on NFS lands.

Most data describing rangeland condition or health of Federal rangelands analyzed by Joyce (1989) and Mitchell (2000) have either become obsolete or were not collected in a comprehensive or timely manner sufficient for deriving meaningful inferences about rangeland health for the current report. For these reasons, this chapter will evaluate health of Federal rangelands through analysis of data collected by the BLM, while non-Federal rangelands are characterized through synopsis of publications (for example, Herrick and others 2010) (http://www.nrcs.usda.gov/wps/portal/nrcs/main/national/home) based on data from the NRI. These recent works summarizing NRI data combined with other information permit focus on attributes of rangeland health, afforestation (or woody encroachment), and invasive species' abundance and distribution.

Health of Lands Managed by BLM

Since 1978, as mandated by the Public Rangelands Improvement Act, the BLM has been monitoring the ecological status of rangelands using predominantly the Ecological Site Inventory (ESI) and the Soil-Vegetation Inventory Method (SVIM) to report on the condition of rangelands. Since inventorying and monitoring using the ESI and SVIM procedures began, rangeland condition of BLM lands has been classified into four ecological status categories. Each category represents percent similarity of the Potential Natural Community (PNC) (Habich 2001) species assemblages on a biomass basis (Mitchell 2000). These classes, expressed as percent similarity to PNC vegetation conditions are: 76-100 percent PNC, 51-75 percent—late seral, 26-50 percent—mid seral, and 0-25 percent—early seral.

While the ESI and SVIM methods permit characterization of rangeland condition, they are not suitable for evaluating other phenomena that are linked to rangeland health (such as ecological processes). Thus, in response to the changing philosophies regarding rangeland health and the need to evaluate other metrics than merely vegetation composition, the BLM created the Standards for Rangeland Health (DOI BLM 2001). Originally, the standards were written to evaluate four fundamentals of rangeland health as they are affected by livestock grazing practices, but later included the effects of other land use activities such as recreation and mineralogical exploration. The four standards promote:

1. keeping ecological processes in order;
2. water quality that complies with state standards;
3. habitats of protected species; and
4. watershed function.

Each state where the BLM administers land determines the most appropriate indicators of rangeland health to monitor the selected land health standards. In the following discussion, results of the ESI, SVIM, and sampling related to the Standards for Rangeland Health are summarized. In table 29, greater scores indicate that the region has vegetation that is more similar to the vegetation that the region supported at potential, in other words, vegetation that existed prior to the settlement of the region by Euro-Americans or vegetation that would exist in the future if human influence was removed from now into the future. A greater score suggests that the region exhibits a greater abundance of plant species and a more similar mixture of plant species compared with the vegetation that the region could support at full potential.

Rocky Mountain Assessment Region

As in all reporting regions, the apparent trend change between 2003 and 2004 (table 29) is due to changes in reporting methods. Therefore, trends can only be evaluated between 2004 and 2009. About 90 percent of all rangeland area for which a condition score has been given is found in the Rocky Mountain Assessment Region. Wyoming exhibits the highest percentage of rangelands designated as PNC while Idaho generally supports the least amount since 2004. In contrast, Idaho exhibits the highest proportion of early seral designation. Montana, North Dakota, and South Dakota (evaluated as a single unit) support the least proportion of land designated as early seral. No significant change in condition categories is readily apparent on BLM lands in the Rocky Mountain Assessment Region (table 29).

Table 29—Rangeland condition on BLM rangelands. Numbers in parentheses indicate the acres (ac x 10^{-3}) sampled since 1978. For the apparent change in rangeland condition between 2003 and 2004, see text.

	Condition Class[a]	Year									
		2000	2001	2002	2003	2004	2005	2006	2007	2008	2009
Rocky Mountain AR											
Arizona (6,246)	PNC	8	6	6	6	8	8	8	8	8	9
	Late	33	30	30	32	43	44	43	44	44	42
	Mid	24	25	24	26	38	38	38	38	37	39
	Early	7	7	7	7	11	10	10	11	11	11
Colorado (3,615)	PNC	3	4	5	5	7	7	7	7	7	6
	Late	17	18	20	20	27	27	27	27	27	28
	Mid	30	30	30	30	41	41	41	41	41	41
	Early	20	19	18	18	25	25	25	25	25	25
Idaho (8,536)	PNC	4	4	4	3	3	3	3	2	2	2
	Late	27	31	31	27	25	24	25	25	25	25
	Mid	35	35	36	38	38	38	38	41	41	41
	Early	22	21	23	27	35	35	34	33	33	33
Montana, North and South Dakota (6,135)	PNC	7	7	7	7	8	7	9	8	9	9
	Late	62	55	57	58	66	65	68	68	66	66
	Mid	22	22	21	21	25	26	22	23	24	23
	Early	1	2	1	1	1	2	1	1	1	1
Nevada (17,617)	PNC	2	2	3	3	4	4	4	4	4	4
	Late	22	22	27	27	39	38	38	38	38	38
	Mid	36	36	32	31	45	46	46	46	46	46
	Early	9	10	8	8	12	12	12	12	12	12
New Mexico (9,506)	PNC	2	4	4	4	4	4	4	4	4	4
	Late	35	30	30	30	24	24	24	24	24	24
	Mid	44	42	41	41	43	43	43	43	43	42
	Early	16	22	22	22	30	30	30	30	30	29
Utah (13,383)	PNC	11	11	12	11	12	12	12	12	12	12
	Late	29	29	28	28	30	30	30	30	30	31
	Mid	43	43	42	42	45	45	45	44	44	45
	Early	12	12	12	13	14	14	13	13	13	13
Wyoming (10,405)	PNC	5	6	6	24	27	27	27	27	27	27
	Late	43	43	43	34	38	38	38	38	38	38
	Mid	34	33	33	27	30	30	30	30	30	30
	Early	6	6	6	5	5	5	5	5	5	5
Pacific Coast AR											
California (1,243)	PNC	3	3	3	3	3	3	3	3	3	3
	Late	21	21	20	20	21	21	21	21	21	21
	Mid	42	42	42	43	45	45	45	45	45	45
	Early	30	30	30	30	31	31	31	31	31	31
Oregon and Washington (7,815)	PNC	1	1	1	1	1	1	1	1	1	1
	Late	22	21	21	21	27	27	28	28	28	28
	Mid	45	45	45	45	60	59	59	59	59	59
	Early	11	11	11	11	13	13	13	13	12	12
Total (84,501)											

[a]The BLM defines PNC as "The biotic community that would become established if all successional sequences were completed without interference by man under the present environmental conditions. Natural disturbances are inherent in development. Potential natural communities can include naturalized non-native species" (Habich 2001:1686).

The results for state-level standards for rangeland health are found in table 30. Roughly 72 percent of rangelands within grazing allotments administered by the BLM have been evaluated to determine the appropriate designation in relation to meeting the standards for rangeland health corresponding to 97 million acres. Of these lands, 57.6 million acres have been designated as meeting all standards or making significant progress toward meeting the standard. In contrast, only 2.8 million acres have been designated as not meeting standards or making significant progress toward meeting the standards, and no appropriate action has been taken to ensure significant progress toward meeting the standards where livestock is a significant factor. Of all lands that have been evaluated in the Rocky Mountain Assessment Region, Arizona has the greatest proportion (92 percent, ~7.8 million acres) of land designated as meeting all standards while Idaho has the least (38 percent, ~3.4 million acres). Where livestock is not a significant factor, Colorado exhibits the greatest proportion (13 percent, ~1 million acres) of land designated as not meeting all standards or not making significant progress toward meeting the standards while Arizona exhibits the least amount (<1 percent, ~21,000 acres).

Pacific Coast Assessment Region

On average, since 2004, Oregon and Washington (evaluated as a single unit) have exhibited the lowest proportion of rangelands designated with PNC status, while California supports the highest proportion of early seral designation. Along with the Rocky Mountain Assessment Region (table 29), the Pacific Coast Assessment Region has not exhibited any significant change in rangeland conditions on BLM lands since 2004.

Oregon and Washington exhibit the highest proportion (64 percent, ~5.9 million acres) of lands designated as meeting all standards or making significant progress toward meeting the standard (table 30). California exhibits the highest proportion (11 percent, ~626,000 acres) of lands designated as not meeting all standards or not making significant progress toward meeting the standards due to causes other than livestock grazing.

All BLM Lands

The condition of all BLM lands from 2004 to 2009 has been quite stable when quantified with the ESI and SVIM results (table 31). The 2000 RPA Rangeland Assessment included similar conclusions regarding the condition of rangelands administered by the BLM. Roughly 75 percent of the lands administered by the BLM are in the mid and late seral stages indicating an overall positive situation. Approximately 68 percent of all BLM grazing lands have been evaluated for determining the level to which they are meeting the standards for rangeland health. Of all BLM lands that have been evaluated for rangeland health standards, 89 percent have been designated as meeting all standards or making significant progress toward meeting the standard. This analysis corroborates evidence developed by the ESI and SVIM results and indicates an overall positive picture of lands managed by the BLM.

Table 30—Categorized summary of cumulative accomplishments as of 2009 relating to the inventory and monitoring of standards for rangeland health implemented by the BLM. Area is quantified as acres x 10^{-3}.

Assessment Region	A.[a]		B.[b]		C.[c]		D.[d]		E.[e]		F.[f]		G.[g]	
	Allot. No.	Acres	Allot. No.	Acres	Allot. No.	Acres	Allot. No.	Acres	Allot. No.	Acres	Allot. No.	Acres	Allot. No.	Acres
Rocky Mountain														
Arizona	624	7,756	10	359	15	256	5	21	654	8,391	168	3,025	822	11,417
Colorado	1,613	4,671	245	1,678	26	262	253	1,016	2,137	7,628	269	229	2,406	7,857
Idaho	1,030	3,363	298	4,141	31	260	203	1,124	1,562	8,888	628	2,684	2,190	11,573
Montana/Dakotas	4,198	6,590	316	1,008	75	128	318	416	4,907	8,142	304	46	5,211	8,188
Nevada	300	15,550	95	9,760	17	871	45	1,702	457	27,883	335	15,940	792	43,823
New Mexico	534	2,342	73	429	22	12	93	164	722	2,947	1,569	9,871	2,291	12,818
Utah	752	9,321	145	2,338	9	357	59	1,447	965	13,463	448	8,229	1,413	21,693
Wyoming	1,336	8,062	288	4,997	85	683	100	573	1,809	14,314	1,717	3,291	3,526	17,605
Total	10,387	57,654	1,470	24,711	280	2,830	1,076	6,462	13,213	91,656	5,438	43,316	18,651	134,972
Pacific Coast														
California	363	2,856	68	1,699	20	626	62	626	513	5,808	173	2,305	686	8,113
Oregon/Washington	799	5,851	117	1,737	35	1,014	114	494	1,065	9,096	977	4,481	2,042	13,577
Total	1,162	8,707	185	3,436	55	1,641	176	1,120	1,578	14,903	1,150	6,786	2,728	21,689
BLM total	11,549	66,361	1,655	28,146	335	4,470	1,252	7,582	14,791	106,560	6,588	50,101	21,379	156,661

[a]Rangelands meeting all standards or making significant progress toward meeting the standard.

[b]Rangelands not meeting all standards or making significant progress toward meeting the standards, but appropriate action has been taken to ensure significant progress toward meeting the standards (livestock is a significant factor).

[c]Rangelands not meeting standards or making significant progress toward meeting the standards, and no appropriate action has been taken to ensure significant progress toward meeting the standards (livestock is a significant factor).

[d]Rangelands not meeting all standards or making significant progress toward meeting the standards due to causes other than livestock grazing.

[e]Total number of allotments that have been assessed.

[f]Total number of allotments that have not been assessed.

[g]Total number of allotments.

Table 31—Condition of all BLM lands (2004 to 2009).

All BLM lands	PNC[a]	Late seral	Mid seral	Early seral
		---------------Percent------------------		
2004	7.7	34.0	41.0	17.7
2009	7.7	34.1	41.1	17.9

[a]The BLM defines PNC as "The biotic community that would become established if all successional sequences were completed without interference by man under the present environmental conditions. Natural disturbances are inherent in development. Potential natural communities can include naturalized non-native species" (Habich 2001: 1686).

Health of Non-Federal Rangelands

Many aspects of rangeland health are easy to observe but difficult or expensive to quantify (Herrick and others 2010), making the use of indicators a logical means of systematic rangeland monitoring. The recently produced rangeland health assessments reported on here relied on the rangeland health protocol implemented in the NRI which was fashioned after Pellant and others (2005). The rangeland health protocols used in the NRI and the accompanying analysis performed by Herrick and others (2010) are significant for at least two important reasons. First, they provide a model that land management agencies could consider as part of a rangeland health evaluation strategy on public lands. Second, it is the first effort of its kind in terms of depth and scope of analysis. No other agency has collected such diverse data describing rangeland health on such a wide scale in a spatially explicit manner.

Three attributes are used by the NRI and are reported and summarized by Herrick and others (2010) to describe rangeland health on non-Federal rangelands:

- Soil and site stability—the capacity of a site to limit redistribution of loss of soil resources, including nutrients and organic matter, by wind and water.

- Hydrologic function—the capacity of the site to capture, store, and safely release water from rainfall, run-off, and snowmelt (where relevant); to resist a reduction in this capacity; and to recover this capacity following degradation.

- Biotic integrity—the capacity of a site to support characteristic functional and structural communities in the context of normal variability, to resist loss of this function and structure caused by disturbance, and to recover following such a disturbance.

Each attribute is monitored using a suite of indicators (Pellant and others 2005) (table 32). The NRI program has collected rangeland health information on approximately 10,000 sample sites, but current field-data collection protocols were not employed until 2003 (Herrick and others 2010). We provide a synopsis of key findings from Herrick and others (2010) and the 2007 NRI report (http://www.nrcs.usda.gov/wps/portal/nrcs/main/national/home), which reflects data collected on non-Federal rangelands from 2003 to 2006.

Table 32—Standard Indicators included in the NRI Rangeland Health protocol and attribute (soil and site stability, hydrologic function, and/or biotic integrity) to which each indicator applies (Pellant and others 2005). The "X" indicates that the indicator is applied to the attribute.

Rangeland health indicator	Rangeland health attribute		
	Soil and site stability	Hydrologic function	Biotic integrity
1. Rills	X	X	
2. Water flow patterns	X	X	
3. Pedestals and/or terracettes	X	X	
4. Bare ground	X	X	
5. Gullies	X	X	
6. Wind scoured, blowouts, and/or deposition areas	X		
7. Litter movement	X		
8. Soil surface resistance to erosion	X	X	X
9. Soil surface loss or degradation	X	X	X
10. Plant community composition and distribution relative to infiltration and runoff		X	
11. Compaction layer	X	X	X
12. Functional/structural groups			X
13. Plant mortality/decadence			X
14. Litter amount		X	X
15. Annual aboveground production			X
16. Invasive plants			X
17. Reproductive capability of perennial plants			X

The assessment performed by Herrick and others (2010) revealed that 21.3±1.3 percent of the 392 million acres of rangelands analyzed showed at least moderate departure from reference conditions for at least one of the three forementioned attributes. Similarly, 9.7±1.1 percent of rangelands analyzed showed at least moderate departure for all three attributes (Herrick and others 2010). Biotic integrity exhibited the largest amount of departure, with moderate departure recorded on 18.2±1.1 percent of the land, while hydrologic function was second at 14.9±1.4 percent, followed by soil and site stability at 12.0±1.4 percent (Herrick and others 2010). Biotic integrity appears to be most affected by the presence of non-native species, though invasive native species also contribute to decreased biotic integrity, especially mesquite (*Prosopis* spp.) and juniper (*Juniperis* spp.). Non-native species are now present on roughly 50 percent of non-Federal rangelands and represent over 50 percent of the total plant cover on 5 percent of non-Federal rangelands. It is important to understand that the mere presence of non-native species does not necessarily affect all aspects of rangeland health. For example, a site can be dominated by smooth brome (*Bromus inermus*, an exotic grass species common on many rangelands) and still exhibit a high degree of hydrologic function and soil and site stability.

Table 33 demonstrates the results of the NRI rangeland health assessment. In general, the Northern Great Plains appear more intact in all three attributes than the southwestern United States (Herrick and others 2010). Texas has the largest overall percent of non-Federal rangeland with health attribute ratings of moderate, moderate-to-extreme, or extreme-to-total departures from expected (indicating a lower degree of rangeland health), followed by Utah, Arizona, and New Mexico. Unfortunately, the margins of error were large enough on one or more attributes in California, Florida, Idaho, Louisiana, South Dakota, North Dakota, Nebraska, and Washington to prevent a suitable inter-comparison of rangeland health attributes among these states. Overall, roughly 80 percent of the non-Federal rangelands in the coterminous 48 states are in relatively healthy condition and exhibit no significant soil, hydrologic, or biotic integrity problems (table 33).

Woody Encroachment by Native Species

Woody encroachment has been defined as establishment, development, and spread of tree or shrub species (Hughes and others 2006). We amend the definition to be more specific to rangeland ecosystems; we define "woody encroachment" as the establishment, development, and spread of tree or shrub species onto rangeland sites that are postulated to have hosted less dense cover by woody species in the past.

Table 33—Percent of non-Federal rangeland by state where rangeland health attribute ratings are moderate, moderate-to-extreme, or extreme-to-total departures from expected with margins of error. California had 39.2 (±5.8) percent of non-Federal rangeland not reporting rangeland health. Only 1.7 (±0.3) percent of the area non-Federal rangelands in the United States did not have rangeland health reported. Table adapted from http://www.nrcs.usda.gov/technical/nri/rangeland/health.html#table2.

State	Soil and site stability	Hydrologic function	Biotic integrity	All three attributes	At least one attribute
	----------------------------- Percent -----------------------------				
Arizona	18 (±5.5)	22 (±6.3)	18.5 (±6.6)	12.4 (±5.3)	26.7 (±6.7)
California	0 (NA)	0 (NA)	Trace	0 (NA)	Trace
Colorado	7.8 (±3.4)	12 (±5.0)	13.5 (±4.0)	6.6 (±3.0)	16.7 (±5.4)
Florida	0 (NA)	0 (NA)	Trace	0 (NA)	Trace
Idaho	Trace	Trace	5.3 (±2.0)	Trace	5.6 (±2.1)
Kansas	5.8 (±2.0)	7.6 (±1.9)	6 (±2.2)	2.9 (±1.6)	10 (±2.5)
Louisiana	0 (NA)	0 (NA)	0 (NA)	0 (NA)	0 (NA)
Montana	2.3 (±1.2)	4.1 (±1.8)	3.6 (±1.5)	Trace	6 (±2.0)
Nebraska	3.7 (±2.2)	4.5 (±2.3)	7.9 (±2.4)	1.8 (±1.5)	10.2 (±2.9)
Nevada	Trace	3.9 (±3.0)	12.9 (±6.4)	Trace	13.6 (±6.2)
New Mexico	13.4 (±3.9)	15.9 (±4.0)	17.1 (±3.8)	10.5 (±3.7)	21.2 (±3.7)
North Dakota	Trace	Trace	4.5 (±2.1)	0 (NA)	4.9 (±2.1)
Oklahoma	6 (±3.1)	9.4 (±3.0)	26.6 (±5.2)	3.4 (±1.8)	30.6 (±4.7)
Oregon	4.4 (±2.1)	6.5 (±3.2)	11.4 (±4.8)	3.9 (±2.2)	11.9 (±4.8)
South Dakota	Trace	Trace	5.6 (±3.1)	Trace	5.9 (±3.1)
Texas	24.6 (±4.4)	30.5 (±4.6)	37.7 (±4.1)	23.6 (±4.3)	39.1 (±4.1)
Utah 28.2 (±11.7)	34.5 (±13.3)	33 (±9.3)	19.4 (±7.9)	43.8 (±13.5)	
Washington	Trace	Trace	16.4 (±5.0)	Trace	17.5 (±5.3)
Wyoming	10.2 (±4.5)	9.4 (±4.1)	8 (±3.6)	4.1 (±3.1)	13.6 (±4.2)
Nation	11.6 (±1.3)	14.4 (±1.4)	17.7 (±1.1)	9.4 (±1.1)	20.7 (±1.2)

The frequency and stature of trees and shrubs has increased over the last 200 years, especially in the southwestern United States and globally in arid and semi-arid ecosystems (Archer and others 1995). In some cases, native woody plants are increasing in abundance within their historic geographic ranges; in other cases, non-native woody plants are becoming dominant (Archer and others 1995). Many areas where this phenomenon occurs are classified as grassland, shrub-steppe, or savanna ecosystems that occupy large areas both in the United States and elsewhere. At present, with some exception given to data collected by the NRI, comprehensive data describing historic or modern rate, areal extent, and pattern of woody plant expansion (Hibbard and others 2001) is lacking. However, a large body of literature exists describing effects of invasive woody species.

It is widely postulated that causal mechanisms responsible for expansion of woody species into previously herb-dominated systems involve overgrazing (Briggs and others 2002; Sankey and Germino 2008), decreasing fire frequency, and optimal climate conditions for plant growth (Miller and Rose 1999). Regardless of the causes, the densification and encroachment of woody species can induce significant ecological change. Therefore, evaluation of woody encroachment into U.S. rangelands is important from an ecological and economic perspective.

When increasing woody species abundance transforms grasslands into savannas and savannas into shrublands or woodlands (Hughes and others 2006), substantial alterations can occur in fire regimes (Ansley and Rasmussen 2005; Miller and Rose 1999), nutrient cycling (Rau and others 2010; Strand and others 2008), biodiversity, and forage yield (Miller and others 2005). Ironically, encroachment by some woody species, such as mesquite, lead to increased aboveground carbon storage, which, from a CO_2 mitigation perspective, is considered a beneficial phenomenon. Mesquite has been estimated to increase aboveground C stocks from less than 9800 pounds per acre in low-density stands to more than 39,000 pounds per acre in mature stands on clay loam soils (Hughes and others 2006). Shrub encroachment can also increase soil organic matter, leading to the ultimate effect of increasing sequestered carbon, which is dependent on many factors such as temperature and rainfall with relatively wetter sites receiving a greater amount of sequestered carbon (Knapp and others 2008). Paradoxically, the same encroachment leads to a multitude of economic and ecological concerns.

In arid regions, increases in the abundance of shrubs at the expense of grasses are a type of desertification often accompanied by accelerated rates of wind and water erosion. Likewise, in semi-arid and subhumid areas, encroachment of shrubs and trees into grasslands and savannas may promote primary production and accumulation of soil organic matter but potentially reduce stream flow, ground water recharge, livestock production, and biological diversity (Archer and others 2001). In this section, we provide a brief synoptic overview of the extent and magnitude of woody encroachment by three key genera: *Prosopis*, *Juniperus*, and *Pinus*. Though some positive effects of increased woody populations exist (Ansley and Rasmussen 2005), here we focus on the ecological and economic consequences and magnitude of invasions.

Junipers

The principle *Juniperus* species addressed in this report are *Juniperus occidentalis* (western juniper), *J. ostesperma* (Utah juniper), *J. monosperma* (one-seeded juniper), *J. ashei* (Ashe juniper), and *J. virginiana* (eastern red cedar). Approximately 10 percent of U.S. rangelands are occupied by invasive *Juniperus* species other than *J. virginiana* (table 34). In general, pinyon and juniper woodlands occupy approximately 74 million acres in the western United States (Miller and others 2005). Most of the growth is found between 2000 and 6000 ft in elevation (Gedney and others 1999). Western juniper exists in the western-most domain of junipers discussed here and is found intermittently in California, southern Idaho, and in sparse, scattered stands in south-central and southeastern Washington, eastern Oregon, and the northwest corner of Nevada (figure 44).

The greatest abundance of western juniper occurs in continuous stands in central Oregon and occupies between roughly 7 (Chambers 2008) and 9 million acres (Miller and others 2005) throughout its range. Miller and Rose (1999) report that western juniper expansion began between 1875 and 1885, and Miller and others (2005) indicated that stands dominated by at least 10 percent canopy cover in eastern Oregon have increased from 456,000 acres in 1936 (Cowlin and others 1942) to 2.2 million acres in 1988 (Gedney and others 1999).

Table 34—Percent of non-Federal rangeland by state where selected native invasive species are present (margins of error displayed in parentheses).

State	Eastern redcedar	Juniper species, excluding eastern redcedar	Juniper species, including eastern redcedar	Mesquite species
			Percent	
Arizona	0 (NA)	13.0 ±4.9	13.0 ±4.9	14.0 ±3.6
California	0 (NA)	Trace	Trace	0 (NA)
Colorado	Trace	7.6 ±3.7	8.3 ±4.0	0 (NA)
Florida	0 (NA)	0 (NA)	0 (NA)	0 (NA)
Idaho	0 (NA)	4.0±2.8	4.0±2.8	0 (NA)
Kansas	5.1±1.8	0 (NA)	5.1±1.8	0 (NA)
Louisiana	0 (NA)	0 (NA)	0 (NA)	0 (NA)
Montana	0 (NA)	12.2 ±3.9	12.2±3.9	0 (NA)
Nebraska	4.6 ±1.9	0 (NA)	4.6 ±1.9	0 (NA)
Nevada	0 (NA)	Trace	Trace	0 (NA)
New Mexico	0 (NA)	12.9 ±5.7	12.9 ±5.7	14.1±4.4
North Dakota	0 (NA)	6.8 ±2.5	6.8±2.5	0 (NA)
Oklahoma	20.4±4.7	Trace	21.3±4.1	7.5±4.2
Oregon	0 (NA)	13.3±4.2	13.3±4.2	0 (NA)
South Dakota	Trace	Trace	1.2±1.1	0 (NA)
Texas	2.6±0.8	19.2±4.5	21.5±4.5	47.6±4.5
Utah	0 (NA)	20.3±8.9	20.3±8.9	0 (NA)
Washington	0 (NA)	0 (NA)	0 (NA)	0 (NA)
Wyoming	0 (NA)	3.1±2.3	3.1±2.3	0 (NA)
Nation	1.8±0.3	10.0±1.2	11.8±1.3	14.1±1.2

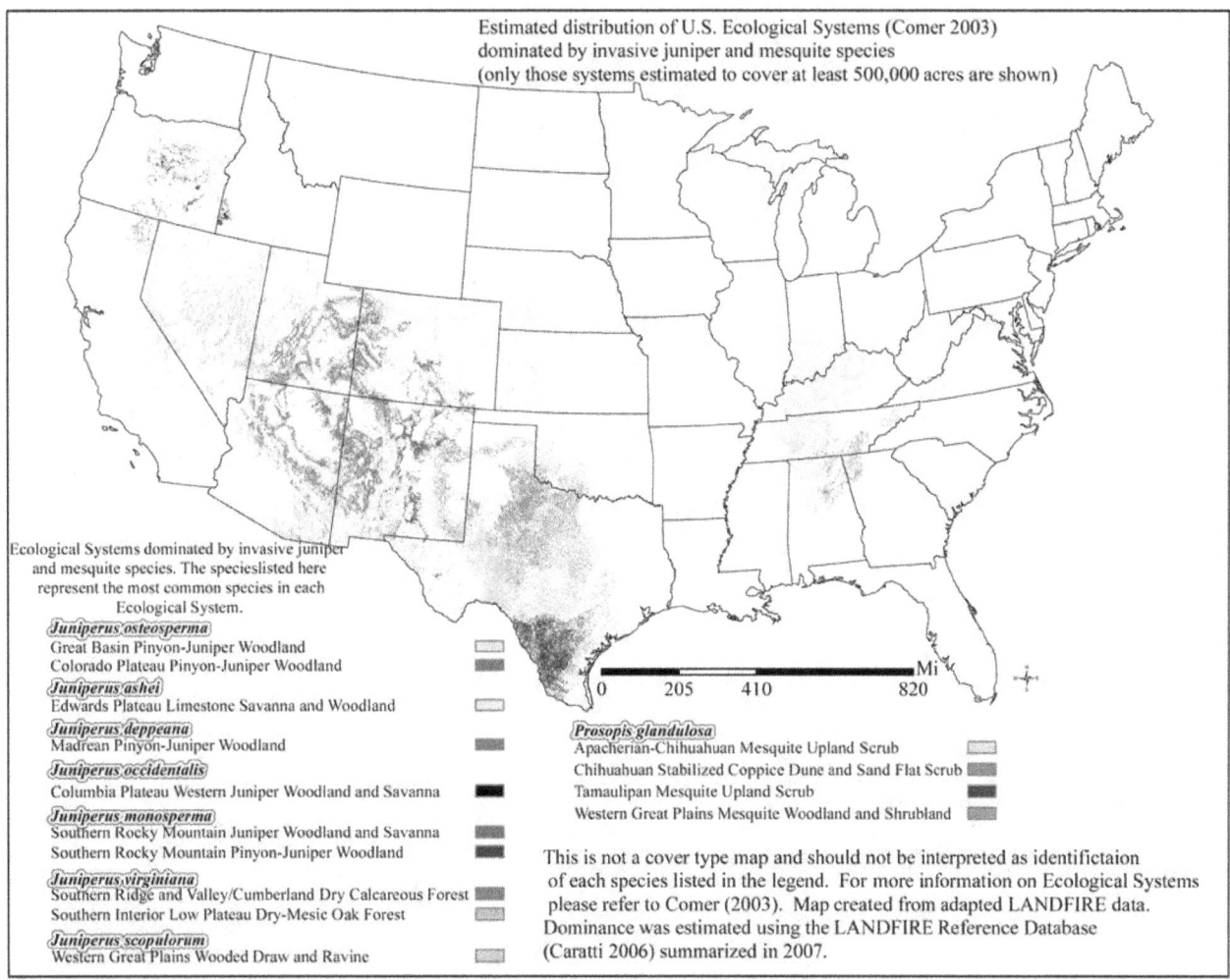

Figure 44—Estimated distribution of U.S. Ecological Systems (Comer 2003) that are dominated by invasive *Juniperus* and *Prosopis* spp. Only those systems estimated to occupy at least 500,000 acres are shown. This map does not reflect the distribution of the species in question but does represent the Ecological Systems dominated by each species.

Figure 45 indicates the general proportion of non-Federal rangelands where *Juniperus* species are present. Note the comparison of figure 45 with the distribution of the Colombia Plateau Western Juniper Woodland (Comer and others 2003; Comer and Schulz 2007) depicted in figure 44. Western juniper has increased the area it occupies by as much as 10-fold throughout much of its range during the past 130 years (Miller and Rose 1999). Between 1985 and 2005, Sankey and Germino (2008) estimated an increase in juniper encroachment of approximately 1.5 percent per year. They also noted that the increases were more dramatic in grazed areas and on intermediate slopes. In the southern extent of the interior northwest, pre-settlement juniper densities averaged 2 to 11 stems per acre, while current densities average 80 to 358 stems per acre—a 10- to 100-fold increase (Miller and others 2008)—most of which were established after 1860 (Johnson and Miller 2008). This pattern of encroachment or densifi-cation is exemplified in figure 46. The estimated amount of non-Federal rangelands where *Juniperus* species other than *J. virginiana* are present is shown in table 34.

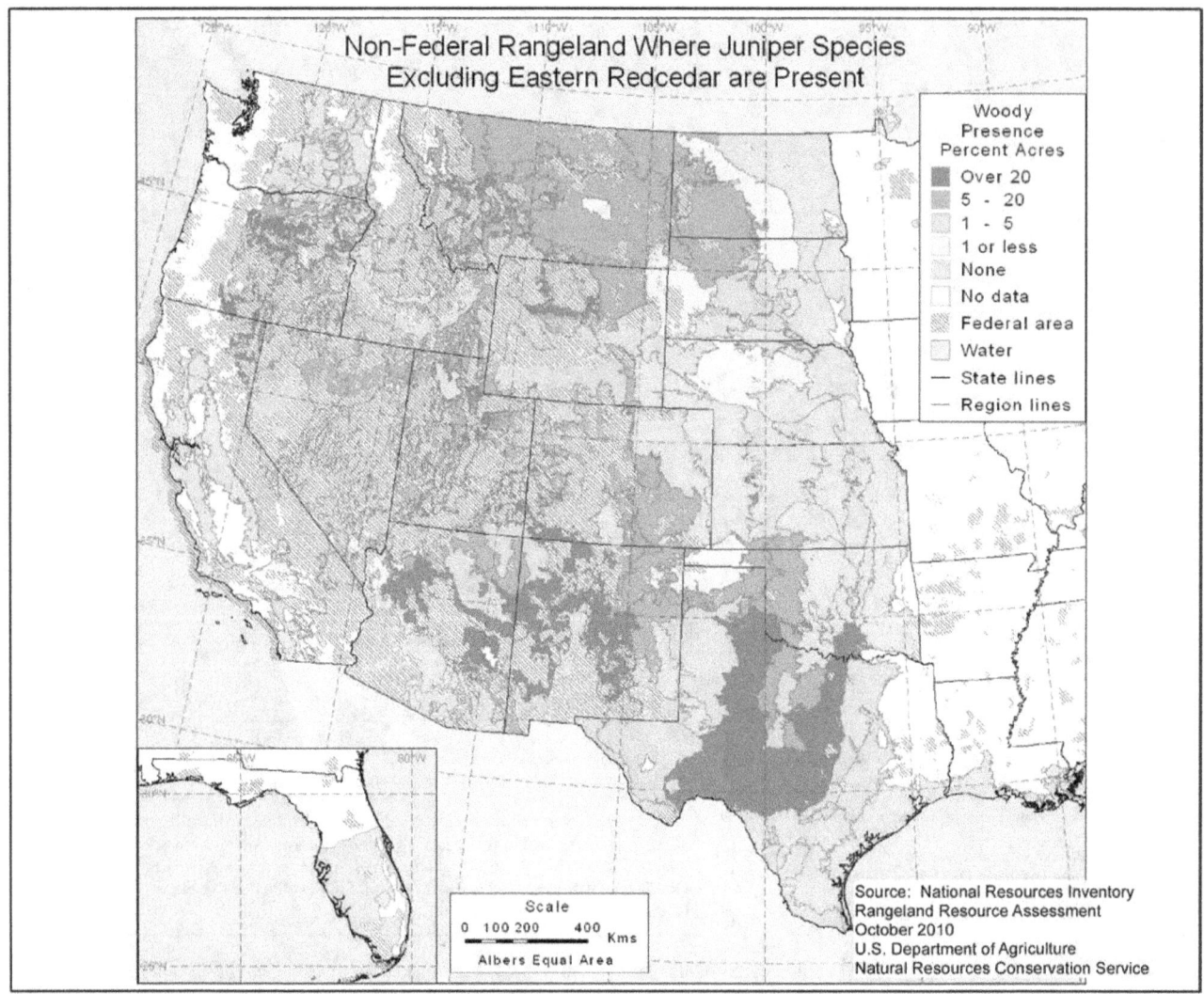

Figure 45—Proportion of non-Federal rangelands where invasive *Juniperus* spp. (excluding *J. virginiana*) are present.

In addition to regionally changing fire and fuel conditions, evidence suggests that the increased abundance of western juniper is also reducing aspen in some stands (loss of aspen is a significant issue discussed in Mitchell [2000]) and decreasing the water available for water-sheds due to increased transpirational demand. Finally, densification of western juniper is also linked to reduced understory biomass and diversity of wildlife and plant species (Wall and others 2001).

Compared with Ecological Systems dominated by western juniper, the Great Basin and Colorado Plateau and Madrean Pinyon-Juniper Woodland Ecological Systems occupy much larger areas (figure 44). These Systems are bounded by an extensive geographic region (figure 44). Although pinyon-juniper woodlands occupy a large area in the United States, less information appears to be available documenting the densification and expansion of individual

A. Keystone Ranch Circa 1890

B. Keystone Ranch Circa 1989

Figure 46—Keystone Ranch east of Prineville, Oregon. Most trees are junipers but a few *Pinus ponderosa* individuals are present. Smaller trees in panel A appear to be about 10 to 25 years old, and larger trees appear to be 60 to 70 years (Miller and others 2005). Panel B represents significant encroachment seen in many parts of the western United States. Photo by Stu Garrett.

species within these areas. Most literature references pinyon-juniper woodlands system as opposed to individual species such as Utah juniper. The following information reflects that distinction.

Blackburn and Tueller (1970) provided estimates near 100 million acres of pinyon-juniper woodlands in the United States. More recent studies indicate less extensive coverage and document that pinyon-juniper woodland area has increased from 7.41 million acres to 74 million acres since the mid 1800s (Miller and Tausch 2001; Miller and others 2008). Further, since 1860, Miller and others (2008) estimated the area occupied by pinyon and/or juniper has increased 125 to 625 percent, varying by location. Following past trends, tree-dominated woodlands are projected to increase from the current 20 to nearly 75 percent of the total woodland area within the next 30 to 50 years (Miller and others 2008). Without disturbance or management, most invaded landscapes will probably become closed woodlands resulting in the loss of understory plant species, decline of sagebrush communities, loss of habitat, decline in herbaceous production, decline of landscape heterogeneity, and increase in restoration costs (Miller and others 2008).

The final *Juniperus* species discussed here are Ashe juniper (*Juniperus ashei*) and eastern red cedar. Ashe juniper occurs in scattered populations in southwestern Missouri and Arkansas and southern Oklahoma. The main population occurs in west-central Texas, largely on the Edwards Plateau (Sullivan 1993), as indicated in figure 44. In a similar fashion to pinyon-juniper woodlands, without fire, Ashe juniper increases and herbaceous biomass decreases at exponential rates until dense canopy woodlands form (Fuhlendorf and others 1996). Ecological thresholds exist, beyond which these conversions may be irreversible (Fuhlendorf and others 1996).

Soil erosion resulting from juniper encroachment is a major concern, and grassland communities in the Great Plains are especially vulnerable (Ansley and Rasmussen 2005). Ashe juniper, unlike species such as *Juniperus pinchotii* (Pinchot's juniper), does not resprout when cut, but expansion rates of the species appear to be exponential (Bidwell and others 1995). Perhaps more troubling is the nature of the expanding individuals. The junipers that establish in over-grazed lands are young, vigorous, dense, multi-trunked, and shallow-rooted, making it difficult for remaining grasses to compete for water. These dense, shallow-rooted shrubs result in less water reaching the soil, thereby decreasing soil yield (Owens and others 2006). Bidwell and others (1995) estimate Ashe juniper and eastern red cedar have increased by 79 percent in some areas over a nine-year period. Expansion rate into Oklahoma rangelands is exponential and estimated at 280,000 acres per year from 1985 to 1994 (Bidwell and others 1995). Eastern red cedar and Ashe juniper now occupy over 6 million acres of rangeland and forestland in Oklahoma (approximately 15 percent of the land area) influencing almost 30 percent of the estimated 21.6 million acres in native plant communities (Bidwell and others 1995).

In contrast to Ashe juniper, eastern red cedar tends to invade more northerly rangelands, especially former tallgrass prairie. The species occurs in nearly every state east of the Rocky Mountains but appears invasive toward the western edge of its range (figure 47). Eastern red cedar is the most widely distributed conifer east of the Mississippi River and pioneers aggressively into abandoned fields and grasslands (Schmidt and Leatherberry 1995). Native tallgrass prairie can be converted to red cedar forest in as little as 40 years with a maximum expansion rate of around 6 percent per year (Briggs and others 2002). Schmidt and Leatherberry (1995) estimated red cedar occupied around 12.4 million acres of forestland in 1993 in the lower Midwest representing a 113 percent increase from two decades earlier.

Relative to other juniper species, invasions by eastern red cedar are particularly problematic because the species threatens tallgrass prairie, one of the most endangered ecosystems in North America (Briggs and others 2005). Invasions by red cedar, like those perpetrated by other *Juniperus* species, elicit ecological consequences. The establishment of red cedar forests or woodlands in areas formerly dominated by grasslands can result in decreased biodiversity (Norris and others 2007), as well as significant changes in fire regimes, productivity, nutrient cycling, forage availability, and soil properties. Horncastle and others (2005) suggested that an increase in overstory cover from 0 percent to 40 percent red cedar can change "a species-rich prairie community" to a community dominated by a single species. In small mammal communities, biodiversity decreases as red cedar increases. Further, even a 5 percent increase in red cedar cover can preclude use by grassland endemic songbirds such as the grasshopper sparrow (Bidwell and others 1995).

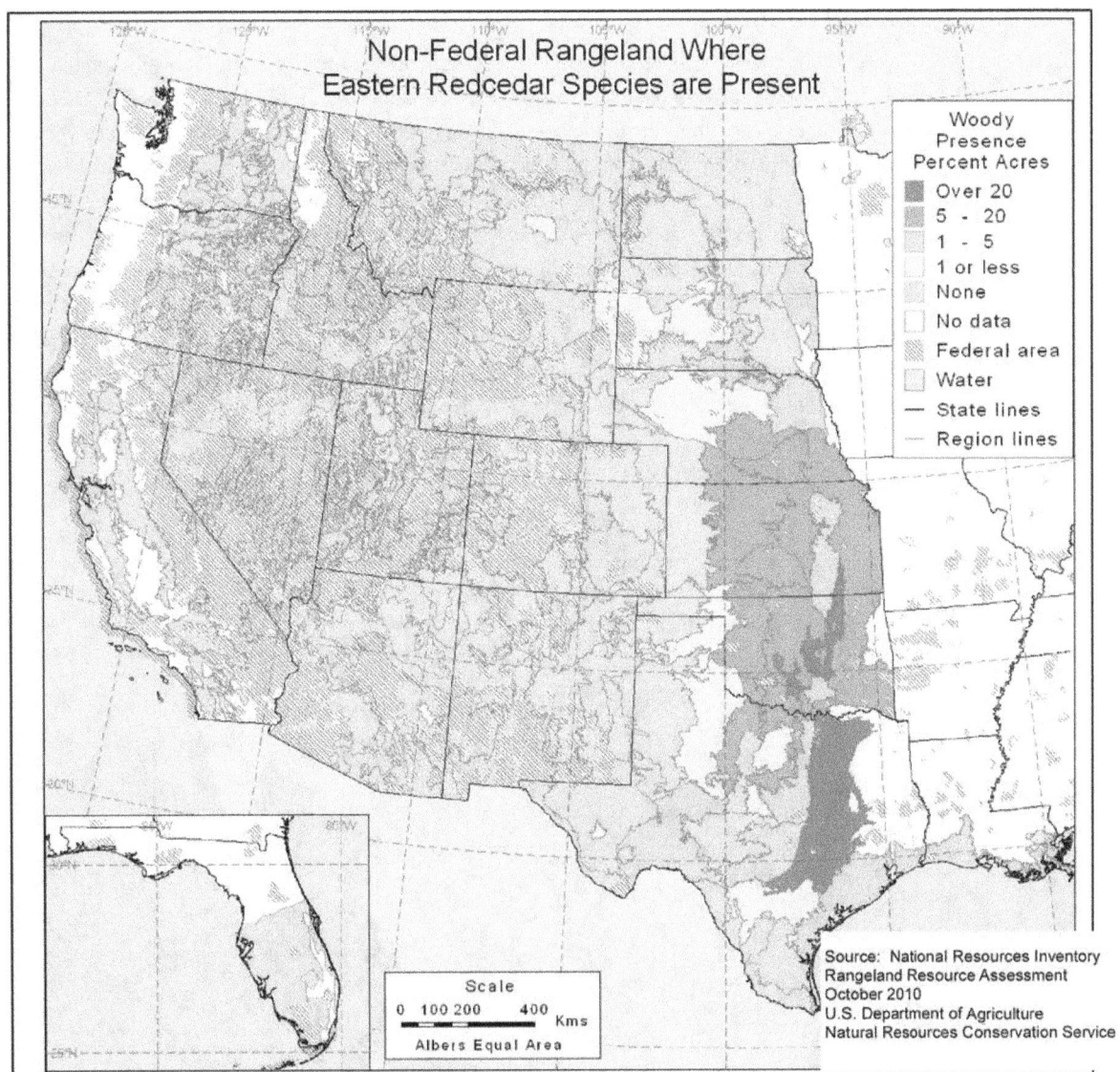

Figure 47—Proportion of non-Federal rangelands where *Juniperus virginiana* is present.

In tallgrass prairie, Norris and others (2007) found that former stands of tallgrass prairie now occupied by red cedar exhibited a 2.5-fold increase in aboveground productivity. The increased productivity is partly due to the two-fold increase in nitrogen-use-efficiency compared with grasses on similar sites. The increase in productivity and stature, in turn, greatly increases the possibility of crown fire, which can permanently alter the site characteristics precluding development by other species, thereby creating a nefarious feedback cycle. Ironically, eastern red cedar has been widely promoted as a species used for conservation purposes with an estimated 2.8 million seedlings distributed by state nurseries in 2001 (Ganguli and others 2008).

Mesquite Species

Overgrazing is widely thought to drive encroachment by *Prosopis* (mesquite) species; but debate still remains as to the exact causes (Kupfer and Miller 2005). Lack of fire has played a role, and evidence suggests that even widespread seed dispersal from increased herbivory via introduction of domestic livestock is largely responsible for the current spread of *Prosopis* species throughout their range (ingestion of mesquite seeds and subsequent digestive processes appear to increase seed germination) (Brown and Archer 1989). Ecological Systems and NVCS alliances dominated by mesquites occupy a large region of the Southwest coterminous United States with significant coverage in Arizona, New Mexico, and Texas. Table 34 indicates the proportion of non-Federal rangelands where invasive *Juniperus* and *Prosopis* species are present. Texas hosts the largest proportion of non-Federal rangelands where mesquite is present; roughly 48 percent are occupied (figure 48). Given that mesquites occupy semi-arid

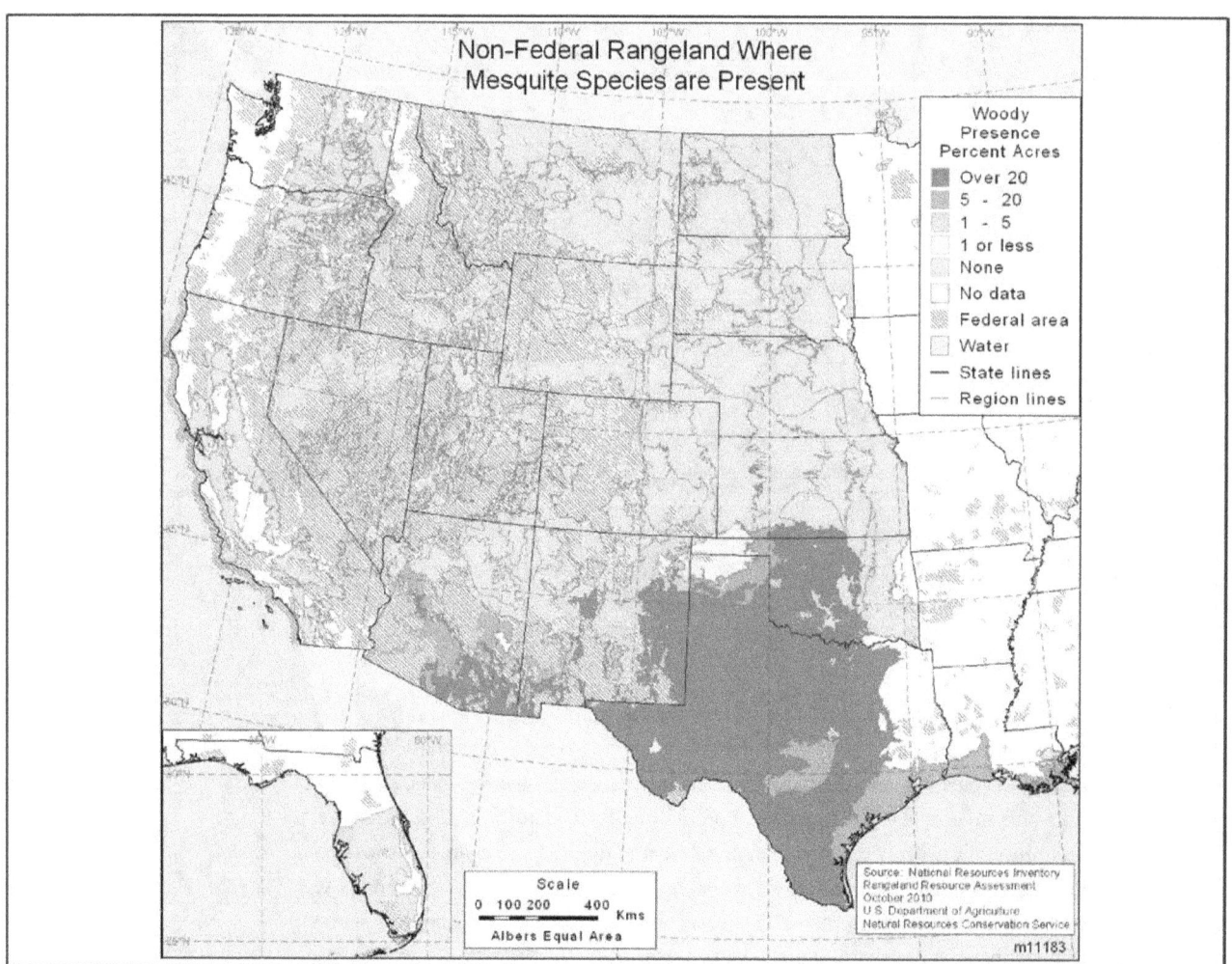

Figure 48—Proportion of non-Federal rangelands where *Prosopis glandulosa* is present.

and arid landscapes, a large focus of current research on encroachment implications is the potential for an increasing area of arid land or desertification. In these landscapes, mesquite can exploit any additional soil moisture that infiltrates under intermittent streambeds and in local areas where water accumulates during runoff (Schlesinger and others 1990).

Mesquite is an ideal woody invader of grasslands due to its production of abundant seed, ability to germinate and establish in a variety of soil types, and ability to fix nitrogen at the seedling and adult stages (Archer and others 1988). These competitive advantages are especially evident outside the natural range of *Prosopis glandulosa* (honey mesquite). Honey mesquite has been introduced in at least six other countries and earned the reputation as one of the top 100 invasive species according to the International Union for Conservation of Nature (IUCN) (http://www.globalspecies.org/ntaxa/778707).

Domestically, *Prosopis* species (*P. glandulosa, P. velutina, P. torreyana, or P. juliflora*) are the dominant woody plant on more than 94 million acres of what has been considered semi-arid southwestern grasslands (Van Auken 2000). Such a large distribution and, in some cases, high stem densities create similar ecological consequences as *Juniperus* species. Much is unknown, however, regarding the long-term implications of mesquite invasions for carbon budgets, primarily due to lack of information regarding distribution and amount of belowground biomass—a critical component of the carbon budget (Jurena and Archer 2003). Encroachment by mesquite can markedly increase the near-surface soil carbon and nitrogen pools and the rapid rates of soil carbon and nitrogen sequestration are now documented (Gill and Burke 1999; Jurena and Archer 2003).

In addition to altering nutrient cycles, mesquite invasions greatly reduce herbaceous forage and thus create an economic burden for working ranches. Warm season herbaceous biomass is linearly related to the amount of mesquite cover (Teague and others 2008). Teague and others (2008) documented a decrease of 12.5 pounds per acre in herbaceous biomass for each 1 percent increase in cover by honey mesquite for a total reduction of up to 73 percent relative to sites where honey mesquite was not significantly present. Reduction in cover of mesquite, usually by herbicide, has been linked to significant increases in forage production (Bedunah and Sosebee 1984).

Though the effect of fire on individual species or systems is well studied, the influence of *Prosopis* species on fuelbed characteristics (and subsequent fire behavior potential) is not. Generally speaking, however, invasion by mesquite generally lowers the potential for wildfire through reduction in fine fuels, especially when the invasion is coupled with intensive grazing, resulting in patchy fuels (Streeks and others 2005) and increased bare ground (Comer and others 2003).

Exotic Plants Abundance and Distribution

Globally, numerous species are spreading outside their historic ranges and causing many types of disruptions across the landscape (Mitchell 2000), including decreases in rangeland health. Exotic or non-indigenous plants are species that have been introduced into ecosystems in which they did not evolve (Mitchell 2000) and may potentially displace or otherwise adversely affect native flora or fauna. Monitoring non-native plant species is a vital component of assessing rangeland health, and developing an understanding of the potential effects of these species is necessary (NISC 2008). The spread of exotic or non-indigenous plants throughout U.S. rangelands has had harmful effects on overall rangeland health and presents management obstacles (Mitchell 2000). It is important both economically and environmentally to address infestations of invasive weeds during early stages of invasion to prevent long-term establishment (Smith and others 1999) (figure 49).

Figure 49—Successful plans for coping with and mitigating invasive species, such as knapweed, will include a combination of strategies. Here, one of the author's goats (A) is eating knapweed, which some goats seem to enjoy. Knapweed root weevils (B), shown infecting a knapweed root, are one of several effective biocontrol agents found on some U.S. rangelands.

The plant invasion process on rangelands can be conceptualized by four primary stages—including introduction, establishment, spread, and impact (Vasquez and others 2010)—each of which results in growing economic, ecological, and human health consequences (Mitchell 2000). Geographical barriers for propagules must be overcome for *introduction* to occur while biotic and abiotic factors (such as competition) must be suitable for *establishment* to occur. Likewise, the *spread* of invasive plants relies on survival and production of propagules that are capable of persisting in new sites. During the *impact* stage, invasive plants are dominant and have noticeable effects on ecosystem processes (Vasquez and others 2010).

Today, an estimated 3310 non-native species occur within the coterminous United States, and of that, 126 million acres are infested by 16 prominent invasive plant species (Duncan and others 2004). The rangelands of the United States have seen increased expansion of invasive plant species and subsequent ecosystem shifts. Non-native species have been shown to degrade natural ecosystem integrity and are now estimated to be present on 48.5±1.4 percent of U.S. rangelands and represent over 50 percent of total plant cover on 5.3±0.5 percent of rangelands (Herrick and others 2010). Invasive plant species have continued to increase in spread and density, and estimates of expansion over time are reflected by the growth in concern over the associated problems.

While the drastic increase in abundance and spread of invasive weeds across U.S. rangelands is often asserted, estimating the total magnitude of expansion is still difficult (Mitchell 2000). Many studies focus only on a subset of invasive species; there is limited collaboration across management entities; and quantifying the extent of spread is difficult. Yet, even a small percentage of non-native species in an ecosystem can cause notable harm and add to shifts in ecosystem functions (NISC 2008).

In 2000, the damage and control efforts resulting from the costs of invasive plant expansion in the United States was approximately $137 billion annually, with costs to the agricultural sector amounting to about $27 billion per year (Stitt and others 2006). These losses are accounted for in decreased yield and lower quality of forage, grazing interference, animal poisonings, and increasing management cost. In addition to these losses, the cost of merely controlling invasive species on rangelands is estimated at $5 billion annually (DiTomaso and others 2010). Some research asserts that the solution to invasive plant species needs to be economic in nature (Perrings and others 2002), but the estimated overall cost of invasive species will continue to change over time. It can be surmised that estimates of costs associated with invasive species are likely to underestimate the problem due to potential quantitative challenges (Perrings and others 2002).

In addition to economic effects, exotic plant invasions pose serious threats to natural systems, often altering ecological functions. Invasive plants reduce the ability of rangelands to provide goods and services that are required by society (Masters and Sheley 2001) and have been known to cause issues such as interruption of processes, including nutrient cycling (Evans and others 2001), pollination, and predator and prey relationships (NISC 2008), reducing biodiversity, increasing soil erosion, degrading wildlife habitat, and reducing the carrying capacity of livestock (Frost and Launchbaugh 2003).

Soil erosion is of particular interest because prior to the establishment of the Soil Conservation Service and the Civilian Conservation Corps, strategies implemented to combat land degradation across U.S. rangelands largely focused on soil stabilization (Herrick and others 2010). Ironically, efforts to control soil erosion, as well as to increase rangeland productivity and stabilize roadsides, often included seeding of invasive plant species, which have since been documented as propellants of erosion (Herrick and others 2010).

Management action and livestock operations enhance the spread of invasive species, and the misuse of grazing practices as weed control may cause additional expansion (Frost and Launchbaugh 2003). However, invasive weed spread is not always linked to a human disturbance, and some invasive species have been found in areas devoid of livestock grazing such as National Parks (Frost and Launchbaugh 2003). The species' ability to invade new areas without human assistance increases the concern regarding the spread potential of invasive plant species as a whole. The National Park Service estimates that non-native species are spreading at a rate of 4000 acres per day on western lands and occupy 8.5 million acres in the Great Basin alone (http://www nps.gov/grba/naturescience/fireregime htm). Such evidence indicates invading plants often out-compete native species for sunlight, nutrients, and space. Most problematic invasive plant species exhibit a host of traits allowing them to spread and maintain a significant presence in the biotic community, including multiple reproductive pathways, rapid dispersion of propagules, fast growth rates, and phenotypic plasticity. These traits enable some invasive species to become aggressively prolific creating unnatural fire regimes that, in turn, create more unfavorable conditions for propagation of native species.

Loss of ecosystem services and biotic integrity remain grave issues facing rangeland health and management, with the exact nature of change across the landscape largely unknown. Difficulties surrounding accounting of ecosystem values add to the barriers associated with estimating the true loss associated with the invasion and replacement of native plants (Hester and others 2006).

Despite the obstacles in synthesizing information regarding invasive species across U.S. rangelands, in the following sections, we discuss the distribution and status of some of the most problematic species that commonly invade rangelands: cheatgrass (*Bromus tectorum*), leafy spurge (*Euphorbia esula*), dalmation toadflax (*Linaria dalmatica*), red brome (*Bromus rubens*), and knapweeds *(Centaurea diffusa, C. maculosa,* and *Acroptilon repens*) (DiTomaso and others 2010). The distributions of these invasive species are debatable, and those provided here were obtained from the Center for Invasive Species (http://www.bugwood.org/). Improvement in the estimates of the distribution of these species requires an intensified, unified, interagency approach, including a publically accessible, spatially explicit database describing the location, magnitude, and composition of infestations.

Cheatgrass

Cheatgrass is considered one of the most abundant invasive plant species in North America (Mitchell 2000) and is known for its ability to successfully out-compete native grasses and forbs. Cheatgrass is found from northern Montana to southern New Mexico and eastern Oregon to western Nebraska in dense populations but exists most prominently in the Great Basin and throughout the western United States (figure 50). The dominance of cheatgrass in

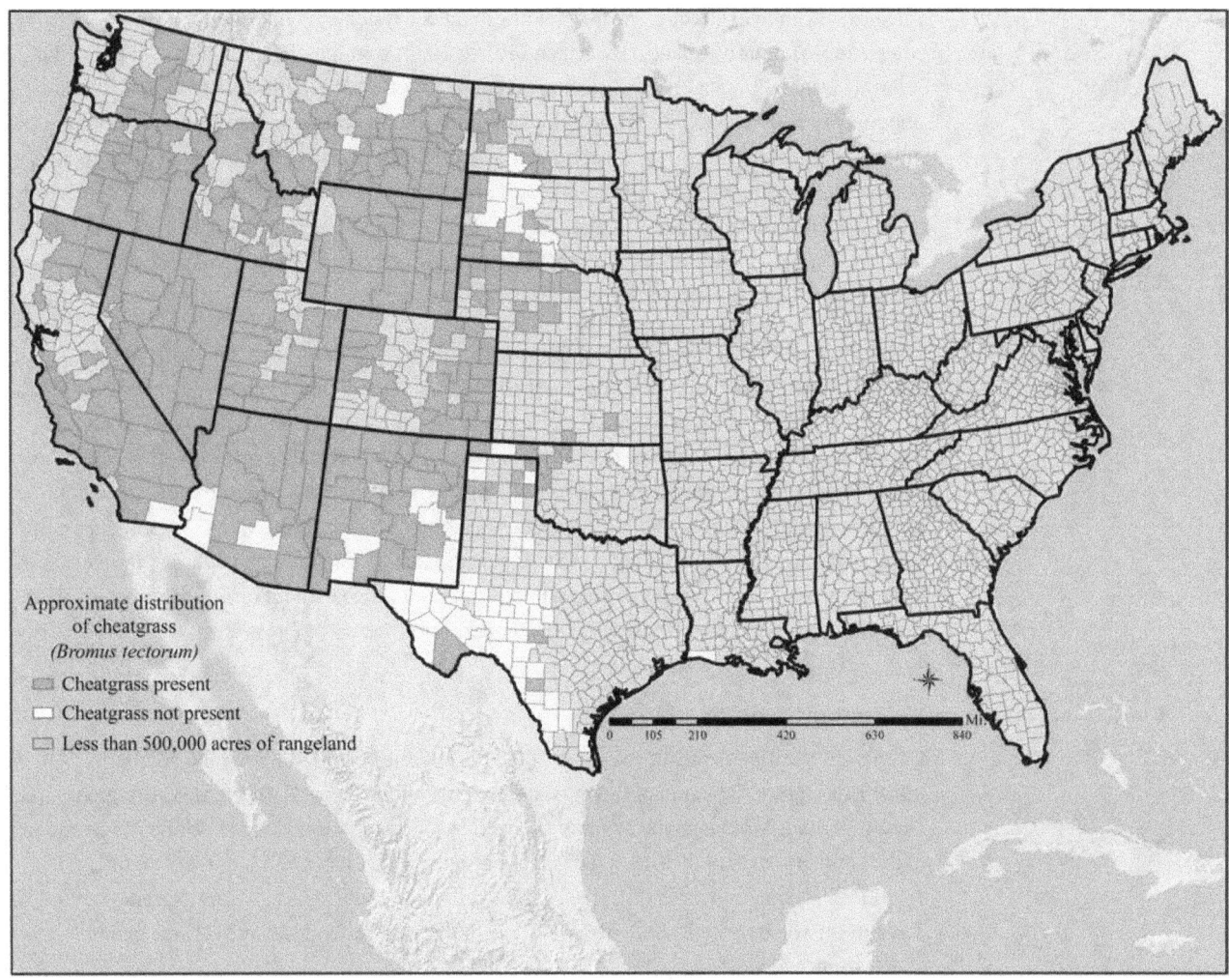

Figure 50—Approximate distribution of cheatgrass (*Bromus tectorum*) across the coterminous United States. Data source: Center for Invasive Species and Ecosystem Health (http://www.bugwood.org/).

the western United States has steadily increased in the last two decades and is expected to continue expansion at the current rate, if not more rapidly (Bradley and others 2006).

In 1994, cheatgrass dominated 3.3 million acres of public lands in the Great Basin Desert with an additional 76.1 million acres either infested or susceptible to invasion (Pellant 1996). Cheatgrass and other annual bromes are highly invasive in communities of sagebrush, pinyon-juniper, and other shrub species. Cheatgrass, with its high local adaptation potential, has expanded into higher elevations during the past 10 to 15 years, signaling that elevation may be an important component of management plan development (Brown and Rowe 2004). The species is an adept invader of previously burned areas and often re-colonizes charred ecosystems more quickly than native species (Bradley and others 2006). Throughout its growing range, cheatgrass competes with native perennials and is good at attaining necessary moisture (Rafferty and Young 2002). Very few species can compete with cheatgrass at the seedling level, and it is likely to thrive in the early stages of development (Reid and others 2008).

Cheatgrass can also affect plant communities and ecosystems by altering fire regimes and competing with native plants (Brown and Rowe 2004) through changing nitrogen dynamics. It has a sizeable impact on sagebrush-grass rangelands, creates a positive feedback in relation to wildfire (Mitchell 2000), and is particularly flammable from late spring until early fall. Cheatgrass expansion will lead to increased frequency and extent of fires (Bradley and others 2006), adding to the difficulties for native plant restoration. Cheatgrass has increased the occurrence of rangeland wildfires throughout the Great Basin, thereby impacting wildfire suppression and overall landscape rehabilitation costs (Pellant 1996). Costs associated with cheatgrass are not limited to fire suppression.

Cheatgrass and the domestic livestock industry interact regularly throughout the West. Livestock managers continue to have a great deal of interest in the relationship between cheatgrass and cattle grazing practices. Also, some research notes a positive impact on livestock operations (Pellant 1996) as cheatgrass is suitable forage at some stages for herbivores (Reid and others 2008). However, the relationship between cheatgrass and fire frequency fluctuations alters forage supply and increases the variability of herbage between wet and dry years (Reid and others 2008), creating livestock management concerns. The widespread invasion of cheatgrass and its deleterious effects on native communities make it one of the most significant plant invaders in North America (Chambers and others 2007).

Dalmation Toadflax

Dalmation toadflax is most prominent in the northwestern United States and southern California (figure 51; some of the most noted infestations are in California, Washington, Oregon, Idaho, Montana, and Wyoming (Erskine Ogden and Renz 2005). While not common in the southern and southeastern states, dalmation toadflax can be found in all continental states (Wilson and others 2005). It is estimated that the species infects approximately 399,197 acres in the western states but only 499 acres in the eastern United States (Duncan and others 2004) (figure 51).

Dalmation toadflax has been observed to easily dominate native plant communities (Wilson and others 2005) and alter the ecosystem dynamics. With high seed production and the ability to colonize quickly, it is often able to dominate and persist on newly established sites (Wilson and others 2005) from early stages. A single plant can produce up to 500,000 seeds annually; and once established, the extensive root system is very difficult to control or eradicate (Erskine Ogden and Renz 2005). Early prevention methods are found to be most effective at controlling or managing infestations.

In addition to rangeland managers, members of the livestock industry are interested in monitoring the spread of this species. Dalmation toadflax contains a poisonous glucoside in its stem liquid that should not be consumed by cattle in large amounts due to potential health risks (Erskine Ogden and Renz 2005). Although cattle have been observed to eat dalmatian toadflax, it is not preferable forage (Jacobs and Sing 2006) and there is concern regarding the toxic potential to grazing animals.

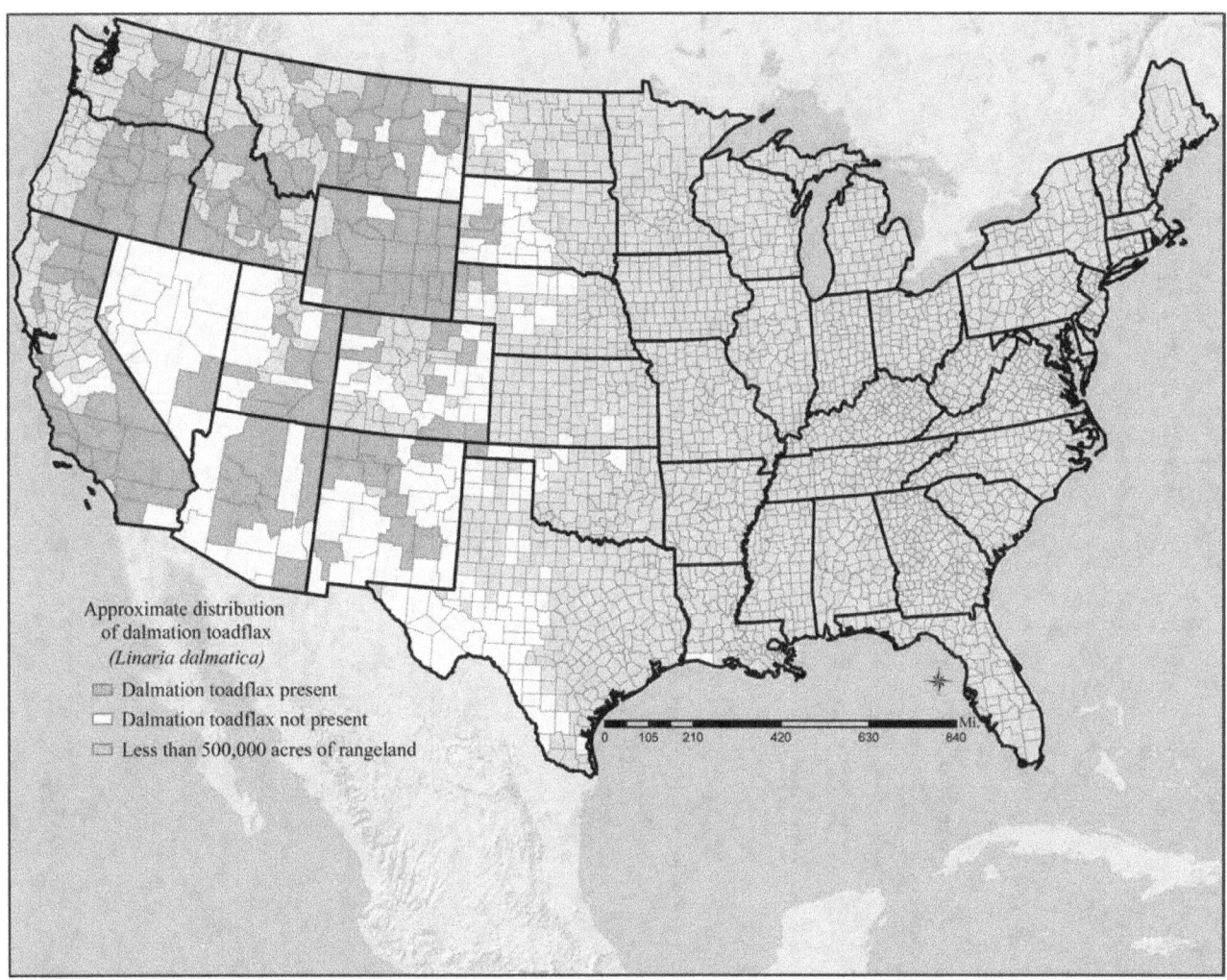

Figure 51—Approximate distribution of toadflax (*Linaria dalmatica*) across the coterminous United States. Data source: Center for Invasive Species and Ecosystem Health (http://www.bugwood.org/).

Knapweed

Knapweed species (*Centaurea* and *Acropitolon* spp.) are mostly found in the western United States with very dense populations in the Southwest and Intermountain regions (figure 52). Knapweed is one of the most commonly identified and acknowledged invasive plant species. It is estimated to infest approximately 5 million acres across the United States (Wilson and Randall 2005). Many species of knapweed are found across the entire United States, but three of the most prolific are spotted (*Centaurea maculosa*), diffuse (*C. diffusa* Lam.), and Russian (*Acroptilon repens* [L.] DC) knapweed. Russian knapweed is estimated to infest 1,200,188 acres in the West and 250 acres in the East; diffuse knapweed infects approximately 1,840,560 acres in the West and 4997 acres in the East, and spotted knapweed infects about 5,231,000 acres in the West and 1,712,308 acres in the East (Duncan and others 2004).

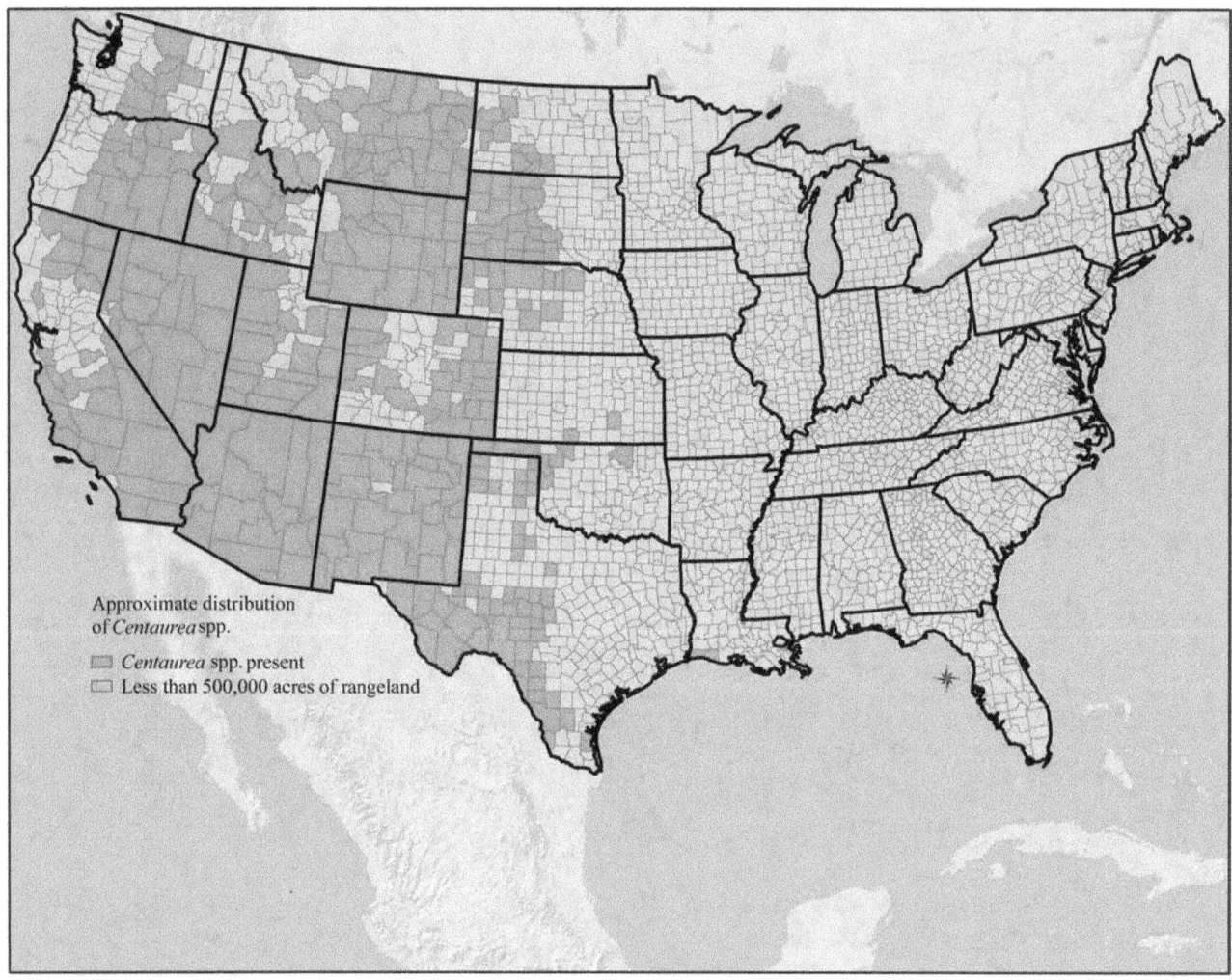

Figure 52—Approximate distribution of knapweeds and starthistles (*Centaurea* spp.) across the coterminous United States. Data source: Center for Invasive Species and Ecosystem Health (http://www.bugwood.org/).

Spotted knapweed is the most widely distributed of the *Centaurea* species and occurs in all but four states (Wilson and Randall 2005), prolifically throughout the Northern Intermountain Region. It has been observed to displace native plant species, even in undisturbed areas has been spreading at a rate of approximately 27 percent per year over the last 80 years across the rangelands of Montana (Jacobs and Sheley 1999). Spotted knapweed is often associated with increased runoff and sediment yield and loss of topsoil, leading to the sedimentation of reservoirs and other water sources (Lacey and others 1989). Reductions in wildlife habitat, biodiversity, and livestock forage have often been associated with spotted knapweed expansion (Jacobs and Sheley 1999). Knapweeds have the potential to alter native habitat, causing declines in both native flora and fauna. In 2008, it was estimated that spotted knapweed infested over 7.4 million acres of grassland habitat in North America (Broennimann and Guisan 2008) and over 1,976,000 acres in Montana alone (Smith and others 1999).

Diffuse and Russian knapweeds are both present, predominantly in western states, and have caused additional woes for native plant communities and related animal species. Diffuse knapweed has been found in over 100 counties and on over 2 million acres of land in the western United States (Sheley and others 1997) and is expected to expand at an increasing rate. Russian knapweed has been associated with reduced livestock carrying capacity, reduced wildlife habitat, and soil and water imbalances (Jacobs and Denny 2006).

The *Centaurea* species are harmful to rangelands and have been found to invade both grazed sites and relatively healthy ecosystems (Mitchell 2000). In addition, the roots of some knapweeds produce a toxin that stunts the growth of many native plant species and causes a noticeable decline in native perennial populations, drastically altering these communities and impacting the food supply, protection, and habitat of other species (Ortega and others 2006).

The livestock industry could be impacted through loss of forage, as well as the threat of poison from knapweed. For example, prolonged ingestion of Russian knapweed by horses has been observed to lead to a fatal neurodegenerative disorder (Jacobs and Denny 2006). With millions of affected acres of rangelands, the species has the potential to cause increasingly severe economic impacts due to the costs of protection, mitigation, and eradication.

Leafy Spurge

The latter half of the Twentieth Century saw exponential increase in leafy spurge populations across the United States. While the increase has been drastic, some experts assert that it already occurs in areas of the United States in which it is best adapted (Mitchell 2000). Leafy spurge is found most predominantly in the northwestern United States with dense populations in eastern Montana and Wyoming (figure 53). The species has become the most abundant weed in the Northern Great Plains (Everitt and others 1995) and has invaded approximately 3,673,475 acres in the western states and 926,630 acres in the East (Duncan and others 2004). Observed in 35 states and 10 Canadian provinces, leafy spurge is considered a serious problem in Colorado, Idaho, Iowa, Minnesota, Missouri, Montana, Nebraska, North Dakota, South Dakota, and Wyoming (Sandell and Knezevic 2010) as it leads to the loss of valuable grassland habitat.

Leafy spurge is a quick invader and is very difficult to remove once it has established in a community. Leafy spurge has been named among the top 10 worst weed problems (Dunn 1979), and its presence has become increasingly unmanageable. Its deep roots make it highly competitive with native species. In the Great Plains, leafy spurge is causing dramatic negative effects on rangeland and pasture carrying capacity (Sandell and Knezevic 2010). Through competition with forages, leafy spurge has reduced carrying capacity by as much as 75 percent with the potential for even greater changes (Sandell and Knezevic 2010). It has been known to reduce species richness of an ecosystem and disrupt numerous natural processes (Butler and Cogan 2004) as well as displace native plants in riparian areas and rangelands alike (Williams and Hunt 2002). In the badlands ecosystem, it forms monocultures with the potential to completely displace entire native communities (Stitt and others 2006). Some wildlife species are negatively impacted by the plant species composition shifts resulting from leafy spurge colonization. In a simple stand sampling comparison, stands infested with leafy spurge averaged 61 percent less species richness than their non-infested counterparts (Butler and Cogan 2004).

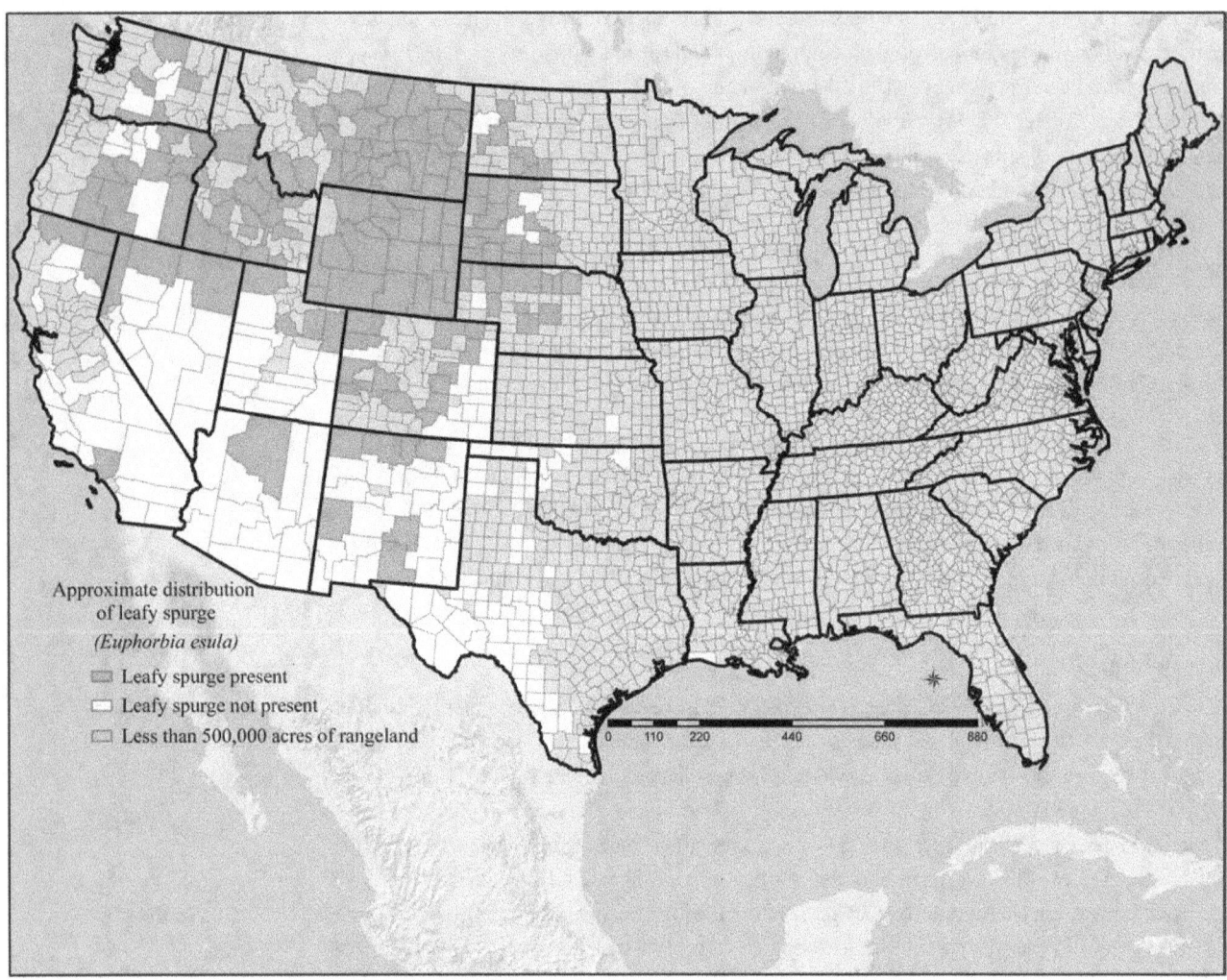

Figure 53—Approximate distribution of leafy spurge (*Euphorbia esula*) across the coterminous United States. Data source: Center for Invasive Species and Ecosystem Health (http://www.bugwood.org/).

In addition to ecological integrity, the economic stability of rangeland is of growing concern due to invasive plant species. Many invasive species, including leafy spurge, create costs for rangeland owners and managers through both decreased grazing capacity and wildlife habitat (Mitchell 2000). Leafy spurge adds to the reduction of livestock carrying capacity on rangelands (Butler and Cogan 2004), and through displacement of other vegetation, leafy spurge forms single-species stands that reduce once desirable forages. Potential economic impacts of leafy spurge invasion are: loss of income for stock growers and landowners, reduced production by ranchers, reduced recreation, and increased concerns surrounding water conservation and habitat integrity (Leitch and others 1994).

Duncan and others (2004) revealed that the direct and secondary impacts of leafy spurge in Montana, North and South Dakota, and Wyoming alone were about $130 million. By 2006, the estimated cost for the same four states had risen to $144 million per year (Stitt and others 2006). The reduced business activity and economic loss in the Northern Great Plains attributed to leafy spurge invasion is estimated at $120 million annually (Bourchier and others 2006). Leafy spurge has invaded approximately 900,000 acres in North Dakota, causing direct and indirect losses exceeding $100 million annually. In Nebraska, with a leafy spurge invasion estimated around 321,000 acres, the direct and indirect losses exceed $16 million per year (Sandell and Knezevic 2010).

Reduction in land value due to the spread of leafy spurge is of great interest to land managers and home owners alike. Due to increased expansion, environmental threats, and potential economic disruption, leafy spurge invasion will continue to be a pressing factor of rangeland health.

Red Brome

Red brome is found predominantly in the southwestern United States, especially in southern California, Nevada, and Arizona (figure 54). Red brome is found to occur from British Columbia to Mexico and from California to western Texas. In the past 50 years, red brome has occupied fewer new areas overall, yet has expanded its range into eastern Arizona and southwestern New Mexico (Reid and others 2008). This spread into new areas indicates that red brome may not be contained to its current range.

The invasion of red brome continues to threaten native plant communities and has been found to significantly alter fire frequency and intensity, causing harmful effects on native species (Reid and others 2008) such as the fire-intolerant, iconic Saguaro cactus (*Carnegiea gigantea*). Red brome produces finer fuels than other annual bromes, such as cheatgrass, fostering an increase in fire behavior that adds to the threat posed to native species (Reid and others 2008).

Observations show that during El Niño Southern Oscillation events, red brome can become the dominant annual species in parts of the Sonoran and Mojave deserts, and it may still be expanding in this area (Reid and others 2008). The species has been very successful at outcompeting native species for light and nitrogen, posing an increasing threat to southwestern communities (Salo and others 2005). Expected CO_2 enrichment could increase red brome's ability to dominate native plants as it has been observed to grow faster, larger, and have higher seed production than native species in instances of atmospheric CO_2 enrichment (Nagel and others 2004).

Overall, the invasive species discussed here will continue to pose economic and ecological hardships and increasingly problematic management concerns. Vigilant management, appropriate financial resources and, most importantly, interagency focus toward inventorying, monitoring, and controlling new populations are critical to reduce the impact of these invasive species. There is an increasing need for better methods of monitoring invasive populations that enable compilation of the necessary data for future assessments (Williams and Hunt 2002).

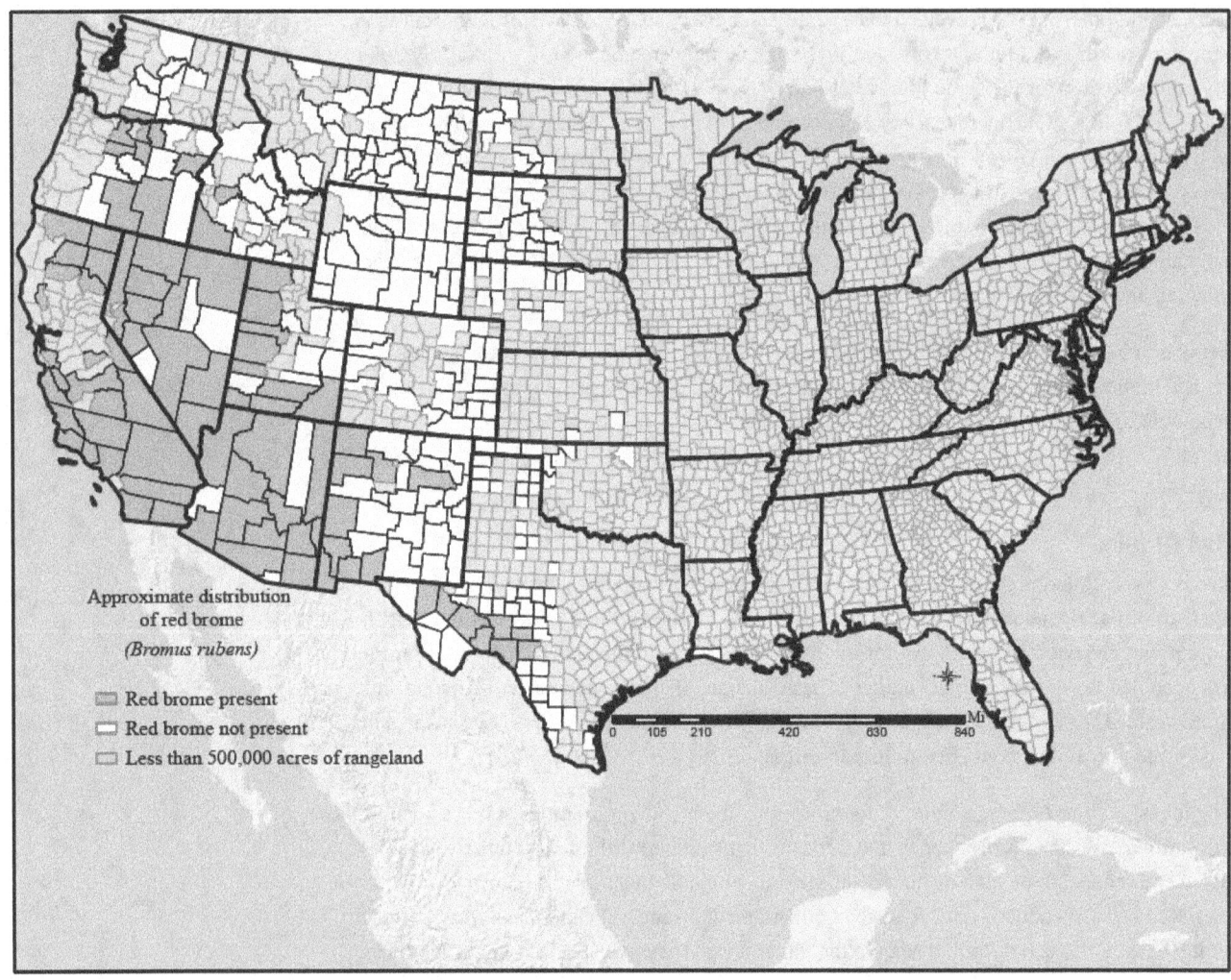

Figure 54—Approximate distribution of red brome (*Bromus rubens*) across the coterminous United States. Data source: Center for Invasive Species and Ecosystem Health (http://www.bugwood.org/).

Federal Management Response to Invasive Species

Despite the economic and ecological effects of invasive species on rangelands, little interagency coordination exists at the national level that is aimed at mapping and systematically monitoring invasive species. Since the 2000 RPA Assessment, progress has been made on the issue and several notable programs and projects have arisen, but most lack an interagency, national perspective. Table 35 exemplifies just a few of the many programs in place (these are just examples; dozens, perhaps hundreds of programs exist) specializing in various aspects of the invasive species problem. However, research and management communities still lack an easily accessible, publically available, spatially explicit, centralized database describing the location and extent of key invasive species for the United States.

Table 35—Examples of the multitude of projects aimed at compiling and characterizing information regarding invasive species.

Project	Website	Agency/organization
USFS Invasive Species Program	http://www.fs.fed.us/invasivespecies/	USFS
National Invasive Species Council	http://www.invasivespecies.gov/	Interagency
USGS Invasive Species Program	http://biology.usgs.gov/invasive/	USGS
The National Invasive Species Council	http://www.invasivespecies.gov/	Interagency
The Global Invasive Species Program	http://tncinvasives.ucdavis.edu/	The Nature Conservancy
Union of Concerned Scientists: Invasive Species	http://www.ucsusa.org/invasive_species/	Non-profit
National Institute of Invasive Species Science	http://www.gisin.org/cwis438/websites/niiss/Home.php?WebSiteID=1	Interagency, administered by USGS
Ecology and Management of Invasive Plants Program	http://www.invasiveplants.net/	Cornell University
Center for Invasive Species and Ecosystem Health	http://www.invasive.org/	University of Georgia
RMRS Invasive Species Working Group	http://www.rmrs.nau.edu/invasive_species/iswg.php	USFS, RMRS
USDA National Invasive Species Information Center	http://www.invasivespeciesinfo.gov/	USDA

The lack of cohesiveness makes developing a report on the status and trends of invasive species on U.S. rangelands problematic. There is hope, however, as recognition of the need for better coordination, inventory, and monitoring has improved. For example, in 2010, the Office of Inspector General developed an audit of the USFS Invasive Species Program and concluded that the agency needed to improve its monitoring strategy, reduce confusion, and improve efficacy of internal databases. Progress is being made at the national level to increase the amount of interagency focus. The Agriculture, Interior, Transportation, Defense, and Energy Departments combined with the EPA have created the Federal Interagency Committee for the Management of Noxious and Exotic Weeds. These efforts will increase the availability of data and, as a result, our ability to characterize the status of invasive species across rangelands will be improved. In addition, substantial efforts have materialized toward combating invasive species. In 2010, the USFS treated 309,228 acres infested with invasive plant species. Merely reporting acres treated, however, falls short of describing the total level of effort dedicated to combating invasive species. For example, much effort is dedicated to decontaminating vehicles and equipment as well as to conducting inventories and surveys, but there is no national performance metric enabling credit for the work so little information is available regarding the costs associated with these activities. In addition, there is more work on education, inventorying, surveying, and monitoring than on controlling (for example, spraying) invasive species (Ielmini, personal communication).

New research is providing information and tools for management of invasive species. In addition, increased public awareness has resulted in citizens participating in weed pulls and educational activities at the local level. One of the more promising products is the concept of the "citizen scientist," which provides a venue for the public to inform management agencies regarding invasive species infestations for which treatments could be prescribed. In an era of decreasing budgets, such a system could become increasingly necessary in our fight against invasive species.

Successful management programs will need to include a host of intervention techniques, including bio-control, prescription grazing (Frost and Launchbaugh 2003) (such as use of alternative livestock during a specific season and for a specific duration to reduce cover of invasive species such as knapweed) (figure 49), herbicide application, and suitable management practices.

Summary

Despite the critical need for information describing rangeland health to support policy and management, little interagency collaboration aimed at characterizing and providing such information in a systematic, cohesive manner exists. Scientific advances in the ability to describe rangeland health have not been incorporated into land management agencies' inventory and monitoring protocols on a meaningful scale. There are effectively four widespread protocols aimed at characterizing rangeland health employed by the BLM and the NRCS. The ESI, SVIM, and standards of rangeland health are used by the BLM while the NRCS employs the indicators of rangeland health. The analysis of the health of U.S. rangelands relies mostly on data summaries from these four systems. Of all lands evaluated by the BLM using the ESI and SVIM protocols, 90 percent of all rangeland area for which a condition score has been given are found in the Rocky Mountain Assessment region. Wyoming exhibits the highest percentage of rangelands designated as PNC while Idaho generally supports the least since 2004. Overall, no significant change in condition categories has been readily apparent on BLM lands in the Rocky Mountain Assessment region since 2004.

Roughly 72 percent of rangelands within BLM grazing allotments have been evaluated using the standards for rangeland health, resulting in 57.6 million acres designated as meeting all standards or making significant progress toward meeting the standard. Only 2.8 million acres have been designated as not meeting standards or making significant progress toward meeting the standards. Of all lands that have been evaluated in the Rocky Mountain Assessment Region, Arizona has the greatest proportion of land (92 percent, ~7.8 million acres) designated as meeting all standards while Idaho has the least (38 percent, ~3.4 million acres) where livestock is a significant factor. From the standpoint of standards for rangeland health, BLM lands in the Rocky Mountain Assessment region are in reasonably good status.

As with the Rocky Mountain Assessment region, BLM lands in the Pacific Coast region do not exhibit any notable changes in relation to PNC status. Approximately 30 percent of rangelands administered by the BLM in California are in early seral status reflecting an overall lower condition than Washington and Idaho. Similarly, California exhibits the highest proportion (11 percent, ~626,000 acres) of lands designated as not meeting all standards or not making significant progress toward meeting rangeland health standards.

At least 75 percent of rangelands under BLM jurisdiction are in mid to late seral stages indicating, from a national perspective, the health of these rangelands is reasonably good and has changed little since 2000. In addition, roughly 89 percent of BLM lands evaluated are meeting or making progress toward the standards for rangeland health, providing further evidence for the positive picture that has emerged over the last decade. Some areas are in very poor condition and require additional resources and changes in management, but from a synoptic perspective, the rangeland health situation for most BLM lands is good.

The rangeland health situation for non-Federal rangelands is somewhat similar to lands managed by the BLM. Roughly 80 percent of non-Federal rangelands show no significant departure from reference conditions, and only 10 percent of rangelands showed significant departure in all three health attributes. Texas exhibits the greatest degree of departure from reference conditions, followed by Utah, Arizona, and New Mexico. Biotic integrity is the largest factor contributing to declines in rangeland health owed mostly to the presence of invasive species.

The expansion of invasive species, particularly by exotics, could pose the largest threat to the future health of U.S. rangelands and cause a serious financial burden to society. In 2000, the damage and control efforts resulting from the costs of invasive plant expansion in the United States was approximately $137 billion annually. Today, an estimated 3310 non-native species occur within the coterminous United States. In addition, 126 million acres are infested by 16 prominent invasive plant species, and non-native species are estimated to be present on 49 percent of U.S. rangelands and represent over 50 percent of total plant cover on 5 percent of non-Federal rangelands.

However, not all invasive species are exotic; invasions by shrubs such as mesquite and juniper species have also created negative consequences. The frequency and stature of trees and shrubs has increased over the last 200 years in arid and semi-arid ecosystems. At present, with some exception given to data collected through the NRI, comprehensive data describing historic or modern rate of expansion, areal extent, and pattern of woody plant expansion (Hibbard and others 2001) are lacking. Overgrazing, decreasing fire frequency, and optimal climate conditions for plant growth are top factors thought to aid the increased density of invasive shrub species. Juniper species have increased rapidly over the last 100 years and in many cases have increased 10- to 100-fold. The increase in eastern red cedar is particularly troubling because it threatens the sustainability (and perhaps the existence) of the tallgrass prairie—one of the most endangered grassland systems in North America. The situation for mesquite is similar, and Texas hosts the largest population of mesquite, with 48 percent of its non-Federal rangelands occupied by mesquite.

While the situation is critical, efforts are underway to control invasive species at the Federal and non-Federal level. For example, in 2010, the USFS treated 309,228 acres infested with invasive plant species. Merely reporting acres treated, however, falls short of describing the total level of effort dedicated toward combating invasive species. For example, much effort is dedicated to decontaminating vehicles and equipment and to conducting inventories and surveys, but little information is available regarding the costs associated with these activities. In addition, there is more work on education, inventorying, surveying, and monitoring than on controlling (for example, spraying) invasive species (Ielmini, personal communication).

New research on tools, education, biocontrol, grazing management, and education offer significant promise for the future. The concept of the "citizen scientist" could prove to be especially valuable and necessary component of the fight against invasive species. In fact, some of the information in this report was compiled using the work of citizen scientists.

Finally, the situation is being elevated to include an interagency focus—the Agriculture, Interior, Transportation, Defense, and Energy Departments and EPA have created the Federal Interagency Committee for the Management of Noxious and Exotic Weeds, which should improve interagency collaboration and data collection and sharing. Hopefully, the increase in education, tools, research, and programs will coalesce into an effective system for dealing with invasive species.

Literature Cited

Adler, P.R.; Sanderson, M.A.; Weimer, P.J.; Vogel, K.P. 2009. Plant species composition and biofuel yields of conservation grasslands. Ecological Applications 19: 2202-2208.

Ansley, R.J.; Rasmussen, G.A. 2005. Managing native invasive juniper species using fire. Weed Technology 19: 517-522.

Archer, S.; Schimel, D.S.; Holland, E.A. 1995. Mechanisms of shrubland expansion: land use, climate or CO2? Climate Change 29: 91-99.

Archer, S.; Scifres, C.; Bassham, C.R.; Maggio, R. 1988. Autogenic succession in a subtropical savanna: conversion of grassland to thorn woodland. Ecological Monographs 58: 111-127.

Archer, S.A.; Boutton, T.W.; Hibbard, K.A. 2001. Trees in grasslands: biogeochemical consequences of woody plant expansion. In: E. Schulze, S.P. Harrison, M. Heimann, E.A. Holland, J. Lloyd, I.C. Prentice, and D. Schimel (eds.). Global Biogeochemical Cycles in the Climate System. San Diego, CA: Academic Press. 363 p.

Bai, Z.G.; Dent, D.L.; Olsson, L.; Schaepman, M.E. 2008. Proxy global assessment of land degradation. Soil Use and Management 24: 223-234.

Barbarika, A. 2009. Conservation Reserve Program: Annual Summary and Enrollment Statistics—FY 2009. Assisted by Skip Hyberg, Rich Iovanna, and Catherine Feather with EPAS/FSA. Washington, DC: U.S. Department of Agriculture, Natural Resources Analysis Group, Economic and Policy Analysis Staff (EPAS), Farm Service Agency (FSA). 78 p.

Bedunah, D.J.; Sosebee, R.E. 1984. Forage response of a mesquite-buffalograss community-following range rehabilitation. Journal of Range Management 37:483-490.

Behnke, R.H.; Scoones, I. 1993. Rethinking range ecology: implications for rangeland management. In: Behnke, R.H.; Scoones, I.; Kerven, C. (eds.). Range Ecology at Disequilibrium. Overseas Development Institute, London, UK: 1-30.

Bidwell, T.G.; Engle, D.M.; Moseley, M.E.; Masters, R.E. 1995. Invasion of Oklahoma rangelands and forests by eastern red cedar and ashe juniper. Oklahoma State University: 1-12.

Bies, L. 2006. The biofuels explosion: is green energy good for wildlife? Wildlife Society Bulletin 34: 1203-1206.

Bird, L.; Bolinger, M.; Gagliano, T.; Wiser, R.; Brown, M.; Parsons, B. 2005. Policies and market factors driving wind power development in the United States. Energy Policy 33: 1397-1407.

Black and Veatch. 2008. Renewable energy options. Overland Park, KS: Black and Veatch Corporation.

Blackburn, W.H.; Tueller, P.T. 1970. Pinyon and juniper invasion in black sagebrush communities in East-Central Nevada. Ecology 51: 841-848.

Bourchier, R.; Hansen, R.; Lym, R.; Norton, A.; Olson, D.; Randall, C.B.; Schwarzlander, M.; Skinner, L. 2006. Biology and biological control of leafy spurge. In: U.S. Forest Service (eds.): Forest Health Technology Enterprise Team: 1-125.

Bradley, B.A.; Houghton, R.A.; Mustard, J.F.; Hamburg, S.P. 2006. Invasive grass reduces aboveground carbon stocks in shrublands of the western US. Global Change Biology 12:1815-1822.

Briggs, J.M., Hoch, G.A.; Johnson, L.C. 2002. Assessing the rate, mechanisms, and consequences of the conversion of tallgrass prairie to Juniperus virginiana forest. Ecosystems 5:578-586.

Briggs, J.M.; Knapp, A.K.; Blair, J.M.; Heisler, J.L.; Hoch, G.A.; Lett, M.S.; McCarron, J.K. 2005. An ecosystem in transition: causes and consequences of the conversion of mesic grassland to shrubland. BioScience 55:243-254.

Broennimann, O.; Guisan, A. 2008. Predicting current and future biological invasions: both native and invaded ranges matter. Biology Letters 4: 585-589.

Brown, C.S.; Rowe, H. 2004. The unwelcome arrival of *bromus tectorum* to high elevations. Fort Collins, CO: Colorado State University. 12 p.

Brown, J.R.; Archer, S. 1989. Woody plant invasion of grasslands: establishment of honey mesquite (*Prosopis glandulosa* var. *glandulosa*) on sites differing in herbaceous biomass and grazing history. Oecologia 80: 19-26.

Brown, L.R. 2002. World's rangelands deteriorating under mounting pressure. Earth Policy Institute (February 5, 2002). Update 6. Bulletin 34: 1203-1206.

Buenemann, M.; Martius, C.; Jones, J.W.; [and others]. 2010. Integrative geospatial approaches for the comprehensive monitoring and assessment of land management sustainability: rationale, potentials, and characteristics. Land Degradation & Deveopment. 14 p.

Butler, J.L.; Cogan, D.R. 2004. Leafy spurge effects on patterns of plant species richness. Journal of Range Management 57: 305-311.

Caratti, J.F. 2006. The LANDFIRE reference database. In: The LANDFIRE prototype project: nationally consistent and locally relevant geospatial data and tools for wildland fire management. Gen. Tech. Rep. RMRS-GTR-175. Fort Collins, CO: U.S. Department of Agriculture, Rocky Mountain Research Station, Missoula Fire Sciences Laboratory, Missoula, MT: 69-98.

Carpenter, F.R. 1981. Establishing management under the Taylor Grazing Act. Rangelands 3: 105-115.

Chambers, J.C. 2008. Sagebrush steppe: a story of encroachment and invasion. Joint Fire Science Program: 1-6.

Chambers, J.C.; Roundy, B.A.; Blank, R.R.; Meyer, S.E.; Whittaker, A. 2007. What makes Great Basin sagebrush ecosystems invasible by *Bromus tectorum*? Ecological Monographs 77: 117-145.

Chow, J.; Kopp, R.J.; Portney, P.R. 2003. Energy resources and global development. Science 302: 1528-1531.

Comer, P.; Faber-Langendoen, D.; Evans, R.;[and others]. 2003. Ecological systems of the United States: a working classification of U.S. terrestrial systems. Arlington, VA. 75 p.

Comer, P.J.; Schulz, K.A. 2007. Standardized ecological classification for mesoscale mapping in the southwestern United States. Rangeland Ecology and Management 60: 324-335.

Cook, J.H.; Beyea, J.; Keeler, K.H. 1991. Potential impacts of biomass production in the United States on biological diversity. Annual Reviews: Energy and Environment 16: 401-431.

Cooley, P. 2010. Personal communication. Phone call/email correspondence to M. Reeves.

Costanza, R.; d'Arge, R.; de Groot, R.; Farberk, S.; Grasso, M.; Hannon, B.; Limburg, K.; Naeem, S.; O'Neill, R.V. 1997. The value of the world's ecosystem services and natural capital. Nature 387: 259-260.

Coulombe, M. J. 1995. Sustaining the world's forests: the Santiago Agreement. Journal of Forestry 93: 18-21.

Coulson, D.P.; Joyce, L.A.; Price, D.T.; McKenney, D.W.; Siltanen, R.M.; Papadopol, P.; Lawrence, K. 2010a. Climate scenarios for the conterminous United States at the 5 arc minute grid spatial scale using SRES scenarios A1B and A2 and PRISM climatology. Fort Collins, CO: U.S. Department of Agriculture, Forest Service, Rocky Mountain Research Station. Available: http://www.fs fed.us/rm/data_archive/dataaccess/US_ClimateScenarios_grid_A1B_A2_PRISM.shtml [2010, August 2].

Coulson, D.P.; Joyce, L.A.; Price, D.T.; McKenney, D.W. 2010b. Climate scenarios for the conterminous United States at the 5 arc minute grid spatial scale using SRES scenario B2 and PRISM climatology. Fort Collins, CO: U.S. Department of Agriculture, Forest Service, Rocky Mountain Research Station. Available: http://www.fs fed.us/rm/data_archive/dataaccess/US_ClimateScenarios_grid_B2_PRISM.shtml [2010, August 2].

Cowlin, R.W.; Briegleb, R.A.; Moravets, F.L. 1942. Forest resources on the ponderosa pine region of Washington and Oregon. Miscellaneous Publication.

Curry, A. 2009. Deadly flights. Science 325: 386-387.

De La Torre Ugarte, D.G.; Walsh, M.E.; Hosein, S.; Shapouri, H.; Slinsky, S.P. 2003. The economic impacts of bioenergy crop production on U.S. agriculture. Agricultural Economic Report No. 816. Washington, DC: U.S. Department of Agriculture.

Denholm, P. 2006. Improving the technical, environmental and social performance of wind energy systems using biomass-based energy storage. Renewable Energy 31: 1355-1370.

DiTomaso, J.M.; Masters, R.A.; Peterson, V.F. 2010. Rangeland invasive plant management. Rangelands 2:43-47.

Duncan, C.A.; Jachetta, J.J.; Brown, M.L.; Carrithers, V.F.; Clark, J.K.; Ditomaso, J.M.; Lym, R.G.; McDaniel, K.C.; Renz, M.J.; Rice, P.M. 2004. Assessing the economic, environmental, and societal losses from invasive plants on rangeland and wildlands. Weed Technology 18: 1411-1416.

Duncan, R.C. 2001. World energy production, population growth, and the road to Olduvai gorge. Population and Environment 22:503-522.

Dunn, P.H. 1979. The distribution for leafy spurge (*Euphorbia esula*) and other weedy *Euphorbia* spp. in the United States. Weed Science 27: 509-516.

Dyksterhuis, E.J. 1949. Condition and management of rangeland based on quantitative ecology Journal of Range Management 2: 104-115.

Ellis, J.E. 1994. Climate variability and complex ecosystems dynamics: implications for pastoral development. In: Scoones, I. (ed.). Living with uncertainty. London, UK: Intermediate Technology Publications: 37-46.

Energy Information Administration [EIA]. 2010. Natural gas annual 2009. DOE/EIA-0131(09). Washington, DC: Office of Oil, Gas, and Coal Supply Statistics, U.S. Department of Energy. 260 p. Available: http://www.eia.doe.gov/iea/overview html [2010, February 2].

Epstein, H.E., W.K. Lauenroth, I.C. Burke, and D.P Coffin. 1997. Productivity patterns of C3 and C4 functional types in the U.S. Great Plains. Ecology 78:722-731.

Erickson, W.P.; Johnson, G.D.; Strickland, M.D.; Young, D.P.; Sernka, K.J.; Good, R.E. 2001. Avian collisions with wind turbines: a summary of existing studies and comparison to other sources of avian collision mortality in the United States. National Wind Coordinating Committee Resource Document. Cheyenne, WY: Western Ecosystems Technology, Inc. 62 p.

Erskine Ogden, J.A.; Renz, M.J. 2005. Dalmation toadflax (*Linaria genistifokia* spp. *Dalmatica*): New Mexico State University Weed-Factsheet. New Mexico State University. 5 p.

Evans, R.D.; Rimer, R.; Sperry, L.; Belnap, J. 2001. Exotic plant invasion alters nitrogen dynamics in an arid grassland. Ecological Applications 11: 1301-1310.

Everitt, J.H.; Anderson, G.L.; Escobar, D.E.; Davis, M.R.; Spencer, N.R.; Andrascik, R.J. 1995. Use of remote sensing for detecting and mapping leafy spurge (*Euphorbia esula*). Weed Technology 9: 599-609.

Fargione, J.; Hill, J.; Tilman, D.; Polasky, S.; Hawthorne, P. 2008. Land clearing and biofuel carbon debt. Science 319: 1235-1237.

Fensholt, R.I.; Sandholt, M.S.; Rasmussen, S.; Stisen, S.; Diou, A. 2006. Evaluation of satellite based primary production modeling in the semi-arid Sahel. Remote Sensing of Environment 105: 173-188.

Follett, R.F.; Reed, D.A. 2010. Soil carbon sequestration in grazing lands: societal benefits and policy implications. Rangeland Ecology and Management 63: 4-15.

Food and Agriculture Organization of the United Nations [FAO]. 2009. FAO statistical yearbook 2009: Table A.4 Land Use. Available: ftp://ext-ftp.fao.org/ES/Reserved/essb/ess/ftp_essb/yearbook_2009_cd/20091109_cd_final/pdf/a04.pdf:2.

Friedl, M.A.; McIver, D.K.; Hodges, J.C.F.;[and others]. 2002. Global land cover mapping from MODIS: algorithms and early results. Remote Sensing of Environment 83: 287-302.

Frost, R.A.; Launchbaugh, K.L. 2003. Prescription grazing for rangeland weed management: a new look at an old tool. Rangelands 25: 43-47.

Fuhlendorf, S.D.; Smeins, F.E.; Grant, W.E. 1996. Simulation of a fire-sensitive ecological threshold: a case study of Ashe juniper on the Edwards Plateau of Texas, USA. Ecological Modelling 90: 245-255.

Gaines, E.M.; Campbell, R.S.; Braisington, J.J. 1954. Forage production on longleaf pine lands in southern Alabama. Ecology 35: 59-62.

Gale, F. 2002. China's food and agriculture: Issues for the 21st Century. Washington, DC: U.S. Department of Agriculture. 64 p.

Ganguli, A.C.; Engle, D.M.; Mayer, P.M.; Fuhlendorf, S.D. 2008. What are native species inappropriated for conservation plantings? Rangelands 30: 27-32.

Gedney, D.R.; Azuma, D.L.; Bolsinger, C.L.; McKay, N. 1999. Western juniper in eastern

Oregon. In: U.S. Department of Agriculture (eds.). Portland, OR: U.S. Department of Agriculture, Forest Service, Pacific Northwest Research Station. 64 p.

Geist, H.J.; Lambin, E.F. 2004. Dynamic causal patterns of desertification. BioScience 54: 817-829.

Gill, R.A.; Burke, I.C. 1999. Ecosystem consequences of plant life form changes at three sites in the semiarid United States. Oecologia 121: 551-563.

Groom, M.J.; Gray, E.M.; Townsend, P.A. 2008. Biofuels and biodiversity: principles for creating better policies for biofuel production. Conservation Biology 22: 602-609.

Grossman, D.H.; Faber-Langendoen, D.; Weakley, A.S.;[and others]. 1998. International classification of ecological communities: terrestrial vegetation of the United States. Volume I. The National Vegetation Classification System: Development, Status, and Applications. Arlington, VA: The Nature Conservancy.

Groundwater Protection Council [GWPC]. 2009. Modern shale gas development in the United States: a primer. U.S. Department of Energy, Fossil Energy & National Energy Technology Laboratory, Award #DE-G26-04NT15455.

Gunter, W.D.; Gentzis, T.; Rottenfusser, B.A.; Richardson, R.J.H. 1997. Deep coalbed methane in Alberta, Canada: a fuel resource with the potential of zero greenhouse gas emissions. Energy Conservation and Management 38: S217-S222.

Habich, E.F. 2001. Ecological site inventory. Denver, CO: U.S. Department of the Iinterior, Bureau of Land Management. 112 p.

Hansen, M.C.; DeFries, R.S.; Townshend, J.R.G.; Sohlberg, R. 2000. Global land cover classification at the 1km spatial resolution using a classification tree approach. International Journal of Remote Sensing: 1331-1364.

Harris, G.A. 1977. Changing philosophies of rangeland management in the United States. Journal of Range Management 30: 75-78.

Heimlich, R.E. 1995. Financial and structural characteristics of CRP enrollees, 1991. Washington, DC: U.S. Department of Agriculture, Economic Research Service. 15 p.

Heimlich, R.E.; Kula, O.E. 1990. Grasslands: the future of CRP land after contracts expire. Journal of Production Agriculture 3: 7-12.

Herrick, J.E.; Lessard, V.C.; Spaeth, K.E.; Shaver, P.L.; Dayton, R.S.; Pyke, D.A.; Jolley, L.; Goebel, J.J. 2010. National ecosystem assessments supported by scientific and local knowledge. Frontiers in Ecology and the Environment 8: 403-408.

Hester, S.M.; Sinden, J.A.; Cacho, O.J. 2006. Weed invasions in natural environments: toward a framework for estimating the cost of changes in the output of ecosystem services. University of New England: 2-35.

Hibbard, K.A.; Archer, S.; Schimel, D.S.; Valentine, D.W. 2001. Biogeochemical changes accompanying woody plant encroachment in a subtropical savanna. Ecology 82: 1999-2011.

Hobbs, N.T.; Galvin, K.A.; Stokes, C.J.; Lackett, J.M.; Ash, A.J.; Boone, R.B.; Reid, R.S.; Thornton, P.K. 2008. Fragmentation of rangelands: implications for humans, animals, and landscapes. Global Environmental Change 8: 776-785.

Holmgren, M.; Scheffer, M. 2001. El Niño as a window of opportunity for the restoration of degraded arid ecosystems. Ecosystems 4: 151-159.

Holmgren, M.; Stapp, P.; Dickman, C.R.;[and others]. 2006. A synthesis of ENSO effects on drylands in Australia, North America and South America. Advances in Geosciences 6: 69-72.

Horncastle, V.J.; Hellgren, E.C.; Mayer, P.M.; Ganguli, A.C.; Engle, D.M.; Leslie, D.M. 2005. Implications of invasion by *juniperus virginiana* on small mammals in the southern great plains. Journal of Mammology 86: 1144-1155.

Hughes, F.R.; Archer, S.R.; Asner, G.P.; Wessmann, C.A.; McMurtry, C.; Nelson, J.; Ansley, J.R. 2006. Changes in aboveground primary production and carbon and nitrogen pools accompanying woody plant encroachment in a temperate savanna. Global Change Biology 12: 1733-1747.

Hunt, E.R.J.; Kelly, R.D.; Smith, W.K.; Fahnestock, J.T.; Welker, J.M.; Reiners, W.A. 2004. Estimation of carbon sequestration by combining remote sensing and net ecosystem exchange data for northern mixed-grass prairie and sagebrush-steppe ecosystems. Environmental Management 33: S432-S441.

Ielminin, M. 2011. Personal communication. Email communication.

International Energy Agency [IEA]. 2008. World energy outlook 2008. Paris, France: Organization for Economic Co-Operation and Development/IEA.

Jacobs, J.; Denny, K. 2006. Ecology and management of Russian knapweed [*Acroptilon repens* (L.) DC]. U.S. Department of Agriculture, Natural Resources Conservation Service. 9 p.

Jacobs, J.; Sing, S. 2006. Ecology and management of dalmatian toadflax (*Linaria dalmatica* (L.) Mill.). U.S. Department of Agriculture, Natural Resources Conservation Service. 9 p.

Jacobs, J.S.; Sheley, R.L. 1999. Grass defoliation intensity, frequency, and season effects on spotted knapweed invasion. Journal of Range Management 52: 626-632.

Jinguo, Y.; Zheng, N.; Wang, C. 2006. Vegetation NPP distribution based on MODIS data and CASA model—a case study of northern Hebei Province. Chinese Geographical Science 16: 334-341.

Johnson, D.D.; Miller, R.F. 2008. Intermountain presettlement juniper: distribution, abundance, and influence on postsettlement expansion. Rangeland Ecology and Management 61.

Jones, K.G. 2004. Trends in the U.S. sheep industry. Washington, DC: U.S. Department of Agriculture, Economics Research Service. 40 p.

Jordan, N.; Boody, G.; Broussard, W.;[and others]. 2007. Sustainable development of the agricultural bio-economy. Science 316: 1570-1571.

Joyce, L.A. 1989. An analysis of the range forage situation in the United States: 1989-2040. A technical document supporting the 1989 USDA Forest Service RPA Assessment. Gen. Tech. Rep. RM-GTR-180. Fort Collins, CO: U.S. Department of Agriculture, Forest Service, Rocky Mountain Forest and Range Experimental Station.

Joyce, L.A.; Mitchell, J.E.; Loftin, S.R. 2000. The applicability of Montreal Process Criterion 3—maintenance of ecosystem health—to rangelands. International Journal of Sustainable Development and World Ecology 7: 107-127.

Jurena, P.N.; Archer, S. 2003. Woody plant establishment and spatial heterogeneity in grasslands. Ecology 84: 907-919.

Karl, M. 2010. Personal communication. Bureau of Land Management BLM, National Operations Center. Numerous phone calls and emails.

Knapp, A.K.; Briggs, J.M.; Collins, S.L.; [and others]. 2008. Shrub encroachment in North American grasslands: shifts in growth form dominance rapidly alters control of ecosystem carbon inputs. Global Change Biology 14: 615-623.

Knapp, A.K., J.M. Briggs, and J.K. Koelliker. 2001. Frequency and extent of water limitation to primary production in a mesic grassland. Ecosystems 4:19-28.

Krohn S.; Damborg, S. 1999. On public attitudes towards wind power. Renewable Energy 16: 954-960.

Kucera, C.L.; Dahlman, R.C.; Koelling, M.R. 1967. Total net productivity and turnover on an energy basis for tallgrass prairie. Ecology 48: 536-541.

Kunz, T.H.; Arnett, E.B.; Erickson, W.P.; Hoar, A.R.; Johnson, G.D.; Larkin, R.P.; Strickland, M.D.; Thresher, R.W.; Tuttle, M.D. 2007. Ecological impacts of wind energy development on bats: questions, research needs, and hypotheses. Frontiers in Ecology and the Environment 5: 315-324.

Kupfer, J.A.; Miller, J.D. 2005. Wildfire effects and post-fire responses of an invasive mesquite population: the interactive importance of grazing and non-native herbaceous species invasion. Journal of Biogeography: 453-466.

Kuuskraa, V.A.; Godec, M.L.; Reeves, S.R. 2007. Outlook for unconventional gas: the next decade. OGJ Unconventional Gas Article #6. Houston, TX: Advanced Resources International, Inc. Available: http://www.adv res.com/pdf/ARI%20OGJ%206%20 Unconventional%20Gas%20Next%20Decade%207_24_07.pdf.

Lacey, J.R.; Marlow, C.B.; Lane, J.R. 1989. Influence of spotted knapweed (*Centaurea maculosa*) on surface runoff and sediment yield. Weed Technology 3: 627-631.

Langer, L. In review. Future scenarios and assumptions: a technical document supporting the Forest Service 2010 RPA Assessment. U.S. Department of Agriculture, Forest Service.

Leinwand, I.F.; Theobald, D.M.; Mitchel, J.; Knight, R.L. 2010. Landscape dynamics at the public-private interface: a case study in Colorado. Landscape and Urban Planning. 12 p.

Leitch, J.A.; Leistritz, F.L.; Bangsund, D.A. 1994. Economic effect of leafy spurge in the upper Great Plains: Methods, models, and results. Fargo, ND: Department of Agricultural Economics. 10 p.

Lepers, E.; Lambin, E.F.; Janetos, A.C.; DeFries, R.; Achard, F.; Ramankutty, N.; Scholes, R.J. 2005. A synthesis of information on rapid land-cover change for the period 1981-2000. BioScience 55: 115-124.

Luginbuhl, J.M.; Green, J.T.; Poore, M.H.; Conrad, A.P. 2000. Use of goats as biological agents for the control of unwanted vegetation. Sheep and Goat Research Journal 16: 124-135.

Lund, G.H. 2007. Accounting for the worlds rangelands. Rangelands: 3-10.

Lyon, A.G.; Anderson, S.H. 2003. Potential gas development impacts on sage grouse nest initiation and movement. Wildlife Society Bulletin 31: 486-491.

Masters, R.A.; Sheley, R.L. 2001. Invited synthesis paper: principles and practices for managing rangeland invasive plants. Journal of Rangeland Management 54: 502-517.

Matheson, J. 2010. Personal communication. Assistant Director National Bison Association. Email to M. Reeves.

Mathews, J.A. 2008. Carbon-negative biofuels. Energy Policy 36: 940-945.

McLaughlin, S.B.; Kszos, L.A. 2005. Development of switchgrass (*Panicum virgatum* L.) as a bioenergy feedstock in the United States. Biomass and Bioenergy 28: 515-535.

McPeak, J.G. 2003. Analyzing and addressing localized degradation. Land Economics 79: 515-536.

Meehl, G.A.; Stocker, T.F.; Collins, W.D.; [and others]. 2007. Global climate projections. In: Solomon, D., D. Qin, M. Manning, Z. Chen, M. Marquis, K.B. Averyt, M. Tignor, H.L. Miller (eds.). Climate Change 2007: The Physical Science Basis. Contribution of Working Group I to the Fourth Assessment Report of the Intergovernmental Panel on Climate Change. Cambridge University Press, Cambridge, United Kingdom.

Milbrandt, A. 2005. A geographic perspective on the current biomass resource availability in the United States. Technical Report NREL/TP-560-39181. Golden, CO: National Renewable Energy Laboratory. 62 p.

Millennium Ecosystem Assessment [MEA]. 2005. Ecosystems and Human Well-being: Synthesis. Washington, DC: Island Press. 155 p.

Miller, R.F.; Bates, J.D.; Svejcar, T.J.; Pierson, F.B.; Eddleman, L.E. 2005. Biology, ecology, and management of western juniper. Oregon State University: 1-82.

Miller, R.F.; Rose, J. 1999. Fire history and western juniper encroachment in sagebrush steppe. Journal of Range Management 52: 550-559.

Miller, R.F.; Tausch, R.J. 2001. The role of fire in pinyon and juniper woodlands: a descriptive analysis. Fire Conference 2000: the First National Congress on Fire Ecology, Prevention, and Management: Tallahassee, FL: 15-30.

Miller, R.F.; Tausch, R.J.; McArthur, E.D.; Johnson, D.D.; Sanderson, S.C. 2008. Age structure and expansion of piñon-juniper woodlands: a regional perspective in the Intermountain West. U.S. Department of Agriculture, Forest Service. 15 p.

Minson, D.J.; McLeod, M.N. 1970. The digestibility of temperate and tropical grasses. Proceedings International Grassland Congress 11: 719-722.

Mitchell, J.E. 2000. Rangeland resource trends in the United States. A technical document supporting the 2000 USDA Forest Service RPA Assessment. Gen. Tech. Rep. RMRS-GTR-68. Fort Collins, CO: U.S. Department of Agriculture, Forest Service, Rocky Mountain Research Station. 84 p.

Mitchell, J.E.; Joyce, L.A.; Bryant, L.D. 1999. Applicability of Montreal process criteria and indicators to rangelands. In: People and rangelands building the future: proceedings of the 6th International Rangeland Congress; Townsville, Queensland, Australia: 183-185.

Morgan, J.A., A.R. Mosier, D.G. Milchunas, D.R. LeCain, J.A. Nelson, and W.J. Parton. 2004. CO2 enhances productivity, alters species composition, and reduces digestibility of shortgrass steppe vegetation. Ecological Applications 14: 208-219.

Morgan, J.A., D.G. Milchunas, D.R. LeCain, M. West, and A.R. Mosier. 2007. Carbon dioxide enrichment alters plant community structure and accelerates shrub growth in the shortgrass steppe. Proceedings of the National Academy of Sciences USA. 104: 14724-14729.

Nagel, J.M.; Huxman, T.E.; Griffin, K.L.; Smith, D. 2004. CO2 enrichment reduces the energetic cost of biomass construction in an invasive desert grass. Ecology 85: 100-106.

Naki☐enovi☐, N.A.; Davis, J.; de Vries, G.; [and others]. 2000. Emissions scenarios. A special Report of Working Group III of the Intergovernmental Panel on Climate Change. Cambridge University Press, Cambridge, United Kingdom. 599 p. Available:http://www. grida no/climate/ipcc/emission/index htm.

National Invasive Species Council [NISC]. 2008. 2008-2012 National invasive species management plan. 35 p.

National Research Council [NRC]. 1994. Rangeland Health: New Methods to Classify, Inventory and Monitor Rangelands. National Academy Press. 180 p.

National Research Council [NRC]. 2007. Environmental impacts of wind-energy projects. Committee on Environmental Impacts of Wind-Energy Projects, Board on Environmental Studies and Toxicology, Division on Earth and Life Studies, National Research Council of the National Academies. Washington, DC: The National Academy Press.

Norris, M.D.; Blair, J.M.; Johnson, L.C. 2007. Altered ecosystem nitrogen dynamics as a consequence of land cover change in tallgrass prairie. American Midland Naturalist 158:432-445.

Nusser, S.M.; Breidt, F.J.; Fuller, W.A. 1998. Design and estimation for investigating the dynamics of natural resources. Ecological Applications 8: 234-245.

Ortega, Y.K.; McKelvey, K.S.; Six, D.L. 2006. Invasion of an exotic forb impacts reproductive success and site fidelity of a migratory songbird. Oecologia 149: 340-351.

Owens, M.K.; Lyons, R.K.; Alejandro, C.J. 2006. Rainfall partitioning within semiarid juniper communities: effects of event size and canopy cover. Hydrological Processes 20: 3179-3189.

Papanastasis, V.P. 2009. Restoration of degraded grazing lands through grazing management: can it work? Restoration Ecology 17: 441-445.

Paruelo, J.M., and W.K. Lauenroth. 1996. Relative abundance of plant functional types in grasslands and shrublands of North America. Ecological Applications 6: 1212-1224.

Parikka, M. 2004. Global biomass fuel resources. Biomass and Bioenergy 27: 613-620.

Pellant, M. 1996. Cheatgrass: the invader that won the West. Boise, ID: Bureau of Land Management, Idaho State Office. 23 p.

Pellant, M.; Pyke, D.A.; Shaver, P.; Herrick, J.E. 2005. Interpreting indicators of rangeland health. Technical Reference 1734-6. Denver, CO: U.S. Department of the Interior, Bureau of Land Management. 119 p.

Perlack, R.D.; Wright, L.L.; Turhollow, A.F.; Graham, R.L.; Stokes, B.J.; Erback, D.C. 2005. Biomass as feedstock for a bioenergy and bioproducts industry: the technical feasibility of a billion-ton annual supply. ORNL/TM-2005/66. Oakridge, TN. Available: http://www.osti.gov/bridge.

Perrings, C.; Williamson, M.; Barbier, E.B.; Delfino, D.; Dalmazzone, S.; Shogren, J.; Simmons, P.; Watkinson, A. 2002. Biological invasion risks and the public good: an economic perspective. Conservation Ecology 6: 7.

Pimentel, D.; Rodrigues, G.; Wang, T.; [and others]. 1994. Renewable energy: economic and environmental issues. BioScience 44: 536-547.

Poling, M. 1991. Legal milestones in range movement. Renewable Resources Journal Summer 1991 9: 7-10.

Polley, H.W., H.B. Johnson, and J.D. Derner. 2003. Increasing CO2 from 4 subambient to superambient concentrations alters species composition and increases above-ground biomass in a C3/C4 grassland. New Phytologist 160:319-327.

Polley, H.W., C.R. Tischler, and H.B. Johnson. 2006. Elevated atmospheric CO2 magnifies intra-specific variation in seedling growth of honey mesquite: an assessment of relative growth rates. Rangeland Ecology and Management 58: 128-134.

Prince, S.D.; Becker-Reshef, I.; Rishmawi, K. 2009. Detection and mapping of long-term land degradation using local net production scaling: application to Zimbabwe. Remote Sensing of Environment 113: 1046-1057.

Rafferty, D.L.; Young, J.A. 2002. Cheatgrass competition and establishment of desert needle-grass seedlings. Journal of Range Management 55: 70-72.

Ragauskas, A.J.; Williams, C.K.; Davison, B.H.;[and others]. 2006. The path forward for bio-fuels and biomaterials. Science 311: 484-489.

Rahman, S. 2003. Green power: what is it and where can we find it? IEEE, Power and Energy 1: 30-37.

Rapport, D.J.; Regier, H.A.; Hutchinson, T.C. 1985. Ecosystem behavior under stress. American Naturalist 125:617-640.

Rau, B.M.; Tausch, R.; Reiner, A.; Johnson, D.W.; Chambers, J.C.; Blank, R.R.; Lucchesi, A. 2010. Influence of prescribed fire on ecosystem biomass, carbon, and nitrogen in a pinyon juniper woodland. Rangeland Ecology and Management 63: 197-202.

Reeves, M.C.; Zhao, M.; Running, S.W. 2006. Applying improved estimates of MODIS productivity to characterize grassland vegetation dynamics. Journal of Rangeland Ecology and Management 59: 1-10.

Reeves, M.; Ryan, K.C.; Rollins, M.G.; Thompson, T. 2009. Spatial fuel data products of the LANDFIRE project. International Journal of Wildland Fire 18: 250-267.

Reeves, M.R.; Mitchell, J.E. 2011. Extent of coterminous US rangelands: quantifying implications of differing agency perspectives. Accepted for publication in Rangeland Ecology and Management.

Reich, P.F.; Numbem, S.T.; Almaraz, R.A.; Eswaran, H. 2001. Land resource stresses and desertification in Africa. In: Bridges, E.M.; Hannam, I.D.; Oldeman, L.R.; Pening de Vries, F.W.T.; Scherr, S.J.; Sompatpanit, S. (eds.). Responses to Land Degradation. New Delhi, India: Oxford Press.

Reid, C.R.; Goodrich, S.; Bowns, J.E. 2008. Cheatgrass and red brome: history and biology of two invaders. In: U.S. Forest Service (eds.): 27-32.

Resources for the Future. 2005. Energy policy in the 21st Century. Resources, Issue 156. Washington, DC: Resources for the Future.

Rice, C.A.; Bullock, J.H., Jr. 2000. Water co-produced with coalbed methane in the Powder River Basin, Wyoming: preliminary compositional data. Open-File Report 00-372. Denver, CO: U.S. Geological Survey.

Riitters, K.H. 2010. Spatial patterns of land-cover in the United States: a technical document supporting the Forest Service 2010 RPA Assessment. Research Triangle Park, NC: U.S. Department of Agriculture, Forest Service.

Rollins, M. 2009. LANDFIRE: a nationally consistent vegetation, wildland fire and fuel assessment. International Journal of Wildland Fire 18: 235-249.

Running, S.W.; Nemani, R.R.; Heinsch, F.A.; Zhao, M.; Reeves, M.; Hashimoto, H. 2004. A continuous satellite-derived measure of global terrestrial primary production. Bioscience 54: 547-560.

Salo, L.F.; McPherson, G.R.; Williams, D.G. 2005. Sonoran Desert winter annuals affected by density of red brome and soil nitrogen. American Midland Naturalist 153: 95-109.

Sandell, L.D.; Knezevic, S. 2010. Leafy spurge: noxious weeds of Nebraska. Lincoln Extension. University of Nebraska: Nebraska Department of Agriculture. 12 p.

Sankey, T.T.; Germino, M.J. 2008. Assessment of juniper encroachment with the use of Satellite Imagery and Geospatial Data. Rangeland Ecology and Management 61: 412-418.

Sanderson, M.A.; Adler, P.R.; Boateng, A.A.; Casler, M.D.; Sarath, G. 2006. Switchgrass as a biofuels feedstock in the USA. Canadian Journal of Plant Science 86: 1315-1325.

Sawyer, H.; Nielson, R.M.; Lindzey, F.; McDonald, L.L. 2006. Winter habitat selection of mule deer before and during development of a natural gas field. Journal of Wildlife Management 70: 396-403.

Scarnecchia, D.L. 1985. The animal-unit and animal-unit-equivalent concepts in range science. Journal of Range Management 38: 346-349.

Schlesinger, W.H.; Reynolds, J.F.; Cunningham, G.L.; Huenneke, L.F.; Jarrell, W.M.; Virginia, R.A.; Whitford, W.G. 1990. Biological feedbacks in global desertification: explains why nutrient cycling is so slow in desert. Science 247: 1043-1048.

Schmidt, T.L.; Leatherberry, E.C. 1995. Expansion of eastern red cedar in the lower Midwest. Northern Journal of Applied Forestry 12: 180-183.

Schroeder, M. A.; Matthew, W.; Haegen, V. 2006. Use of conservation reserve program fields by greater sage-grouse and other shrubsteppe-associated wildlife in Washington state. Final report to U.S. Department of Agriculture, Farm Service Agency, Washington Department of Fish and Game: Olympia, WA: 4-39.

Schuman, G.E.; Janzen, H.H.; Herrick, J.E. 2002. Soil carbon dynamics and potential carbon sequestration by rangelands. Environmental Pollution 116: 391-396.

Scoones, I. 1994. New directions in pastoral development in Africa. In: Scoones, I. (ed.). Living with Uncertainty. London, UK: Intermediate Technology Publications: 1-36.

Serageldin, I. 1999. Biotechnology and food security in the 21st Century. Science 285: 387-389.

Sere, C.; Steinfeld, H. 1996. World livestock production systems: current status, issues and trends. Rome, Italy: Food and Agriculture Organization of the United Nations. 89 p.

Sheley, R.L.; Olson, B.E.; Larson, L.L. 1997. Effect of weed seed rate and grass defoliation level on diffuse knapweed. Journal of Range Management 50: 39-43.

Skaggs, R.K.; Kirksey, R.E.; Harper, W.M. 1994. Determinants and implications of post-CRP land use decisions. Journal of Agricultural and Resource Economics 19: 299-312.

Smil, V. 2000. Energy in the Twentieth Century: resources, conversions, costs, uses, and consequences. Annual Review of Energy and the Environment 25: 21-51.

Smith, H.A.; Johnson, W.S.; Shonkwiler, J.S.; Swanson, S.R. 1999. The implications of variable or constant expansion rates in invasive weed infestations. Weed Science 47: 62-66.

Society for Range Management [SRM], Glossary Update Task Group. 1998. Glossary of terms used in range management. 4th ed. Denver, CO: Society for Range Management. 32 p.

Solaiman, S.G. 2007. Assessment of the meat goat industry and future outlook for U.S. small farms. Tuskegee, AL: Animal and Poultry Sciences Tuskegee University. 29 p.

Spottiswoode, C.N.; Wondafrash, M.; Gabremichael, M.N.; Dellelegn, Y.; Mwangi, M.A.K.; Collar, N.J.; Dolman, P.M. 2009. Rangeland degradation is poised to cause Africa's first recorded avian extinction. Animal Conservation: 1-9.

Stitt, S.; Root, R.; Brown, K.; Hager, S.; Mladinich, C.; Anderson, C.L.; Dudek, K.; Bustos, M.R.; Kokaly, R. 2006. Classification of leafy spurge with earth observing-1 advanced land imager. Rangelands Ecology and Management 59: 507-511.

Stoddart, L.A.; Smith, A.D. 1943. Range Management. New York: McGraw-Hill Book Co. 547 p.

Stokes, C.J.; McAllister, R.R.J.; Ash, A.J. 2006. Fragmentation of Australian rangelands: processes, benefits and risks of changing patterns of land use. The Rangeland Journal 28: 83-96.

Strand, E.K.; Vierling, L.A.; Smith, A.M.S.; Bunting, S.C. 2008. Net changes in aboveground woody carbon stock in western juniper woodlands, 1946-1998. Journal of Geophysical Research- Biogeosciences 113: 13.

Streeks, T.J.; Owens, K.M.; Whisenant, S.G. 2005. Examining for behavior in mesquite-acacia shrublands. International Journal of Wildland Fire 14: 131-140.

Stubbs, M. 2007. Land conversion in the northern Plains. Congressional Research Service: Washington D.C. 16 p. Available: http://lugar.senate.gov/services/pdf_crs/ag/12.pdf.

Sullivan, J. 1993. Juniperus ashei. In: Fire Effects Information System. [Online]. U.S. Department of Agriculture, Forest Service, Rocky Mountain Research Station, Fire Sciences Laboratory. Available: http://www.fs fed.us/database/feis/ [2010, October 20].

Sullivan, P.; Daniel, H.; Hansen, L.; Johansson, R.; Koenig, S.; Lubowski, R.; McBride, W.; McGranahan, D.; Roberts, M.; Vogel, S.; Bucholtz, S. 2004. The Conservation Reserve Program: Economic Implications for Rural America. U.S. Department of Agriculture, Economics Research Service.

Teague, W.R.; Ansley, J.R.; Pinchak, W.E.; Dowhower, S.L.; Gerrard, S.A.; Waggoner, J.A. 2008. Interannual herbaceous biomass response to increasing honey mesquite cover on two soils. Rangeland Ecological Management 61: 496-508.

Tilman, D.; Hill, J.; Lehman, C. 2006. Carbon-negative biofuels from low-input high-diversity grassland biomass. Science 314: 1598-1600.

Theobald, D.M. 2005. Landscape patterns of exurban growth in the USA from 1980 to 2020. Ecology and Society 10(1): 32. Available: http://www.ecologyandsociety.org/vol10/iss1/art32/ [2012, February 2].

Wear, David N. 2011. Forecasts of county-level land uses under three future scenarios: a technical document supporting the Forest Service 2010 RPA Assessment. Gen. Tech. Rep. SRS-141. Asheville, NC: U.S. Department of Agriculture Forest Service, Southern Research Station. 41 p.

Wilson, J.R., and R.H. Brown. 1983. Influence of leaf anatomy on the dry matter digestibility of C4, C3 and C3/C4 intermediate types of Panicum species. Crop Science 23: 141-146.

Winslow, J.C., E.R. Hunt, and S.C. Piper. 2003. The influence of seasonal water 1 availability on global C3 versus C4 grassland biomass and its implications for climate change research. Ecological Modelling 163: 153-173.

U.S. Department of Agriculture [USDA]. 2009. Summary report: 2007 national resources inventory. Washington, DC: Natural Resources Conservation Service and Center for Survey Statistics and Methodology. Ames, IA: Iowa State University. 123 p.

U.S. Department of Agriculture, Economic Research Service [USDA ERS]. 2008. 2008 Farm bill side-by-side: Title II: conservation (November 14, 2008). Available: http://www.ers.usda.gov/FarmBill/2008/Titles/TitleIIConservation.htm#conservation [2011, May 25].

U.S. Department of Agriculture, Economic Research Service [USDA ERS]. 2009. International agricultural baseline projections to 2007: beef. Washington, DC: U.S. Department of Agriculture: 151-160. Available: http://www.ers.usda.gov/publications/aer767/aer767g.pdf.

U.S. Department of Agriculture Forest Service [USDA FS]. 1980. An assessment of the forest and rangeland situation in the United States. Washington, DC. 631 p.

U.S. Department of Agriculture, Forest Service [USDA FS]. 2008. Field instructions for the annual inventory of California, Oregon and Washington. Field Instructions. FIA Program, PNW Research Station, USDA Forest Service 348 p. Available: http://www fs.fed.us/pnw/fia/publications/fieldmanuals.shtml.

U.S. Department of Agriculture, Forest Service [USDA FS]. 2000 to 2008. Grazing statistical summaries. Available: http://www.fs fed.us/rangelands/reports/index.shtml [2010, September 28].

U.S. Department of Agriculture, Forest Service [USDA FS]. 2012. Future scenarios: a technical document supporting the Forest Service 2010 RPA Assessment. Gen. Tech. Rep. RMRS-GTR-272. Fort Collins, CO: U.S. Department of Agriculture, Forest Service, Rocky Mountain Research Station. 34 p.

U.S. Department of Agriculture, Forest Service [USDA FS]. 2010. Interior West Forest Inventory & Analysis P2 field procedures. Washington, DC, USA: USDA Forest Service.370 p.

U.S. Department of Agriculture, Farm Service Agency [USDA FSA]. 2011. Conservation programs: conservation reserve program (Updated April 1, 2011). Available: http://www.fsa.usda.gov/FSA/webapp?area=home&subject=copr&topic=crp [2008, November 30].

U.S Department of Agriculture, National Agricultural Statistics Survey [USDA NASS]. 2009. 2007 Census of agriculture: United States summary and state data. U.S. Department of Agriculture. 739 p.

U.S Department of Agriculture, National Agricultural Statistics Survey [USDA NASS]. 2010. National Agricultural Statictics Survey and census. Available: http://www nass.usda.gov/Data_and_Statistics/Quick_Stats/index.asp [2010, September 27].

U.S. Department of Agriculture, Natural Resources Conservation Service [USDA NRCS]. 2009. The Conservation Reserve Program Enhances Landscape-level Grassland Bird Species Richness. Natural Resources Conservation Service: Washington, D.C.: 1-4.

U.S. Department of Agriculture, Natural Resources Conservation Service [USDA NRCS]. 2011. Conservation Reserve Program (updated March 9, 2011). U.S. Department of Agriculture. [Online]. Available: http://www.nrcs.usda.gov/programs/CRP/ [October 23, 2008].

U.S. Department of Agriculture, Natural Resources Conservation Service [USDA NRCS]. 2007. National Range and Pasture Handbook. Revised December 2003. U.S. Department of Agriculture: Washington, DC. Eleven Chapters and appendices (individually numbered). Available: http://www.glti nrcs.usda.gov/technical/publications/nrph html.

U.S. Department of Agriculture, Soil Conservation Service [USDA SCS]. 1988. Forage utilization by game species. Washington, DC: U.S. Department of Agriculture, Soil Conservation Service. 4 p.

U.S. Department of Energy. 2005. Biomass as feedstock for a bioenergy and bioproducts industry: The technical feasibility of a billion-ton annual supply. Oakridge, TN: Office of Science and Technical Information. Available: http://www.osti.gov/bridge.

United Nations Environment Programme [UNEP]. 1991. Status of desertification and implementation of the United Nations plan of action to combat desertification United Nations Environment Programme: Nairobi, Kenya.

U.S. Department of Interior Bureau of Land Management [DOI BLM]. 2000 to 2009. Public land statistics (PLSS). Washington, DC. 122 p.

U.S. Department of the Interior, Bureau of Land Management [DOI BLM]. 2001. Rangeland health standards. Washington, DC: Healthy Rangeland Initiative, BLM Manual H-4180-1. 51 p. Available: http://www.blm.gov/public_land_statistics/index htm.

Van Auken, O.W. 2000. Shrub invasions of North American semiarid grasslands. Annual Review of Ecology, Evolution, and Systematics 31: 197-215.

Van Tassell, L.W.; Phillips, C.; Hepworth, W.G. 1995. Livestock to wildlife is not a simple conversion. Rangelands 17: 191-193.

Vasquez, E.A.; James, J.J.; Monaco, T.A.; Cummings, D.C. 2010. Invasive plants on rangelands: a global threat. Rangelands 2: 3-5.

Vogelmann, J.E.; Howard, S.M.; Yang, L.; Larson, C.R.; Wylie, B.K.; Driel, J.N.V. 2001. Completion of the 1990s national land cover data set for the conterminous United States. Photogrammetry Engineering and Remote Sensing 67: 650-662.

Wall, T.G.; Miller, R.F.; Svejcar, T.J. 2001. Juniper encroachment into aspen in the Northwest Great Basin. Journal of Range Management 54: 691-698.

Walsh, M.E.; De La Torre Ugarte, D.G.; Shapouri, H.; Slinsky, S.P. 2003. Bioenergy crop production in the United States. Environmental and Resource Economics 24: 313-333.

Washington-Allen, R.A.; Ramsey, R.D.; West, N.E.; Efroymson, R.A. 2006. A remote sensing- based protocol for assessing rangeland condition and trend. Rangeland Ecology and Management 59: 19-29.

Wear, D.N. 2011. Forecasts of county-level land uses under three future scenarios: a technical document supporting the Forest Service 2010 RPA Assessment. Gen. Tech. Rep. SRS-141. Asheville, NC: U.S. Department of Agriculture, Forest Service, Southern Research Station. 41 p.

Wessels, K.J.; Prince, S.D.; Carroll, M.; Malherbe, J. 2007. Relevance of rangeland degradation in semiarid northeastern South Africa to the nonequilibrium theory. Ecological Applications 17: 815-827.

Westoby, M.; Walker, B.; Noy-Meir, I. 1989. Opportunistic management for rangelands not at equilibrium. Journal of Range Management 42: 266-274.

Williams, A.P.; Hunt, E.R, Jr. 2002. Estimation of leafy spurge cover from hyperspectral imagery using mixture tuned matched filtering. Remote Sensing of Environment 82: 446-456.

Wilson, L.M.; Randall, C.B. 2005. Biology and biological control of knapweed. In: U.S. Forest.

Service (eds.), Department of Plant, Soil and Entomological Sciences, University of Idaho: 1-89.

Wilson, J.R., and R.H. Brown. 1983. Influence of leaf anatomy on the dry matter digestibility of C4, C3 and C3/C4 intermediate types of *Panicum* species. Crop Science 23:141-146.

Wilson, L.M.; Sing, S.E.; Piper, G.L.; Hansen, R.W.; Clerck-Floate, R.D.; MacKinnon, D.K.; Randall, C. 2005. Biology and biological control of dalmation and yellow toadflax. In: U.S. Forest Service (eds.): 1-116.

World Wind Energy Association [WWEA]. 2011. World Wind Energy report 2010: 10th World Wind Energy conference and renewable energy exhibition. Greening energy: converting deserts to power houses. Cairo, Egypt. 23 p. Available: http://www.wwindea.org/home/images/stories/pdfs/worldwindenergyreport2010_s.pdf.

Zhao, M.; Running, S.W. 2010. Drought induced reduction in global terrestrial net primary production from 2000 to 2009. Science: 1-3.

Zhu, Z.; Ohlen, D.; Kost, J.; Chen, X.; Tolk, B. 2006. Mapping existing vegetation composition and structure for the LANDFIRE Prototype project. In: The LANDFIRE Prototype Project: nationally consistent and locally relevant geospatial data and tools for wildland fire management. Gen. Tech. Rep. RMRS-GTR-175. Missoula, MT: Missoula Fire Sciences Laboratory: 197-215.